1 July 74

The
Russian Revolution
and
Bolshevik Victory

PROBLEMS IN
EUROPEAN CIVILIZATION

Under the editorial direction of
John Ratté
Amherst College

The Russian Revolution and Bolshevik Victory

Causes and Processes

Second Edition

Edited and with an introduction by

Arthur E. Adams
The Ohio State University

D. C. HEATH AND COMPANY
Lexington, Massachusetts Toronto London

International Standard Book Number: 0-669-81745-7

Library of Congress Catalog Card Number: 72-5151

CONTENTS

INTRODUCTION   vii
THE CONFLICT OF OPINION   xvii

I THE MARCH REVOLUTION: ITS CAUSES AND ITS LEADERS

George F. Kennan
THE AUTOCRACY'S MANY SHORTCOMINGS BROUGHT ITS
COLLAPSE   3

Bernard Pares
RASPUTIN AND THE EMPRESS ALEXANDRA   19

Peter I. Lyashchenko
ECONOMIC AND SOCIAL CONSEQUENCES OF THE WAR   30

William H. Chamberlin
THE MARCH REVOLUTION WAS SPONTANEOUS   44

Leon Trotsky
BOLSHEVIK WORKINGMEN LED THE REVOLT   53

II FROM MARCH TO OCTOBER: THE SEARCH FOR EVER MORE RADICAL SOLUTIONS

Adam B. Ulam
DEMOCRACY FAILED TO SOLVE RUSSIA'S PROBLEMS   71

Nicholas N. Golovine
A DEMORALIZED ARMY SPREAD DISSATISFACTION AMONG
THE PEOPLE   86

David Mitrany
A PRIMITIVE PEASANTS' WAR GAINED MOMENTUM   97

Launcelot A. Owen
THE PEASANT BECAME "AUTOCRAT OF RUSSIA"   99

Richard Pipes
NATIONAL MINORITIES SOUGHT AUTONOMY AND INDEPEN-
DENCE   110

Isaac Deutscher
BOLSHEVIKS LED WORKERS TOWARD RADICAL REVOLUTION 123

III THE BOLSHEVIK VICTORY: WHY THE PROVISIONAL GOVERNMENT FELL AND WHY THE BOLSHEVIKS WERE SUCCESSFUL

Alexander Kerensky
BOTH LEFT AND RIGHT BETRAYED THE PROVISIONAL GOV-
ERNMENT   137

Leonid I. Strakhovsky
KERENSKY BETRAYED RUSSIA   148

Robert V. Daniels
LENIN GAMBLED WILDLY AND WON   167

The Communist Party of the Soviet Union
THE BOLSHEVIK PARTY LED THE MASSES   186

SUGGESTIONS FOR ADDITIONAL READING   192

INTRODUCTION

There are several warnings to which anyone proposing to study the Russian Revolution must listen before setting out on what is certain to be a fascinating but perplexing intellectual expedition. It is essential first to understand that this revolution was an incredibly complex historical event. Acted out on a nationwide stage it presents an almost limitless panorama of suffering humanity caught up in a series of swiftly evolving crises no one seemed able to prevent. Passions and pressures built up through many generations of frustration were concentrated in a social and political upheaval that may be likened to a long-continuing explosion which tossed men and ideas about like matchsticks, crumbling traditions and institutions to dust. It is not easy to comprehend such phenomena.

There is another major problem. Inevitably, the upheaval, so crucial for Russia, so crammed with bitterness and bloodshed and change in the years that followed, so significant for subsequent events in the rest of the world, provoked a flood of writings. Great piles of documents, eyewitness accounts, polemics, scholarly studies, and deliberate distortions have resulted. Most have some usefulness. Very few are completely reliable or unbiased. Somewhere in the multitude of books, articles and documents lies the truth about the revolution. But here we face a dilemma. Painstaking, objective scholarly investigation has only just begun. The slow, tedious culling of fact from fiction that is essential to the forming of reliable generalizations has still to be carried out. Accomplishment of this work requires scholars with profound knowledge of Russia's history, her ideologies, institutions, and people, and a total commitment to the truth. From such scholars must come long lists of monographs dealing exhaustively with specialized and narrow topics until we know more of the facts about the revolution. Only upon the foundation of such detailed studies can other scholars tie the events together into sound hypotheses. First the patient researchers who examine every salient problem; then powerful creative minds, like those which have worked on the French Revolution, to pull out the great explanations—until this process is completed we seek to understand without being able to learn enough to understand. Our hypotheses remain guesses. We cannot explain but must be satisfied with suggesting relationships and theories which may or may not be true.

Given this unsatisfactory state of our knowledge and desiring to understand better one of the most complex and significant social and political upheavals of modern times, one must follow a careful plan of study. True, there are many interpretations of the events of 1917, and none of these can legitimately claim to be the exhaustive and final summation. Nonetheless, judgments can be made, for some materials are demonstrably more valuable than others. It is the first aim of this book to provide an acquaintance with those interpretations which are most rational and perceptive or which have been most favorably considered by thoughtful, well-informed men.

If the reader is to evaluate and relate the differing interpretations intelligently, he must possess considerable detailed information about the events of 1917. He must comprehend the awesome political and moral passions which then raged through Russia and which continue to influence even the most objective scholars today. It is the second purpose of this book to present information that will aid this process of evaluation.

There is also a need for a useful conceptual approach to the study of the revolution. Can an effective analysis of these complex events be made in simple terms? Or is the very truth itself embedded in the chaos and intricacy of revolutionary events, in the innumerable actions and interactions of men and ideas with the realities of an exhausted and disintegrating social order? Most significant historical processes defy simple explanations; their causes, manifestations, and consequences seem to repel neat classification. Comprehension of such events is usually best gained by studying them from many sides and from many levels. The student must examine the history, the institutions, the ideas, the characters of the men involved; he must even seek to make himself sensitive to the almost intangible tenor of a whole social climate. Somewhere in his study of the matrix of forces and events, he will begin to perceive relationships between one event and another which may be formulated as tentative hypotheses to be tested by further examination of the evidence. From this process comes understanding. The third purpose of this book, therefore, is to provide materials which make possible a many-sided examination of the revolution, so that each reader may form his own hypotheses and begin the process of testing them.

In order to catch hold of the subject and build a conceptual framework that can guide us through the maze of detail, it is helpful to ask several specific questions about the revolution, even though they cannot be finally answered. All students of the Russian Revolution agree that some events and processes in 1917 were more significant than others. It is, for example, much more necessary to examine the impact of World War I upon Russia than to study the operation of the Russian secondary school system in 1917. The studies presented in this book, therefore, focus upon the significant problems, and the partial answers given by different authorities are offered because they provide meaningful insights into events which appear to have had predominant influence.

The first specific problem we examine focusses on the February/ March Revolution, and the conflict of opinion centers around questions related to its causes and its leadership. Three scholars discuss the problem of causes. George Kennan has been a profound scholar of Russia's history for many years and has reflected carefully on the problem. Sir Bernard Pares was one of Great Britain's most learned Russian scholars; and Peter Lyashchenko is a Marxist economic historian and Soviet citizen. It is significant that these three differ not so much in the rejection of one another's views as in their emphases upon the influence of different factors.

Discussing the question of the leadership of the February/March Revolution, William Henry Chamberlin seeks to establish the complete lack of any organized leadership. Leon Trotsky virulently attacks this point of view by systematically attacking *all* its adherents; then Trotsky boldly argues that the leaders of the revolution were the workers of Petrograd who had been strongly indoctrinated by the Bolshevik party. In all, the five selections of Part I fill out a dramatic picture of the era just prior to 1917 and describe the events of the February/March Revolution.

In the months following March, Russia hurtled at an ever-increasing pace toward more radical solutions of its problems, toward ultimate rejection of the achievements of February/March. The materials in Part II of this book attempt to explain the causes and the manifestations of this process of radicalization. The continuing breakdown of political and social institutions and the growth of more extreme attitudes, on the Right as well as the Left, were the consequences of many distinct but related factors. Here it becomes clear that what is habitually referred to as *The Revolution* was in reality several revolutions, and that each of these more or less followed its own course and moved at its own speed, although there were many points of contact and interaction. Thus there was a social revolution of urban workers and idle soldiers and a political revolution in the capital cities, an agrarian revolution, and separate revolutions developed by the strong national minorities previously held in subjection by tsarist authority. Another kind of political revolutionary movement was patiently organized and nurtured by Lenin and his Bolshevik party. These developing revolutions were accompanied by counter-movements, as well as worsening military and economic conditions, which heightened the tensions and hurried the rush toward what Alexander Kerensky calls the "catastrophe" of October. The six selections in Part II trace the courses followed by the several clearly definable revolutions and offer evidence concerning their most important interrelationships.

In Part III four studies attempt to explain why the Provisional Government fell and why the Bolsheviks were able to seize power. These are fiercely controversial problems, and as yet there is little agreement about the proper answers. The four studies presented here represent the considered judgments of outstanding representatives of the principal interpretations. The first article, by Alexander Kerensky, who was in 1917 the principal figure in the series of coalition governments roughly defined as the Provisional Government, argues that the Provisional Government was betrayed by the moderates and rightists, who should have supported it. Leonid Strakhovsky, an avowed monarchist scholar and defender of the military honor of Russia's generals, sets forth other evidence which asserts that Kerensky himself betrayed the Provisional Government and thus made its downfall inevitable. The brilliant American political scientist, Robert Daniels, argues that despite all Lenin's efforts to drive the Bolshevik party to revolution, it resorted to violence only in self-defense against attack by forces of the Provisional Government, so that Bolshevik victory occurred more because of a vigorous defense than because of its aggressive determination to seize power. And the final account—from the official explanation of the Russian Communist party—holds that Marxist-Leninist political philosophy and close relationship with workers and poor peasants guided the Bolsheviks to victory and made such victory (given Lenin's leadership) inevitable. Clearly, the diversity of views could not be more wide. It is for the reader to study and compare and decide for himself where the truth lies, insofar as final decision is possible.

Besides addressing themselves to the major controversial questions, most of the excerpts in this book contain various additional attributes of value for the reader who is attempting to form valid judgments about the revolution. Several of them, while being the considered opinions of scholarly authorities, are also valuable original sources, offering deep insights into the general climate of opinion which characterized certain social groups during the revolution. Thus, for example, the work of Leon Trotsky, represented here by an excerpt from his *History of the Russian Revolution*, is a valuable source. It is the work of a man who was simultaneously a scholar of tremendous intellectual power, one of the world's great polemicists, and a leader of the Bolshevik party. Trotsky's analysis of the facts penetrates to the deepest social and historical roots; sometimes with no more than a glance he sees far more deeply than the best of our professional scholars. Yet, every word and every line of his thought is saturated with his profound faith in the Marxist doctrine and with the amazing intellectual arrogance which persuaded him that only he, Lenin and their adherents could understand history accurately. To read Trotsky is to see how the mind of one of the greatest of the Bolshevik leaders functioned. It is an impressive experience.

In Part III, Alexander Kerensky, so long and so bitterly maligned by all sides, speaks for himself. Through all the years of his life outside of Russia, he brooded over the events of 1917. In his later years he joined with the young American professor, Robert Browder, to

examine the records of the Provisional Government with the purpose
of summing up the history of that institution. But in the article presented here, Kerensky develops an argument often reiterated in his
books and articles. He speaks with the tortured pride of a man who
is accused of the most heinous of modern crimes—betrayal of his
country—and who believes that on the contrary *he was betrayed*.
His argument, repeated desperately, almost hopelessly, and long
rejected by many, is today being reconsidered more sympathetically.
It would surely be a major shortcoming if this book deprived the
reader of the opportunity to judge the character of the man who lost.

The last excerpt of the book, from *History of the Communist Party
of the Soviet Union* (1969) possesses its own special significance as
an expression of the official Soviet view. This is Communist propaganda, of course, stated with a simple and somewhat awkward sin-
cerity, and undoubtedly reflecting the explanation Soviet citizens
believe to be accurate. In this interpretation, the Bolsheviks are said
to have succeeded in October because they were guided by the only
theory of historical change that is scientifically right, because Lenin
knew how to make the best use of the Marxist-Leninist doctrine, and
because urban workers and poor peasants recognized the party's
legitimacy as their true leader. This explanation in its several varia-
tions has been multiplied many millions, perhaps billions, of times
in several successive versions of the official *History of the Party* and
in innumerable other Soviet publications. It is, in short, the official
line of the Communist party of the Soviet Union today and has been
for many years.

Implicit in all the materials included and in the problems raised
about the revolution are many issues of immense significance for
the present day. For example, there is reason to believe that Russian
democracy may have failed because its defenders were too much
dedicated to constitutional procedures and moderation. Does this
mean that other democratic societies may be destroyed by their
belief in constitutional government and doomed by their moderation?
On the other hand, some of the evidence appears to indicate that
the Bolsheviks won because of their superior political organization
and their ruthless and uncompromising determination to gain power
at any cost. Must political success in the twentieth century invariably
go to the political group that stops at nothing? The belief of Marxist-

Leninist followers that they have new and superior ways to achieve age-old human goals challenges the older theories and methods of the Western world. What will be the outcome of this competition? These questions, of course, underline only a few of the most obvious points about the impact of the revolution upon our world. Its continuing influence is visible on every hand.

A Note on Technicalities

Through 1917 Russia employed the old Julian calendar, which in this century is thirteen days behind our own. Because some of the authors presented here use the old style dates and others the new, I have included a chronology of principal events, giving their dates in both old and new styles. Also because different writers use different methods of transliterating Russian words into English, and because these different methods are sometimes hotly defended by their adherents, I have not ventured to revise my authors. It seems necessary, however, to advise the reader that Miliukov, Milyukov, and Miljukov are not three different men but only one whose name has been variously transliterated.

Chronology, 1917

Old Style	New Style	
February 22–March 2	March 7–15	The February/March Revolution
February 27	March 12	Formation of the Duma Committee and the Petrograd Soviet
March 2	March 15	Abdication of Nicholas II and formation of First Provisional Government
April 3	April 16	Lenin arrives in Petrograd
May 2	May 15	Milyukov's resignation as minister of foreign affairs
May 5	May 18	Organization of First Coalition Government
June 18	July 1	The Kerensky offensive
July 3–5	July 16–18	The July Days: unsuccessful Bolshevik demonstrations
July 24	August 6	Kerensky becomes prime minister in Second Coalition Government
August 25–30	September 7–12	The Kornilov revolt
September 1	September 14	Kerensky establishes the Directorate of Five
September 23	October 6	Trotsky becomes president of Petrograd Soviet
September 25	October 8	Formation of Third Coalition Government
October 12	October 25	Military Revolutionary Committee of the Soviet placed under Trotsky's direction
October 25	November 7	Seizure of power in Petrograd
October 26	November 8	Organization of the Bolshevik Government

The Conflict of Opinion

The March Revolution

. . . what occurred in Russia in February–March 1917 was, precisely, a breakdown of the autocracy under a fortuitous combination of momentary strains—not the overthrow of the existing order by revolutionary forces.

GEORGE F. KENNAN

While the empress's letters wipe clean away all the scandalous charges made against her personal character . . . they also prove that she and, through her, Rasputin were the prime authors of the collapse of the empire and of Russia.

SIR BERNARD PARES

The war was, in Lenin's expression, 'a mighty accelerator' of the process of revolutionization . . .

PETER LYASHCHENKO

The collapse of the Romanov autocracy in March 1917 was one of the most leaderless, spontaneous, anonymous revolutions of all time. While almost every thoughtful observer in Russia in the winter of 1916–1917 foresaw the likelihood of the crash of the existing regime no one, even among the revolutionary leaders, realized that the strikes and bread riots which broke out in Petrograd on March 8 would culminate in the mutiny of the garrison and the overthrow of the government four days later.

WILLIAM H. CHAMBERLIN

To the question, Who led the February Revolution? we can . . . answer definitely enough: Conscious and tempered workers educated for the most part by the party of Lenin. But we must here immediately add: This leadership proved sufficient to guarantee the victory of the insurrection, but it was not adequate to transfer immediately into the hands of the proletarian vanguard the leadership of the revolution.

LEON TROTSKY

From March to October

From June on, those who hoped for a democratic conclusion and peace had to work with increasing bitterness and despair in their hearts. There was no longer even an appearance of national unity or of "revolutionary democracy."

ADAM ULAM

. . . from the beginning of the revolution a desire to end the war, along with the political, economic, and social stimuli at work in every revolution, spread rapidly in both the army and the people.

N. N. GOLOVINE

What is plain, and relevant to our subject, is that it was a double revolution—a peasant revolution and a political one . . .

DAVID MITRANY

[Chernov's] declaration that "the peasantry itself was the real autocrat of Russia" . . . was a statement the truth of which was never more evident than in the succeeding October, when he himself was hurled from power by those who utilized the forces that had placed his party in office.

L. A. OWEN

The outbreak of the Russian Revolution had, as its initial consequence, the abolition of the tsarist regime and, as its ultimate result, the complete breakdown of all forms of organized life throughout Russia. One of the aspects of this breakdown was the disintegration of the empire and the worsening of relations between its various ethnic groups. In less than a year after the tsar had abdicated, the national question had become an outstanding issue in Russian politics.

RICHARD PIPES

The Bolsheviks were becoming the masters in the working-class suburbs of Petersburg. . . . The Bolsheviks met the new coalition with grim hostility; but in opposing it they displayed a tactical imagination and subtlety which could not fail to yield massive and quick rewards.

ISAAC DEUTSCHER

The Bolshevik Victory

Only by way of conspiracy, only by way of a treacherous armed struggle was it possible to break up the Provisional Government and stop the establishment of a democratic system in Russia after the revolution.

ALEXANDER KERENSKY

. . . let the facts in this case speak out the truth, and let history pronounce its verdict of guilty in betraying Russia against the former prime minister of the Provisional Government, to whom the dubious gains of the March Revolution were dearer than the welfare, the future, and the very existence of his country and its people.

LEONID STRAKHOVSKY

The stark truth about the Bolshevik Revolution is that it succeeded against incredible odds in defiance of any rational calculation that could have been made in the fall of 1917. The shrewdest politicians of every political coloration knew that while the Bolsheviks were an undeniable force in Petrograd and Moscow, they had against them the overwhelming majority of the peasants, the army in the field, and the trained personnel without which no government could function.

ROBERT DANIELS

A decisive circumstance that made the victory of the revolution possible was the fact that the masses of the people were headed by the well-tried, militant and revolutionary Bolshevik party, a party guided by the advanced theory of the working class, the theory of Marxism-Leninism.

COMMUNIST PARTY OF THE SOVIET UNION (1969)

I THE MARCH REVOLUTION: ITS CAUSES AND ITS LEADERS

George F. Kennan

THE AUTOCRACY'S MANY SHORTCOMINGS BROUGHT ITS COLLAPSE

George Kennan is one of the wisest and most thoughtful American students of Soviet affairs. Years of diplomatic experience in Russia, combined with an inexhaustible scholarly interest in the reasons for Russia's unique development, have given him profound insights into the processes of Russian history. Since 1950 (with time out to serve as ambassador to Russia and to Yugoslavia) he has worked at the Institute for 'Advanced Study at Princeton, where he has continued to study the Communist world and American foreign policy. Among his principal published works are: Decision to Intervene; Russia Leaves the War; Russia and the West under Lenin and Stalin; *and* Memoirs 1925–1950. *In the essay that follows, he examines Russia's past and offers a sophisticated, complex analysis of the reasons for the autocracy's breakdown in March 1917.*

The discussion that follows proceeds from the premise that what occurred in Russia in February–March 1917 was, precisely, a *breakdown* of the autocracy under a fortuitous combination of momentary strains—not the overthrow of the existing order by revolutionary forces. In essence, the regime may be said to have collapsed because it was not able to muster sufficient support to enable it to withstand this sudden combination of strains. In quarters whose support would have been essential to enable it to do this, there was either distrust, indifference, outright hostility, or, in the particular case of the bureaucracy and the army, a mixture of disorientation, demoralization, and ineptness. The central question involved is therefore the question as to which of the regime's policies—that is, what elements of its behavior, what errors of commission or omission, or possibly what circumstances outside its control—were decisive or outstandingly important in bringing it to the helpless and fatal predicament in which it found itself at the beginning of 1917.

Such an inquiry presents special difficulty in view of the bewildering interaction of long-term and short-term causes. One is compelled

Excerpted by permission of the publishers from George F. Kennan, "The Breakdown of the Tsarist Authority," in *Revolutionary Russia,* ed. Richard Pipes (Cambridge, Mass.: Harvard University Press, 1968), pp. 1–15. Copyright © 1968 by Richard Pipes.

to ask not just what were the long-term weaknesses that rendered the regime susceptible to the danger of collapse under relatively trivial pressures in the first place, but also what it was that caused the collapse to come at this particular moment.

I should like to begin with an examination of some of the long-term weaknesses and failures of the regime and then conclude with some brief reflections about the developments of the final wartime period just preceding its fall.

Long-term Weaknesses and Failures of the Regime

When one looks for those more basic mistakes and failings that undermined the tsarist autocracy and caused it to lose what the Chinese would call the "mandate of Heaven," one is obliged first to deal with certain broadly held misimpressions on this score— misimpressions that Soviet historians, in particular, have been at no pains to dispel. One of these is that the autocracy lost the confidence and respect of the people because it failed to bring a proper degree of modernization to Russian society in the economic, techno-logical, and educational fields—that it made no adequate effort to overcome Russia's backwardness. Another is that the regime was intolerably cruel and despotic in its treatment of the populace gen-erally; and that a revolution was required to correct this situation. In each of these impressions there are, of course, elements of truth; but both represent dangerous, and in general misleading, oversimpli-fications. That this is true is so well known to experts in the field that it needs, I think, no great elaboration here. But I shall just men-tion briefly, to avoid unclarity, my own impressions of the situation.

Let us take first the subject of industrialization. Here, it seems to me, we have one of those fields in which the tsar's regime had least to be apologetic about from the standpoint of responsibility for the modernizing of the country. The rates of industrial growth achieved in Russia in the final decades of tsardom would appear to compare not at all unfavorably with those achieved in Western countries at comparable stages of development. The 8 per cent growth rate that I understand to have been achieved in the 1890s, and the comparable 6 per cent figure for the period from 1906 to 1914, are respectable

figures, to say the least. One must doubt that the pace of industrialization could have been pushed much further without producing adverse social consequences out of all proportion in seriousness to the
gains involved. Nor does there seem to be any reason to suppose
that if revolution had not intervened, and if the dynamics of growth
observable in the final decades of tsardom had been projected into
mid-century, the results achieved would have been significantly inferior to those that have actually been achieved under Soviet power.
This is, of course, only another way of saying that if industrialization
was the main concern then no revolution was needed at all: there
were easier and no less promising ways of doing it.

It has often been pointed out by way of reproach to the tsar's
regime—both at the time and since—that this growth was achieved
only by an excessive acceptance of investment and equity participation by foreigners in Russian industry, as well as by excessive state
borrowing from other governments. Certainly, the proportion of foreign equity participation in Russian industrial concerns was very
high, particularly in mining and metallurgy; and it is perfectly true
that the Russian government was the most heavily indebted, ex-
ternally, of any government in the world at the time. But I am not
sure how well these charges stand up as reproaches to the policies
of the tsar's government. Whether the high rate of foreign industrial
investment was a bad thing depends on whether one accepts the
Marxist thesis that any important degree of such external financing
represented a form of enslavement to the foreign investors. The experience of the United States, where foreign capital also played a
prominent part in nineteenth-century industrial development, would
not suggest that this is the case. And as for the government borrowing: much of this, of course, found its way, directly or indirectly, into
the process of industrialization, and particularly into the building of
railways. But the main stimulus to such borrowing was not the need
for industrial capital but rather the effort by the government to maintain a military posture, and to engage in military ventures, that were
far beyond its means. These practices, and the heavy indebtedness
to which they led, were indeed among the significant weaknesses
of the regime; but they do not constitute a proper source of reproach
to the regime in connection with its program of industrialization.
Had the foreign borrowings of the government been restricted to

what it required in order to do its share in the stimulation of the growth of industry, the resulting burden of debt would surely have been well within its means.

Another reproach often leveled at the tsar's government in this connection was that industrialization was given precedence over agriculture and that it was partially financed by the exploitation of the peasantry through such devices as high indirect taxation, rigged prices for agricultural products, forced exportation of grain, and so on. Certainly there is much substance in these charges. The program of rapid industrialization was indeed put in hand long before any attack of comparable vigor was made on the problems of the peasantry, and the peasant was made to contribute heavily to its costs. But these circumstances seem to me to be illustrative less of any error or unfeeling quality on the part of tsarist statesmen than of the cruelty of the dilemmas with which they were faced. Without at least a certain prior development of industry, and particularly without the construction of railway network, no modernization of Russian agriculture would have been conceivable at all. And while somewhat more might perhaps have been extracted from the upper classes through ruthless taxation, there is no reason to suppose that this could have changed basically the logic of the situation, which was that the cost of industrialization, to the extent it was not covered by foreign borrowing, had to be covered by limitations on consumption by the great mass of the Russian people—which meant, in fact, the peasantry. To have tried, through the device of heavy taxation, to switch this entire burden to the relatively well-to-do or property-owning classes would merely have tended to destroy existing possibilities for the accumulation of private industrial capital; but such private accumulation was precisely what the government was concerned, and for a very respectable reason, to stimulate and promote.

The truth is that the tsar's government, if it wished to get on in a serious way with the industrial development of the country, had no alternatives other than foreign borrowing and an extensive taxation of the peasantry. The claim that it should have avoided one or the other of these devices is thus equivalent to the allegation that it moved not too slowly but much too fast in the whole field of industrialization. For this there might be much to be said. But this is not the way the reproach is usually heard.

In the case of agriculture, the pattern is obviously more complex. Certainly, the reform of the 1860s left much to be desired: it was not properly followed through; the burdens resting on the peasantry down to 1905 were inordinate; the economic situation of large portions of the peasant population remained miserable. In all this there were just grounds for reproach to the regime; and I have no desire to minimize its significance. It seems reasonable to suppose that the additional burden of bitterness that accumulated in peasant minds in the final decades of the nineteenth century contributed importantly both to the peasant disorders of the first years of the new century, and to that spirit of sullen contempt for the dynasty, an indifference to its fate, that manifested itself at the time of the revolution.

Against these reflections must be set, however, two compensatory considerations. One has, first, the fact that the most important single factor involved in producing the land hunger and economic misery of the central-Russian village in these decades was nothing having to do with governmental policy but simply the enormous increase in the rural population that occurred at that time—a doubling, and more, just in the years between the emancipation and the outbreak of the world war. Second, there is the fact that after 1906 the government did finally address itself vigorously, intelligently, and in general quite effectively to the problems of the Russian countryside. The fact that this effort came late—too late to be successful in the political and psychological sense—should not blind us to its imposing dimensions. What was achieved in those final years from 1907 to 1914 in a whole series of fields affecting the peasant's situation—in the purchase of land by small peasant holders; in the break-up of the peasant commune and the facilitating of the transition from communal to hereditary tenure; in the consolidation of strip holdings, with all the enormous labor of surveying and adjudicating this involved; in resettlement and in colonization of outlying regions of the empire; in the development of the cooperative movement in the countryside—strikes me as impressive in the extreme.

One can truthfully say that the tsar's government deserved reproach for its failures in relation to the peasant throughout most of the nineteenth century. And there can be no doubt that the price of these failures figured prominently in the reckoning the autocracy had to face in 1917. No one would deny, in particular, the importance of the impact that the spectacle of all this rural misery and degradation had on the growth of the Russian revolutionary movement in the nineteenth century. And one can well say that such efforts as were made to improve the situation of the peasantry came much too late in the game. What one cannot say is that they did not come at all or that revolution was necessary because the tsar's government, as of 1917, had still done nothing effective about agriculture. The fact is that the revolution came precisely at the moment when the prospects for the development of Russian agriculture, the war aside, had never looked more hopeful.

Similar conclusions could be drawn, I should think, with relation to education. That Russia was slow in coming to popular education no one would deny. But that the progress made in this field in the final years of tsardom was rapid and impressive seems to me equally undeniable. If, as I understand to be the case, enrollments in primary schools throughout the empire more than doubled in the final two decades before 1914; if in this same period enrollments in institutions of higher learning more than tripled and those in secondary schools nearly quadrupled; or if, for example, the incidence of literacy among military recruits increased from 38 percent in 1894 to 73 percent in 1913—then it may be argued, I think, that all this might have been done earlier; but it cannot be said that nothing consequential was being done at all. The official goal, as adopted five or six years before the outbreak of the world war, was the achievement of universal, compulsory primary school education. The tsarist authorities hoped to achieve this goal by 1922. The rate of progress made prior to the war suggests that it would probably have been achieved at the latest by the mid-1920s had not war and revolution intervened. This is certainly no later than the date at which it was finally achieved by the Soviet regime. Again, one simply cannot accept the thesis that the old regime kept the Russian people in darkness to the end and that a revolution was necessary in 1917 to correct this situation.

In all these fields of modernization, the pattern is in fact much the same: initial backwardness, long sluggishness and delay, then a veritable burst of activity in the final years. If it was in these fields that one was to look for the decisive failures of the autocracy and the reasons for revolution, then it would have to be said that there was much less reason for an overthrow of the regime in 1917 than there was in 1905. Had the 1905 Revolution succeeded, one might well have concluded that the tsar's regime had been overthrown because it failed to bring the Russian people into the modern age. To account for an overthrow coming in 1917, one has to look for other and deeper causes.

The first and most decisive of these causes seems to me to have been, unquestionably, the failure of the autocracy to supplement the political system in good time with some sort of a parliamentary institution—the failure, in other words, to meet the needs of the land-owning nobility and then, increasingly, of the new intelligentsia from all classes for some sort of institutional framework that would associate them with the undertakings of the regime, give them a sense of participation in the governmental process, and provide a forum through which they, or their representatives, could air their views and make their suggestions with regard to governmental policy. In the absence of any such institution, literally hundreds of thousands of people—student youth, commoners *(raznochintsy),* sons of priests, members of the national minorities, members of the gentry, even members of the land-owning nobility itself—people bursting with energies and the love of life in all its forms; people vibrating with intellectual excitement under the flood of impressions that swept over Russian society as its contacts with the West developed during the nineteenth and early twentieth centuries; people passionately concerned with public affairs, intensely aware of Russia's backwardness, and possessed by no more consuming passion than the desire to contribute to its correction—all these people found themselves, insofar as they did not become associated with the armed forces or the administrative bureaucracy, repelled by the regime, held at a distance from its doings and responsibilities, condemned either to a passive submissiveness in public affairs that did violence to their consciences as well as their energies or to the development of forms of association and political activity that could not, in the circumstances, appear to the regime as other than subversive. What was required, initially, was not a widely popular assembly. There was much to oe said for the view that the Russian people at large were not yet ready for this. At any time in the nineteenth century, even a central assembly of the local government boards *(zemstva)* would have constituted an important safety valve, and in fact a very suitable one, insofar as it would have enlisted as collaborators in the tasks of government at the central level not mere theorists devoid of practical experience but people who had had the best sort of preparation: namely, experience at the local, provincial level in the fields of administration intimately connected with the lives and interests of common people. To attempt, with relation to so great and complex a process as that of the loss of public confidence by the Russian autocracy, to identify any single error as a crucial one is, of course, always to commit an act of oversimplification; but if one were to inquire what, by way of example, might appear as outstanding historical errors of the regime, I should think one would have to name such things as the flat repulsion by Alexander II in 1862 of the initiative taken by the gentry of Tver, under the leadership of Unkovskii, in favor of a central *zemstvo* organ; or the rebuff administered by Nicholas II to the representatives of the *zemstva* and the nobility who called on him in 1895 to urge—if only in the mildest of language—the recognition of the need for a more representative system of government. In the entire record of the last decades of tsarist power, I can think of no mistakes more calamitous than these.

There was, of course, eventually, the Duma; and it was, as an institution, not really so bad as it has often been portrayed. Its initial members could, as Vasilii Maklakov pointed out, have made much better use of it than they actually did. The franchise was indeed a limited one, but it was not so severely limited as to prevent both First and Second Dumas from being violently oppositional, and even extensively revolutionary, in spirit. Nor can I develop any lively sympathy for the great unhappiness manifested by the Cadets over the fact that the Duma was not given the right to appoint and control the government. For an American, in particular, it is hard to regard a fusing of the legislative and executive powers as absolutely essential to a sound political system. But leaving aside the adequacy of the arrangements governing the constitution and functioning of the Duma, it Is obvious that the granting of it by Nicholas II came far too late and in precisely the wrong way—under pressure, that is, and with obvious reluctance and suspicion on his part. Given the situation that existed at that particular moment, it was natural enough for him to do so. There could have been no more than a minority of the members of the First Duma whose political aspirations, if satisfied, would not have ended in the violent destruction of the autocracy; and the tsar understood this very well. And yet it was Nicholas himself, his father, and his grandfather who were responsible for the fact that this was the way things were. Had they acted earlier—and the 1860s would not have been too soon—they might have had a different, more respectful, and less menacing sort of a parliamentary body before them. And the difference would, I think, have been decisive. The conservative and liberal intelligentsia, from which the dynasty really had something to hope, might have rallied to its side and the radical revolutionary movement, from which it could expect nothing good, would have been split. The effect of waiting forty years and establishing the Duma in 1906 instead of in the 1860s was just the opposite: it unified the radical-revolutionary movement against the regime and split the conservative and liberal intelligentsia, whose united support was essential if the dynasty was to survive.

It was true, of course, that to grant a parliamentary institution would have involved at any time on the tsar's part a readiness to share the power which the dynasty had previously exercised absolutely. But in the mid-nineteenth century, there were still people on the other side who would have been willing to content themselves with this sharing of supreme power. By 1906 there was practically no one left, not only in the revolutionary movement but among the liberals as well, who did not insist, by implication at least, on destroying the tsar's powers entirely rather than just sharing in them. It was the destruction of the autocracy as such, not really its limitation, that was implicit in the demands of the First Duma for a responsible government, for control in effect of the police, and above all for a general amnesty.

In the 1860s the dynasty might still have had before it, in a parliamentary institution, people who were anxious to see it succeed in its tasks and willing to help it do so. By 1906 it was confronted, in every political party to the Left of the Octobrists and even partly in the ranks of that grouping, not by people who constituted a loyal opposition, not by people who really wanted the dynasty to succeed with the tasks of modernization to which I referred earlier on, not by people who wished to have a share in the dynasty's power, but by rivals for the exercise of that power, by people whose chief grievance against the regime was not that it was dilatory or incompetent but that it stood in their own path, whose complaint was not really that the autocracy misruled Russia, but that it prevented *them* from ruling —or misruling, as history would probably have revealed—in its place. With Unkovskii and his associates in 1862, Alexander II might, it seems to me, have come to some sort of political terms. With Miliukov and his associates, decorous and mild-mannered as they outwardly were, this same possibility no longer existed. It had become by that time a case of *kto kogo* (who whom)—either the tsar or they. Yet without their help, as February 1917 revealed, the dynasty itself could not be defended.

In the mid-nineteenth century, in other words, the autocracy could still have opted for the status of a limited monarchy. In 1906 this option no longer remained open to it. And the failure to accept it when it *had been* open left only one possibility, which was its final and total destruction.

This great deficiency—namely the denial of political expression— must be clearly distinguished from the question of physical cruelty and oppression in the treatment of the population. It was suggested, at the outset of this discussion, that it was a misimpression that the regime was intolerably cruel and despotic in this respect. This is, of course, a controversial statement; and I do not wish to make it unnecessarily so. I am well aware of the fact that the tsarist police and prison authorities, as well as the military courts, were guilty of many acts of stupidity, injustice, and cruelty. I am not unmindful of the observations of my distinguished namesake, the elder George Kennan, on the exile system in Siberia. But the standards of the present age are different from those of the latter—unfortunately so. The tsarist autocracy did not engage in the sort of prophylactic terror— the punishment of great numbers of the innocent as a means of frightening the potentially guilty—of which we have seen so much in our age. Its treatment of many individual revolutionaries, including incidentally Chernyshevskii, seems to have been, if anything, on the lenient side. The censorship was irritating and often silly, but it was not sufficiently severe to prevent the appearance in Russia of a great critical literature. Most important of all, one has to distinguish, when one speaks of police terrorism, between that element of it that is spontaneous and the element that is provoked. That the Russian revolutionaries behaved provocatively, and deliberately so, on countless occasions is something that few, I think, would deny. Now, it is a habit of political regimes to resist their own violent overthrow; it is something to be expected of them. Stolypin used harsh measures—yes—in suppressing the disorders of the period following the war with Japan, but measures no more harsh than the situation required from the standpoint of the regime. Had there been a time in the history of the United States when political assassinations—assassinations of public officials—were running at the rate of more than one and a half thousand per annum, as was the case in Russia in 1906, I rather shudder to think what would have been the reaction of the official establishment here. In situations of this nature, where there is a constant interaction between the strivings of revolutionaries and the defensive efforts of a political regime, the question of responsibility for violence becomes a matter of the chicken and the egg. If one abstracts from the behavior of the regime in the administration of justice and in the imposition of political discipline that element that was provided by provocation from the revolutionary side, then the use of police terror cannot be regarded as more than a minor determinant of the alienation of great sectors of society that underlay the breakdown of 1917.

So much for the denial of parliamentary government and political liberty. A second crucial deficiency of the autocracy was one that it shared with a large part of upper-class Russian society, and with a portion of the lower classes as well, and that was for this reason not only much more difficult to recognize at the time but has been more difficult of recognition even in the light of history. This was extreme nationalism—that romantic, linguistic nationalism that was the disease of the age.

The spirit of modern nationalism was pernicious for the Russian autocracy for two reasons: first, because it reflected itself unfortunately on the treatment by the tsar's government of the national minorities; but second, because it led to an adventurous foreign policy, far beyond what the capacities of the Russian state at that time could support.

In an empire of which nearly half, or something more than one half (depending on where the Ukrainians were ranked) of the population was made up of national minorities, an absolute monarchy was confronted, in the age of nationalism, with a basic choice. It could make political concessions to the Great-Russian plurality and thus at least keep the strongest single national element firmly associated with it in an effort to hold down the minorities; or, if it did not wish to do this, it could employ a light touch with the minorities, do everything possible to reconcile them to the Russian state, and play them off against the potentially rebellious central Great-Russian group. The tsar's government did neither. Operating against the background of a sullen Russian peasantry, a frustrated Russian upper class, and a lower-class Russian intelligentsia veritably seething with sedition, it set about to treat the national minorities in the name of Russian nationalism with an utterly senseless provocation of their national cultures and feelings and a rigid repression of all their efforts to establish a separate national political identity. This was a policy calculated to make sure that if there were anyone among the minority elements who was not already alienated from the autocracy by virtue of its general social and political policies, he would sooner or later be brought into the opposition by the offense to his national feelings. . . .

The second manner in which the disease of extreme nationalism manifested itself in tsarist policy was, as already noted, in the field of foreign affairs. Particularly was this true under Nicholas II. The origins of the war with Japan were, from the Russian side, disreputable and inexcusable. There was no need for this involvement; it could easily have been avoided; the attendant military effort was clearly beyond the physical resources of the country at that moment of rapid economic and social transition; and the folly of the venture from the domestic-political standpoint was at once apparent in the events of the Revolution of 1905. . . .

The Franco-Russian alliance served, in Russia's case, a financial interest but not really a political one. The kaiser's Germany may have been a threat to Britain; it was not in great measure a threat to Russia. Some of the more sober statesmen, Witte and even the otherwise nationalistic Stolypin, saw this, and would have tried betimes to avoid the catastrophe to which this alliance, which took no proper account of Russia's internal conditions, was leading. But it was the pervasive nationalism of the age that defeated them; and I am inclined, for this reason, to attribute to that nationalism a major role in the causes of the final collapse of the regime. A tsarist autocracy that saw things clearly and wished to exert itself effectively in the interest of its own preservation would have practiced a rigid abstention from involvement in world political problems generally, and from exhausting foreign wars in particular, at that crucial juncture in its domestic-political development.

The third of the weaknesses of the autocracy that I should like to mention was the personality of the last Russian tsar himself. Poorly educated, narrow in intellectual horizon, a wretchedly bad judge of people, isolated from Russian society at large, in contact only with the most narrow military and bureaucratic circles, intimidated by the ghost of his imposing father and the glowering proximity of his numerous gigantic uncles, helpless under the destructive influence of his endlessly unfortunate wife: Nicholas II was obviously inadequate to the demands of his exalted position; and this was an inadequacy for which no degree of charm, of courtesy, of delicacy of manner, could compensate. It is ironic that this man, who fought so tenaciously against the granting of a constitution, had many of the qualities that would have fitted him excellently for the position of a constitutional monarch and practically none of those that were needed for the exercise of that absolute power to which he stubbornly clung. Time and time again, in the record of his reign, one finds the evidence of his short-sightedness and his lack of grasp of the realities of the life of the country interfering with the political process in ways that were for him veritably suicidal. True, he was the product of the vagaries of genetics; another tsar might not have been so bad. But the experience of his reign only illustrates the fact that these accidents of royal birth, tolerable in earlier centuries where the feudal nobility bore a good portion of the load, and tolerable again in the modern age wherever the main burden is borne or shared by parliamentary institutions, were not tolerable in the age of economic development and mass education and in a political system where the monarch claimed the rights of personal absolutism.

So much for the leading and crucial weaknesses of the autocracy itself in the final decades of its power. Mention must be made, in conclusion, of the Russian revolutionary movement. It was, of course, not the revolutionary parties that overthrew the autocracy in 1917. Nevertheless, there were indirect ways in which their existence and activity affected the situation of the regime; and these must be briefly noted.

First of all, by providing a somewhat romantic alternative to any association with the governing establishment, the revolutionary movement drew many talented youths into an attitude of defiance and revolutionary disobedience to it, thereby impoverishing it in talent, energy, and intelligence. Every time that a young person of ability was drawn into the ranks of its revolutionary opponents, the bureaucracy, deprived of these sources of recruitment, became just that more stupid, unimaginative, and inept.

Second, there was the effect the revolutionary elements had on the development of governmental policy. They obviously had no interest in seeing the modernization of the country proceed successfully under tsarist tutelage, and they did as little as they could to support it. I find it significant that more useful social legislation appears to have been passed by the two final and supposedly reactionary Dumas than by the first two relatively liberal, and partially revolutionary, ones. But more important still was the influence of the revolutionaries in frightening the regime out of possible initiatives in the field of political reform. These revolutionary parties and groupings had, as a rule, no interest in seeing genuine progress made in the creation of liberal institutions. Their aim was generally not to reform the system but to cause it to fall and to replace it. For this reason, the more the regime could be provoked into stupid, self-defeating behavior, the better from their standpoint. They often found themselves, in this respect, sharing the same aspirations and purposes as the extreme right wing of the political spectrum, which also—though for other reasons—did not wish to see any liberalization of the autocracy. And in this respect one has to concede to the revolutionary movement a series of important successes. In one instance after another where there appeared to be a possibility of political liberalization or where the pressures in this direction were intense the timely intervention of revolutionary activity of one sort or another sufficed to assure that no progress should be made. . . .

The War and the Final Crisis

So much, then, for the major weaknesses, failures, and strains that entered into the undermining of the tsarist system of power. It remains only to note the manner in which the effect of all of them was magnified by the world war that began in 1914: magnified to a point where the system could no longer stand the strain. Wartime patriotic fervor, engulfing the liberal-parliamentary circles even more hopelessly than the government itself, brought them in at this point as critics of the government on new grounds: on the grounds that it was not *sufficiently* nationalistic, not *sufficiently* inspired and determined in its conduct of the war effort. And to this there was now added the quite erroneous but heady and dangerous charge that it was pro-German and even treasonable in its relations to the enemy. These charges were utilized by the liberal-parliamentary circles as the excuse for setting up new organizational entities, such as the various war industry councils, which were able to function as rival authorities to the governmental bureaucracy, to provide channels for political activity hostile to the regime, and eventually to contribute significantly to the circumstances surrounding its collapse. Meanwhile, the strictly military aspects of the war effort had a whole series of effects—such as the weakening by losses in battle of the loyal portion of the officer's corps, the stationing of undisciplined garrisons in the vicinity of the capital city, the removal of the tsar himself to field headquarters, and so on—that were to have important connotations, unfavorable to the security of the regime, at the moment of supreme trial. In a number of ways, furthermore, the war effort exacerbated relations between the government and members of the national minorities, who for obvious reasons did not always share the Russian emotional commitment to the war. Finally, not perhaps as a consequence of the war (this is hard to judge), but certainly simultaneously with it, there were the grotesque developments in the tsar's own personal situation,

particularly the ripening and the denouement of the Rasputin affair
—developments that finally succeeded in alienating from his cause
not only large elements of the immediate bureaucratic and military
entourage that had constituted his last comfort and protection, but
even a portion of the imperial family itself, thus completing his isolation and removing, or disqualifying, his last potential defenders.

Conclusions

Prior to the undertaking of this review, I was inclined to feel that
had the war not intervened, the chances for survival of the autocracy
and for its gradual evolution into a constitutional monarchy would not
have been bad. On reviewing once more the events of these last
decades, I find myself obliged to question that opinion. Neither the
tardiness in the granting of political reform, nor the excesses of an
extravagant and foolish nationalism, nor the personal limitations of
the imperial couple began with the war or were primarily responses
to the existence of the war. None of the consequences of these deficiencies were in process of any significant correction as the war
approached. The spectacle of the final years of tsardom prior to 1914
is that of an impressive program of social, economic, and cultural
modernization of a great country being conducted, somewhat incongruously, under the general authority of a governmental system that
was itself in the advanced stages of political disintegration. The
successes in the field of modernization might indeed, if allowed to
continue, have brought Russia rapidly and safely into the modern age.
It is doubtful that they could for long have overbalanced the serious
deficiencies of the political system or averted the consequences to
which they were—even as war broke out—inexorably leading.

Bernard Pares

RASPUTIN AND THE EMPRESS ALEXANDRA

The English-speaking world owes much of its knowledge about Russia to the indefatigable enthusiasm, energy, and intelligence of Sir Bernard Pares (1867–1949). Besides teaching almost continuously from 1908 to 1949 at the Universities of Liverpool and London, and in the United States, he was attached to the Russian army from 1914–1917, visited Russia many times, directed the School of Slavonic and East European Studies, and found time to write and translate numerous excellent works on Russia. In the article here excerpted, Pares describes the destructive influence of the imperial court and its chief actors.

The publication of the letters of the tsaritsa to her husband for the first time showed in black and white Rasputin's enormous political significance. But those who took the trouble to wade through that mass of loose English were probably too overcome by the sweep of the vast tragedy to realize at first the unique importance of the letters as historical material. It is to this aspect of the subject that this article is devoted.

The Rasputin tragedy passed at the time behind closed doors, except for Rasputin's own entire indifference to public scandal. By now almost every one of the persons who could give valuable first-hand evidence on the subject has said his word. M. Gilliard, tutor to the tsarevich, a man of great good sense and good feeling, has given a beautiful picture of the home life of the imperial family, the accuracy of which has been confirmed both by the Provisional and the Soviet governments. We have for what it is worth the Apologia of Madame Vyrubov, the only person who was with the family continually, and Rasputin's chosen go-between for his communications with the empress. A slighter record is given by another friend of the empress, Madame Lili Dehn. The head of the Police Department, Beletsky, has told a typical story of ministerial intrigue centered round Rasputin. The French ambassador, M. Paléologue, has issued

From Sir Bernard Pares, "Rasputin and the Empress: Authors of the Russian Collapse." Reprinted by permission from *Foreign Affairs*, October 1927. Copyright by the Council on Foreign Relations, Inc., New York.

a current record of events, evidently touched up for publication, which gives the atmosphere of grand ducal and higher society, but also connects Rasputin at point after point with political events of the most critical importance. Now we have also the important record of the president of the Third and Fourth Dumas, Mr. Michael Rodzianko, prepared in exile without many materials but preserving the details of his various conversations with the emperor, which were evidently written down with care at the time.

Rasputin, who was under fifty at the time of his death, was born in the village of Pokrovskoe on the Tura, near Tobolsk in Siberia. Like many peasants he had no surname; Rasputin, which means "dissolute," was a nickname early given him by his fellow peasants. He suddenly went off to the Verkhne-Turski Monastery near his home, where were several members of the *Khlysty,* a sect who mingled sexual orgies with religious raptures and who were emphatically condemned by the Orthodox Church. On his return he became a *strannik,* or roving man of God, not a monk, not in orders, but one with a self-given commission from heaven, such as have often appeared in Russian history, especially at critical times. Meanwhile, he lived so scandalous a life that his village priest investigated it with care. That he habitually did much the same things as the *Khlysty* is conclusively proved; but that he was actually one of the sect has not been definitely established. Certainly to the end of his life he alternated freely between sinning and repenting, and professed the view that great sins made possible great repentances. He seduced a large number of women, several of whom boasted of the fact, or repented and confessed it to others. The village priest reported him to Bishop Antony of Tobolsk, who made a more thorough inquiry and found evidence which he felt bound to hand over to the civil authorities. During the inquiry Rasputin disappeared. He went to St. Petersburg, and as a great penitent secured the confidence of Bishop Theophan, head of the Petersburg Religious Academy, and confessor to the empress, a man whose personal sanctity has been recognized by everyone. He secured also the patronage of the Grand Duchess Militsa, daughter of King Nicholas of Montenegro, a lady with a strong taste for the sensational, and also that of her future brother-in-law, the Grand Duke Nicholas. It was these who introduced him to the palace.

The Empress Alexandra, formerly Princess Alix of Hesse Darmstadt, was a daughter of the English Princess Alice and a favorite
granddaughter of Queen Victoria, from whom she may be said to
have taken all the ordinary part of her mental environment. The
unusual feature in her character was her strong mysticism. Her
family was scourged with the hemophilic ailment; all the male children of her sister Princess Irene of Prussia suffered from it. It does
not appear in females, but is transmitted by them to males. Its effect
is that the slightest accident may set up internal bleeding, which
there is no known way of arresting. Children suffering from it may
die at any moment, and on almost any occasion, though if they live
to the age of thirteen they may in some measure overcome it; Rasputin prophesied such an issue for the Tsarevich Alexis. Much of
the tragedy in the position of the empress lay in the fact that after
she had given birth to four charming and healthy daughters, her
only son, the long-desired heir to the throne, suffered from this
scourge, and that she well knew that his disease came through
herself.

In every other domestic respect the family was ideally happy.
Husband and wife literally adored each other; the children were
equally united with them and with each other. The empress was the
pillar of the house, their actual nurse and attendant in time of
sickness. She brought them up entirely in English ideas; they had
cold baths and slept on camp beds; they talked largely in English.
The family as a whole, in its clean-minded life, represented a veritable oasis in the corruption which was so prevalent in higher Russian society, and we may imagine that with that world this aspect of
their isolation was one of their chief offenses. They lived almost as
much apart from it as if they were settlers in Canada.

The empress's nature was singularly narrow and obstinate; Rodzianko rightly describes her as "essentially a creature of will." She
had a fondness for her first "little home" at Hesse Darmstadt, but
a strong antipathy for the Emperor William; indeed the Prussian
monarchy found many of its bitterest critics among the smaller reign-
ing German families. She regarded herself as essentially English,
but she had frankly embraced the country of her adored husband,
and more than that, she had embraced the Russian autocracy. She
repeatedly speaks of herself as "anointed by God," and once as

"Russia's mother." There is on record a conversation between her and Queen Victoria in which she put very strongly this difference between the English monarchy and the Russian. For her, Russia was the Russian people, above all the peasantry. Society she identified with the general corruption which she saw around her. She was always, we may be sure, entirely against the Duma and against the concession of a Russian constitution. Any such suggestion she regarded as a direct wrong to her son, and denounced in the strongest language.

When she married, three of her husband's last five ancestors had perished by assassination. Her first appearance before the Russian public was in the funeral procession of her father-in-law, and the reign from start to finish was soaked in an atmosphere of fatality. She had an antipathy to all court ceremonies. The slightest accident filled her with apprehension. In the period when her most ardent desire was to give an heir to the throne, she met in France a charlatan soul doctor, Philippe, who was brought to Russia but expelled, despite her protection, for meddling in politics during the Japanese War. Philippe gave her a bell as a token that she was to scare away all other counsellors from her husband. She refers to this several times in her letters. Bishop Theophan, when he introduced Rasputin to the court, appears only to have thought that he was substituting a Russian influence for a foreign.

Rasputin at first kept quiet and studied his ground. He saw the imperial family infrequently, and his presence was sought only to comfort the nerves of the empress and her husband, and to reassure them as to the health of their son. M. Gilliard, who was nearly all day with his charge, saw him but once. The meetings ordinarily took place at the little house of Madame Vyrubov outside the palace. Soon, however, Rasputin went on openly with his earlier scandalous life. Toward the end of 1911 sensational happenings attracted public attention to him. Among his former supporters had been the robust bishop of Saratov, Hermogen, a very strong monarchist, and the Monk Heliodor, a notable and popular preacher, also very conservative. An attempt was made to push through the Synod an authorization to ordain Rasputin a priest. This was defeated in view of his well-known dissoluteness. Hermogen was one of its most vigorous opponents. Direct interference from the court obtained at least a partial reversion of the decision of the Synod. Hermogen again was most vigorous in his protests. He and Heliodor, acting together, arranged a meeting with Rasputin which resulted in threats on both sides; Rasputin threw himself on the bishop as if to strangle him, and when pulled off departed threatening vengeance. Hermogen was then banished to his diocese by order of the emperor and, as he still refused to submit, both he and Heliodor were ultimately relegated to monasteries. The emperor had acted illegally in imposing such a sentence on a bishop without trial by a church court.

This was not the end. Shortly afterwards one Novoselov, a specialist on Russian sects who lectured at the Religious Academy near Moscow, issued a pamphlet giving full details of Resputin's seductions, which seemed to be numberless. The book was immediately suppressed, but was widely quoted by Russian newspapers beginning with "The Voice of Moscow," the organ of Guchkov. He was leader of the Duma, and for a short time its president, and he had at first hoped to play the part of tribune of the people at the palace and to carry the emperor with him for reform. But he had been severely rebuffed, and chose this ground for attack. The papers were now forbidden to speak of Rasputin. At this time the preliminary censorship no longer existed, and such orders by the government were therefore illegal. Fines could be imposed after publication, but fines in this case the newspapers were ready to pay. Guchkov led a debate in the Duma on this infraction of the law. Rodzianko, who tried to limit and moderate the debate as much as possible, obtained an audience from the emperor, and speaking with absolute plainness laid a number of data before him. "I entreat you," he ended, "in the name of all that is holy for you, for Russia, for the happiness of your successor, drive off from you this filthy adventurer, disperse the growing apprehensions of people loyal to the throne." "He is not here now," said the emperor. Rodzianko took him up, "Let me tell everyone that he will not return." "No," said Nicholas, "I cannot promise you that, but I fully believe all you say. I feel your report was sincere, and I trust the Duma because I trust you." Next day he authorized Rodzianko to make a full investigation, and the plentiful material in the possession of the Synod was handed over to him. The empress tried to get these papers back, but Rodzianko gave a stout refusal to her messenger, saying that she was as much the subject of the emperor as himself. When he was ready with his conclusions he asked for another audience, but Nicholas put him off. He threatened to resign, and was invited to send in a report. Later he heard that it had been studied by Nicholas and the grand duke of Hesse, brother of the empress, while they were together at Livadia in Crimea. The grand duke, as is known, in no way supported the attitude of the empress.

For the time Rasputin disappeared. In the summer of 1912, while the imperial family was at a hunting box in Poland, the tsarevich fell on the gunwale of a boat; the bruise set up internal bleeding and for some weeks his life was despaired of. All the family were distracted with grief. The best doctors declared themselves impotent. The empress then ordered a telegram to be sent to Rasputin, who replied: "This illness is not dangerous; don't let the doctors worry him." From the time of the reception of the telegram the boy rapidly recovered. There is no doubt as to these facts, which were testified to unanimously by various witnesses. Nor is there evidence of any kind for the supposition that the illness was artificially created.

Stolypin before his death in 1911 had reported in the strongest language against Rasputin. The attitude of his successor, Count Kokovtsev, was practically the same. The empress when she met him turned her back on him, and he was curtly dismissed from the post of premier in January 1914. The aged Goremykin who succeeded him, and who possessed throughout the complete confidence of the empress, summed up the question to Rodzianko in the words, "C'est une question clinique."

When war broke out, Rasputin was lying dangerously ill at Tobolsk, where one of his female victims had tried to assassinate him. He sent a telegram to Madame Vyrubov, "Let papa (the emperor) not plan war. It will be the end of Russia and of all of us. We shall be destroyed to the last man." The emperor was very annoyed at this, and never was he more at one with his people than when he appeared on the balcony of the Winter Palace and the vast crowd kneeled in front of him. For the first period of the war the empress devoted herself to hospital work, and spared herself no labor or unpleasantness in the care of the sick; on matters of administration she only ventured tentative and timid opinions.

The discovery of gross munition scandals in the early summer of 1915 roused a wave of national indignation, and seemed at first to

FIGURE 1. Tsar Nicholas II and Wife Alexandra. (*The Bettmann Archive*)

bring Russia nearer to an effective constitution than ever before. It
must be understood that the constitutional question was still unsettled. The Duma had come to stay, as even the empress at this time
admitted. In spite of a manipulated and limited franchise, it had
more and more come to represent the nation. The limits on its com-
petence, however, remained; it had once succeeded by moral pressure in removing a minister (Timiriazev), but the ministers were not
responsible to it. As is clear from the emperor's talks with Rodzianko,
he certainly did not recognize his famous edict of October 30, 1905,

which gave full legislative powers to the Duma, as the grant of a constitution, and the Duma's rights had been whittled down since then both by limitations imposed at the outset in the fundamental laws of 1906, and also in practice ever since.

The emperor was in entire agreement with his people as to the needs of his army. He appealed for the utmost efforts, and at Rodzianko's request he established a War Industries Committee on which the Duma was to be represented. The Alliance itself worked in the same direction, for democratic France and England desired to see as hearty as possible a cooperation of the Russian people in the prosecution of the war. The war minister, Sukhomlinov, who had been at least criminally negligent, was dismissed; the emperor also got rid of those of his ministers who were at best half-hearted about the war, Nicholas Maklakov, Shcheglovitov and Sabler, and replaced them by men who had the confidence of the country. It looked as if the movement would go a good deal further. The bulk of the Duma, containing nearly all its best brains, had practically formed into one party under the name of the Progressive Bloc, and it asked for the definite adoption of the principle that the ministry as a whole should be such as to possess the public confidence. Those of the ministers who were of the same view, at this time a majority in the cabinet, went even further; they wrote a letter to the sovereign asking that the aged and obviously incompetent prime minister should be changed. If things had not stopped here, Russia would have done what all her Allies were doing at the same time, namely have formed a national and patriotic Coalition Ministry; but, beyond that, she would also have completed the process towards a constitution which, though often interrupted, had been going on since the emancipation of the serfs in 1861.

It was here that the empress intervened, with the assistance and advice of Rasputin. She got the emperor back to Tsarskoe Selo for several weeks and persuaded him to dismiss from the chief command the Grand Duke Nicholas, who was popular with the Duma and the country. This both she and Rasputin regarded as the most essential victory of all. She then obtained the prorogation of the Duma, and its president and the delegates of other public bodies who begged the emperor to reverse this decision were met with the most chilling refusal. She then persuaded her husband that all the ministers who had, so to speak, struck work against Premier Goremykin should be replaced as soon as possible. We thus enter the critical period which changed the war from being an instrument for producing a Russian constitution into the principal cause of the Russian Revolution. From now till the final collapse Russia was governed by the empress, with Rasputin as her real prime minister.

Two incidents in the summer and autumn sharpened the conflict between the court and the public over the influence of Rasputin. In the summer Rasputin varied his dissolute orgies with a severe course of repentance and visited the tombs of the Patriarchs in Moscow. Presumably he overdid the repentance, for he followed it up with a visit to a notorious resort, the Yar, where he got drunk and behaved in the most scandalous way. His proceedings were recorded in detail by the police, who were present, and were reported by them to one of the most loyal servants of the emperor, General Dzhunkovsky, at this time commander of the palace guard. Dzhunkovsky presented the report without comment to the emperor. Next day he was dismissed from all appointments, and the protest of another intimate friend of the Emperor, Prince Orlov, had the same result. The empress flatly refused to believe such reports and persisted in regarding them as machinations of the police.

In 1915 the emperor was starting with his son for the front when the tsarevich was taken violently ill in the train, which thereupon returned to Tsarskoe Selo. Rasputin was summoned at once and from the time of his visit the boy recovered, as in 1912. Rasputin often played on this theme. Once he fell into fervent prayer and when he had ended declared that he had saved the emperor from assassination. He made many happy guesses, some of which were almost uncanny. On the other hand, the empress herself gives several instances, some of them conspicuous, of predictions which went all wrong.

Neither the emperor nor the empress had at this time any thought whatsoever of a separate peace; the emperor, we know, never entertained such an idea even after abdication. Up till December 30, the date of the last of the empress's letters, we know that she regarded victory in the war as a foregone conclusion, that her chief anxiety was that Russian influence might be overshadowed by British when the victorious peace was made, and that her main desire was that the victory of Russia should be entirely the triumph of her husband. Nicholas at times spoke tentatively of reforms, but throughout this period insisted that they could only follow after the war.

In going to the front the emperor had *ipso facto* more or less abandoned the administration to his wife, who definitely describes herself as his "wall in the rear," speaks even of "wearing the trousers" in the struggle against internal enemies, recalls the time when Catherine the Great (who had much more drastically disposed of her husband) received the ministers, and in the end is absolutely certain that she is "saving Russia." Rasputin, who had on several occasions pushed suggestions as to the war, gradually became the ultimate factor in all decisions. Practically no minister could be appointed except on his recommendation or after accepting allegiance to him.

He initiated the period of his power by making himself absolutely supreme in all church affairs. Let me sum up his principal achievements in this domain. He dismisses an adverse minister of religion, Samarin, who had been the elected marshal of the Moscow nobility; he dismisses his successor, Volzhin, appointed at his own desire; he practically appoints a third minister, Raiev; he commands a public prayer-giving throughout the country, insisting that the order should not pass through the Synod; he appoints as metropolitan of Petrograd, Pitirim, a contemptible sycophant of his own; he negatives a project of the Synod to create seven Metropolitan Sees in Russia; through one of his subordinates and in violation of all rules he creates a new saint, St. John of Tobolsk.

But there was hardly any other department of administration with which he did not interfere. He settles at various times and in various ways the administration of the food supply; he orders an absurdly simplified way of dealing with the question of rations; he confers repeatedly with the minister of finance, whose resignation he at first demands and then defers, and he insists on the issue of an enormous loan. He secures that the whole passenger transport of the country should be suspended for six days for the passage of food—a measure which is made futile by the failure to collect the food supplies at the proper places for transport. He repeatedly interferes both in military appointments and in military operations; he secures the suspension of Sukhomlinov's trial; he secures tne dismissal of his successor, Polivanov, who according to all military evidence, including that of Hindenburg, in his few months of office brought about a wonderful recovery of the efficiency of the Russian army; he orders an offensive; he countermands an offensive; he dictates the tactics to be followed in the Carpathians; he even demands to be informed in advance of all military operations, and to know the exact day on which they are to begin, in order that he may decide the issue by his prayers; he arranges the details of the future military entry into Constantinople. He removes the foreign minister, Sazonov, who in Russia was the main arch of the alliance, the trusted friend of the British and French ambassadors. He adjourns and opposes any execution of the emperor's promise to give autonomy to Poland. He dictates telegrams to the King of Serbia and to the King of Greece.

*   *   *

While the empress's letters wipe clean away all the scandalous charges made against her personal character, while they show that up to Rasputin's death she was a fervent Russian patriot who had no thought of a separate peace with Germany, they also prove that she and, through her, Rasputin were the prime authors of the col lapse of the empire and of Russia.

The Bolshevist leaders were far away in Switzerland or Canada, and their not numerous followers were out of the picture. The leaders of the Duma, largely in answer to the pressure of Russia's Allies, were doing all that they could to postpone the explosion till after the war. Up to the intervention of the fatal pair in the late summer of 1915, it seemed that the war itself was only bringing nearer what practically all Russia desired. Apart from the terrible depression that followed on the disillusionment of 1915, Russia was then confronted with a monstrous regime which would have seemed impossible in some small duchy in the Middle Ages. In the midst of a world-wide struggle, in a time of the closest collaboration with the best brains of Western statesmanship, the Russian ministers were selected by an ignorant, blind, and hysterical woman on the test of their subservience to an ignorant, fantastic, and debauched adventurer, a test which they could only satisfy by open-eyed self-abasement or at the best by cynical passivity, and the supreme commands of the adventurer permeated every detail of government in every branch of the administration. Meanwhile, in his drunken revels he babbled publicly of his influence over the empress, held a daily *levée* attended by the worst financial swindlers, and preached views both on the war and on the government of the country, which were shared only by the avowed friends of Germany, who evidently had easier access to him than any one else.

It was under the leadership of such a government that the lives of millions of peasants were thrown into the furnace of the World War.

Peter I. Lyashchenko
ECONOMIC AND SOCIAL CONSEQUENCES OF THE WAR

Peter I. Lyashchenko, a "legal Marxist" and a recognized economic scholar under the imperial regime, continued his studies as a Soviet citizen after 1917. A doctor of political economy and statistics, he taught at several Soviet universities and was for many years Corresponding Member of the USSR Academy of Sciences and Member of the Ukrainian Academy of Sciences. His numerous articles and books brought him many honors, including a Stalin Prize received in 1949. The work from which the following excerpt is taken was first published in 1939 and received official approval for use as a textbook in Soviet institutions of higher education. As the student will see, it is very much a Marxian interpretation.

The War and the Militarization of Russian Industry

The war disrupted both industry and agriculture by altering all normal conditions of production, demand, export, manpower, and other factors. Owing to the heavy mobilization of workers, the output of industries working for the free market began to decline seriously by early 1915.

The position of industry was affected quite radically by the militarization of industry and by the conversion of plants to war requirements, which was at first performed through the private initiative of the entrepreneurs interested in obtaining profitable government orders, and afterward by official compulsion. By the autumn of 1914, military orders had absorbed all facilities of the larger metal-processing and metal-construction plants: the Sormovo, the Bryansk, the Kolomna, and others. As a result, production of locomotives at the Sormovo plant, for example, dropped from 117 in 1913 to 64 in 1916 and to 55 in 1917. From 1915 all more or less suitable metal-processing plants began to be converted for war production, with little quantitative or qualitative results, however, owing to the inflexibility and poor technical equipment of these plants. The same was attempted, with even less success, in the chemical industry, which was converted to the production of explosives and similar military supplies.

These were followed by the leather and shoe industry, and the cotton and wool industries, which were adapted to the production of supplies ordered by the military commissaries.

The results of the first year of war production were quite depressing. By the spring of 1915 it had become obvious that Russian industry was incapable of coping with the tremendous military problems imposed by the world imperialist war. . . .

. . . The low technical equipment of the country's industry, especially in the production of machines and weapons, precluded the possibility of effecting the necessary retooling of its plants for new types of production once imports of machinery from abroad ceased. On the eve of the war, of a total annual consumption of 720 million rubles in technical equipment of capitalist industry, up to 37 percent was satisfied by imports from abroad, and in the case of industrial machinery, as much as 58 percent. In addition the acute shortage of qualified workers, the congestion of transport, the critical condition of the fuel supply, and the general disruption that was steadily spreading throughout all economic and public life completed the hopelessness of the situation. As a result many enterprises were forced to liquidate, and although war conditions gave rise to new industrial undertakings, the number of liquidated companies exceeded the number of those newly established.

Thus 350 enterprises closed as early as 1914 compared to 215 new establishments. In 1915 these figures were 573 closed and 187 newly opened, in 1916, 298 closed and 276 opened, and in 1917, 541 closed compared with 264 opened. The militarization of industry and "survival of the fittest" among enterprises naturally resulted in further concentration of industry. Hence some quantitative successes were achieved in the increase of production. The "war" industries succeeded in increasing their production somewhat by 1916. According to the industrialists' own figures, in one of the main regions engaged in "defense work," the fifteen provinces of the central-industrial region, the number of workers increased by 19 percent in 1916 compared with the prewar period, and in the metal-processing industry of that region specifically, the increase amounted to 190 percent, chiefly as a result of attracting unskilled manpower. The situation was similar in the metal-processing industries of the Petrograd and the Ural regions. Conditions were much worse, however, in the branches of industry not working on war orders. . . .

The most catastrophic influence upon the national economy and in undermining the country's basic production forces was not so much the decline in output but complete absorption in war production. The militarized industry siphoned from the economic life of the country everything available: metal, fuel, financial resources, and manpower. According to the figures of the War Industries Committee, the country's ferrous metal requirements (which before the war amounted to 305 million poods)[1] in 1915 had to be satisfied with an allocation of 48 million poods for the private market and 15.8 million poods for industrial consumption of the total 241.3 million poods of iron produced. Among the various metal products of mass consumption, structural iron, for example, declined in output from 41 million poods to 15.7 million poods. The amount of orders received by the leading distribution syndicate, Prodamet, declined to 79 million poods of iron products of all types in 1916, and to about 48 million in 1917, compared with 148 million poods in 1913.

[1] One pood equals 36 pounds.—Ed.

The Fuel Crisis

Similar results may be observed in the distribution of fuel. With respect to coal, even the expanded production of the Donets-basin region in 1916 could not cover all requirements because of the elimination of the Polish coal region and of the considerable foreign imports of the prewar period.

Fuel production during the war years was as follows (in million poods):

Years	Coal		Petroleum
	In the Whole Empire	Including the Donets Basin	
1913	2,199	1,560	561
1914	2,181	1,684	550
1915	1,919	1,627	568
1916	2,096	1,751	602

The increased Donets-Basin output was not sufficient to compensate for the loss of the entire output of the Dombrovsky coal basin. In 1913 the latter yielded almost 426 million poods of the total coal output of 2,199 million poods, and in 1916 total production could not be raised above 2,096 million poods. Moreover, although a maximum labor supply was thrown into the Donets coal industry (291,000 persons by January 1917, compared to 168,000 in 1913), production per worker declined by January 1917, to 534 poods a month compared to 764 poods a month in 1913.

The situation with regard to petroleum was somewhat better, but here, too, production was far from adequate. The country's oil resources were exploited wastefully. With the increase of oil production in 1916, drilling work declined. By 1917 the number of active oil wells in the Baku region dropped from 3,600 to 1,500, drilling work having declined to about one-tenth of the usual volume. A similar tendency was apparent in the Grozny and Emba regions.

As a consequence of the war and of the mobilization of industry, the consumption of fuel increased to a great extent, especially because some of the country's major industrial regions formerly operating on imported coal were now drawing upon the domestic coal supply. The greatest detriment to industry was not so much the coal deficit as the policy of fuel distribution. The creation of a Special Council for Fuel, and its policy of fuel allocation based on the establishment of categories of privileged (entirely war-connected) and nonprivileged (all other) consumers, brought the country into a state of critical fuel scarcity.

The Crisis and Decline in Agriculture

Most direct and most depressing was the effect of the war and the heavy manpower mobilization upon agriculture. Compared with the prewar army of 1,370,000 persons, Russia mobilized during the war, up to the middle of 1917, a total of 14 million persons. Moreover the first years of the war withdrew from the national economy about 7.4 million persons, most of them adult workers of the agricultural population. According to the census of 1917, no less than a third, and in some cases as much as one-half, of the total number of peasant households were left without workers in a majority of provinces. The forced labor of the war prisoners and refugees brought little relief both because of its limited supply and because of the casual manner in which this type of manpower was distributed. In all, not more than 10 per cent of the losses in labor was replenished from the above source.

Aside from devouring great masses of human labor power, the war seriously undermined all resources of production in agriculture. As a result of the metal scarcity and the policy of distribution of fuel and metal, the production of agricultural machines and implements was thoroughly disrupted. By the end of 1914 some of the largest farm-machinery plants had reduced their output of machinery to one-third of the prewar level, while in 1916, production in 173 of the largest plants amounted to only 25 percent of the prewar output of farm machines. A majority of these plants was converted to war production, while the remaining plants were allowed only 1.3 million poods of metal in lieu of the 15 million poods previously consumed. With a situation of this type prevailing in the large plants, the position of the small repair and maintenance workshops, the village forges, was obviously desperate: because of a lack of metal and fuel and because of the mobilization of manpower into the army, repair work on farm inventory was completely abandoned. Finally, to this should be added the almost complete halt in agricultural machinery imports, which before the war amounted to 9.7 million poods annually and covered about 50 percent of the country's requirements; in 1915 only some 196,000 poods were imported, and 391,000 poods in 1916. Thus, with domestic production reduced to 20 or 25 percent and imports to 4 percent of the prewar level, only 8 to 9 percent of the requirements for agricultural machinery was satisfied. Together with the loss of manpower in rural economy, this decline in farm machinery supply lowered output very seriously. A change in wartime economic policy during 1915–1917 (in 1917 some 1,726,000 poods of farm machines valued at 21.8 million rubles were imported from abroad) was too late to be effective. In any event it could not actually have saved the situation.

Another rather important factor, likewise affected by the reduction of domestic output as well as imports, was mineral fertilizer requirements. Of a total quantity of 42 million poods consumed before the war, only about 11 million poods were produced within the country, while 31 million poods were imported from abroad, chiefly from Germany. While imports dropped to almost zero, domestic production also declined as a result of the conversion of the chemical industry to war, with the result that in 1916 the market could satisfy no more than a similar 8 to 9 percent of consumption needs. A similar situation existed in the supply of improved seeds, which were hitherto imported from abroad.

Finally, the war dealt a most serious blow to another basic element in agricultural production; namely, livestock. The mass mobilization of horses from the peasant economy, without regard for its minimum needs of draft power, left a number of households either without horses or with too few. Altogether, in the second half of 1917 some 2.1 million head of horses were mobilized, and the total number of work horses in the fifty provinces of European Russia declined from 17.9 million in 1914 to 12.8 million in 1917. No less disastrous was the decline in draft cattle generally, and in oxen particularly, caused by increased requisitioning and slaughtering for the army food supply, which consumed about 18 million head. On the whole, taking into account the cattle lost in the provinces occupied by the German army, the total losses in cattle during the first nineteen months of the war amounted to 26 million head. The effect upon the peasant economy was particularly ruinous, since it was incapable of replenishing its losses in livestock, of replacing its worn-out inventory, or of alleviating the shortage of manpower on the farm.

The result of this situation was a steep decline in farm output of all types, especially in the more important market commodities as well as in grain. By 1917 the acreage of the major grains declined to 78 million *dessyatins* compared to 88.6 million in 1914, or by nearly 10 million *dessyatins*.[2] The edible grains dropped from an acreage of 51.2 million to 45.1 million *dessyatins.* The sharpest decline occurred in the major commercial and producing areas (the North Caucasus and the southern steppe provinces) and in the more valuable commercial grains, wheat and barley. With an inevitable decline in yield, the gross harvest of grain dropped even below the level of the reduced acreage. The total harvest of all grains and potatoes was 7 billion poods during 1909–1913 and 6.9 billion in 1914, declining in 1916 to 5.1 billion, and in 1917 to 5 billion poods; of this, the food grains dropped from a total of 2.8 billion poods during the last peace-time five-year period to 2.2 billion poods for 1916–1917, while the fodder grains (barley and oats) declined from 2.1 billion poods for the prewar period to 1.1 billion poods in 1916.

The exportation of agricultural products was almost completely discontinued. . . .

The Food Crisis

Bearing in mind that before the war grain exports alone withdrew from the national food supply between 600 and 750 million poods, with the complete cessation of exports the above-cited decline in harvest should not have resulted in a food crisis. However, by 1916 the country began to experience a critical food shortage. The causes lay not only in the above-mentioned decline in agricultural production but also in the entire combination of a disrupted economic life and the government's food and supply policy. By directing all industrial production into war channels, the government policy deprived

2 One dessyatin equals 2.7 acres.—Ed.

the village of its supply of goods, of both the producer and consumer type. The village lost interest not only in planting but also in selling its grain, especially when the value of the currency began to decline in the face of an increased output of paper money. Beginning with 1915 a food scarcity was clearly in evidence not only in the cities but in army provisioning as well.

In the fields of civilian food supply and of the regulation of agriculture and the agricultural market, an attempt was made, in view of the impossibility of coping with the difficulties by ordinary measures, to establish the same type of regulating agencies that existed in industry and in transport. In August 1915, a Special Council on Food was established, formally endowed with consultative functions only but in reality invested with very broad, almost dictatorial authority in the person of the president and his local "delegates," the governors.

From this time the food procurement for the population (aside from army procurement, which remained under the control of the military authorities) passed into the hands of the government and partly to the local municipal and rural self-administrative agencies. The centralized government apparatus procured 305 million poods during 1914–1915, 502 million in 1915–1916, and 540 million poods in 1916–1917. In other words the government procurement took away nearly the entire volume of commercial grain, destroying the free grain market. A situation of this type was, however, far from a successful solution of the food crisis. Government procurement was based on a system of fixed farm prices, which, with the depreciation of the currency and the wide divergence between farm prices and the price of industrial goods, was very unsatisfactory from the standpoint of the agricultural producers. After partial requisitioning had also failed to alleviate the situation, it was decided in December 1916 to undertake the compulsory allocation of grain, beginning with a pool of 772 million poods of grain. But this measure was not put into force before the coming of the February Revolution. Upon the testimony of Shingarev, the first minister for food of the Provisional Government, the government had no grain reserves of any kind at its disposal by 1917, and in early March of 1917 "there were moments when the flour supply was sufficient for only a few days in Petrograd and Moscow, while there were sectors of the front with hundreds of thousands of soldiers where the bread supply was sufficient to last no more than half a day."

* * *

The Rising Cost of Living

The decline in agricultural production, the disruption of supply, the reduction in consumer-goods output, and the rapid depreciation of the ruble could not fail to cause a rapid rise in the cost of living affecting all articles of consumption, especially foodstuffs. The burden of the high cost of living was made more real by the fact that the nominal increase in money wages, especially during the first years of the war, lagged far behind the rise of prices. The facts most responsible for this situation were the increased amount of currency in circulation and the depreciation of the paper money.

During the first few months of the war, as early as December 1914, food prices increased by 25 percent compared with the prewar level, while other prices rose by 11 percent. Toward the spring of 1917, grain prices increased by 59 percent and industrial goods by 35 percent. During the second year of the war the price of grain rose by 122 percent and that of industrial goods by 145 percent. Finally, by 1917 prices on all goods increased in the course of one year from 40 to 200 percent. Thus, if we take food prices in Moscow for 1916 as 100, the price index for January 1917 would be: bread, 141; meat, 249; vegetables, 328; milk, 191; dairy products, 238; and so forth. The sharpest increase in food prices occurred in the major industrial and urban centers such as Petrograd, Moscow, and others. In Petrograd, prices in late 1916 increased in comparison with 1914: milk, 150 percent; white bread, 500; butter, 830; shoes and clothing, 400 to 600 percent.

The Condition of the Workers

During the war of 1914–1917 the condition of the workers deteriorated substantially as a result of the gap between the wage level and the rising cost of living, poorer conditions of work, and wartime repression of labor, especially in the militarized enterprises. The workday was nearly everywhere lengthened, as a rule, by the compulsory overtime work necessary for the fulfillment of war orders. The number of rest days was reduced, and sanitary conditions at the plants grew worse as a result of overloading the factories and twenty-four-hour production, which increased sickness as well as accidents among the workers. With a great number of male workers recruited into the army, the manufacturers began to utilize a larger proportion of female and child labor, which, although less trained, was less costly. By 1916, despite the fact that industry had not been able to cope successfully with the huge orders placed by the army, unemployment began to increase not only in the textile industry, for example, but in metallurgical production as well. In 1915 the government organized labor exchanges in Petrograd and several other major centers. But during the nine months of their operation only 237,900 workers of the 313,900 workers offering their services obtained work. The industrialists preferred to hire, outside the labor-exchange channels, the cheaper, though less trained, labor of women and children, while the labor exchanges were accumulating masses of unemployed trained workers.

Wages, nominally increased during wartime, were in reality lagging behind the rise of prices. Average annual wages in the Moscow industrial region were as follows (in rubles):

Years	Average for all Industries	Metal Workers	Textile Workers
1913	218	384	210
1914	221	324	202
1915	248	445	221
1916	406	761	320

The nominal wage of all workers in the Moscow region increased by 86 per cent, that of the metal workers, by 98, and textile workers, by 65.6 per cent, but the price of goods had risen by the end of 1916 by 200 to 300 per cent as compared with 1914, and prices on articles of prime necessity in the worker's consumption rose to five or six times the prewar level. The budgetary costs of the worker as of January 1, 1917, had increased by 294 per cent on an average for all Russia, and by 306 per cent for Moscow, in comparison with 1913.

Hence, despite a nominal increase in wages, the workers were on the verge of starvation in 1916. The attempt to place labor in the war industries on a system of payment in kind by the military authorities, along with other measures of the tsarist regime and the bourgeoisie for "combating the high cost of living," ended in failure. The workers soon began to realize that the solution of their "food problem" was to be found in a revolutionary struggle against tsarism and the imperialistic bourgeoisie.

The Labor Movement During the War Period

The military crisis and the disruption of the capitalist economy, which was turning more and more into a general economic, social, and political crisis, could not avoid intensifying and hastening the process of revolutionizing the toiling masses in general and, of course, the progressive ranks of the workers in particular. The war was, in Lenin's expression, "a mighty accelerator" of the process of revolutionization, despite the great quantitative and qualitative changes that occurred in the composition of the working class during the war.

The mobilization of 14 million peasants and workers for service at the front at once withdrew from production a considerable proportion of workers, frequently those best trained, and occasionally replaced them with politically less advanced elements. But this circumstance, which at times affected production unfavorably, was of tremendous political significance: it intensified the propagandistic work of the mobilized progressive workers at the front. At some plants the very first phases of mobilization withdrew about 40 per cent of the skilled labor. Although the government and the bourgeoisie had regarded mobilization of the workers as a device to discourage their revolutionary activity, economic necessity required that some skilled workers be left behind, especially in enterprises engaged in war production, which became systematic after the inauguration of a system of industrial mobilization.

Of particular political significance was the fact that, with the expansion and new construction of large plants, the concentration of industry continued to increase still further during the war. Thus, of a total of 2.5 million industrial workers on January 1, 1915, small enterprises employing up to 100 persons (78.4 per cent of all enterprises) accounted for only 17.8 per cent of the labor force, while the larger enterprises, employing over 500 workers and constituting only 5.6 per cent of the country's enterprises, employed 56.5 per cent of all workers. These huge enterprises, chiefly in the metal-processing industry, became the labor headquarters for the preparation of the revolution.

During the first years following the declaration of war, mobilization provoked serious strikes and labor demonstrations at Petersburg. Because of the wartime regime, however, the labor movement and its leadership had to prepare a new set of tactics. Consequently, during the very first days of the war a type of propagandist-agitational work came into being, of which Lenin said, "It *alone* will bring the fruits of socialism and the fruits of the revolution." . . .

The rising cost of living and the food crisis could not but serve as revolutionary factors among the masses. The explanation of the political significance of the food problem to the worker became one of the most pertinent and easily understood issues, even for the less progressive masses. Gradually the minor issues of food, the price of bread, and the lack of goods turned into general political discussions concerning the entire system of the social order. In this atmosphere political movements and political demands grew feverishly and matured quickly, although they were still limited in form to economic strikes.

The "food riots" that broke out in Petrograd and Moscow in April 1915, slowly spread to various other centers and acquired a political character, laying the foundation for the future civil war. At that time Lenin already considered it necessary to utilize the food difficulties for spreading revolutionary ideas among the masses, so as to "explain to the masses . . . that we are in the presence of an historical impellent of the greatest force which generates disaster, famine, and countless miseries. This impellent is war."

The above statements with respect to the condition of the working class and of all toilers in general during the first years of the war, also explain the character of the labor movement during these years.

Figures on the strike movement (at enterprises subject to factory
inspection) during the war years are presented in the following table:

Years	Number of Strikes	Number of Striking Workers (Thousands)
1914 (August to December)	68	34.7
1915	928	539.5
1916	1,284	951.7
1917 (January and February)	1,330	676.3

The movement in the form of economic strikes was begun by the
textile workers, while the final phase of the political strike movement
was undertaken by the metal-workers. Petrograd became the center
of the labor movement and of its more clearly expressed political
demands. Here, beginning with the second half of 1915, the strikes
had become more tempestuous in character, involving the introduction of political demands and active armed opposition to the police
and the troops. By September 1916, the commander of the Petrograd
military district announced that workers who failed to appear at their
jobs would be sent to courts-martial (that is, actually to the firing
squad). But even this military repression failed to halt the movement.

Beginning with October 1916, the labor movements of Petersburg
and Moscow entered a period of widespread increase in political and
revolutionary demands made under the direct leadership of the
"Leninist underground" and by Bolshevik slogans and propaganda.
During the first months of 1917, the proletariat of Petrograd emerged
fully prepared to deliver the crushing blow to the tsarist regime, and,
further, to the whole system of Russian capitalism.

On February 18, 1917, a strike broke out at Petrograd among the
workers of the Putilov plants, and by February 22 the workers at most
enterprises in the city were on strike. During February 23 and 24 the
city witnessed a number of large political demonstrations, and about
200,000 workers were on strike. By February 25 and 26 the revolu-

tionary movement had spread to all proletarian sections of Petrograd, and the demonstrations began to turn into attempts at an uprising.

In the other industrial centers, including Moscow, the movement was at first limited in scope, with purely economic demands foremost, but here, too, strikes provoked by the high cost of living and marked by purely economic demands evolved into significant political events as a result of the political leadership of the Bolsheviks and the resentment of the workers against military repression by the government. Among such events were the strikes at Kostroma and Ivanovo-Voznesensk in the summer of 1915, at the Tver mills, at the Tula and Bryansk plants in 1916, and at the Nizhny Novgorod factories, all of which ended only after troops fired upon the workers. In the south the labor movement had been developing with equal intensity since 1915–1916, changing rapidly even there, and for the same reasons, from economic forms of struggle to political demands and to active resistance against the police. Such were the strikes at the metallurgical enterprises of Taganrog, at the mines and pits of Mariupol and the Don districts, at the shipbuilding yards of Nikolayev, and at the mines and enterprises of the Bakhmut, Gorlovka, and Baku regions, which ended in bloody clashes. All these strikes, while originating for economic reasons and not always successful from the standpoint of the worker, were vastly significant because they prepared the working masses of the periphery for delivering, in conjunction with the Petrograd workers, the crushing blow against the tsarist regime.

The revolutionary struggle of the worker found sympathy and support among the soldier-peasants in uniform. Thus soldiers called to suppress a strike at the automobile plant of Louis Renault in Petrograd in October 1916 fired not at the workers but at the police.

In the course of the February Revolution, during the first days of the uprising (February 26) the Petrograd garrison joined the side of the revolutionary masses against the autocracy. On the morning of February 27 some 10,000 soldiers were in open rebellion, by the evening of the same day, over 60,000, and by the morning of March 1, 144,700. In the course of that day, as they became better acquainted with the situation, the military detachments of the capital became fully activated and changed to the side of the revolution. By the evening of March 1, 170,000 soldiers had risen against the government.

William H. Chamberlin

THE MARCH REVOLUTION WAS SPONTANEOUS

For many years William Henry Chamberlin was perhaps one of the best-known American authorities on the Russian Revolution. Born in Brooklyn in 1897 and educated at Haverford College, he had a long and brilliant career as journalist, author, and historian. From 1922 through 1934 he was the Moscow correspondent of The Christian Science Monitor, *an experience that helped him gain deep insights into Russian problems. In later years he wrote many books, lectured at various universities and continued to write regularly for several magazines. In* The Russian Revolution, *still one of the best studies of the revolution, Chamberlin diligently tried to examine all the relevant sources and to give a scrupulously unbiased report based on their evidence.*

The collapse of the Romanov autocracy in March 1917 was one of the most leaderless, spontaneous, anonymous revolutions of all time. While almost every thoughtful observer in Russia in the winter of 1916–1917 foresaw the likelihood of the crash of the existing regime no one, even among the revolutionary leaders, realized that the strikes and bread riots which broke out in Petrograd on March 8 would culminate in the mutiny of the garrison and the overthrow of the government four days later.

The tsarina was not distinguished by political perspicacity; and it is not surprising that she should write to her husband, who was at the Headquarters of the General Staff in Moghilev, on March 10, when the capital was in the grip of a general strike: "This is a hooligan movement, young people run and shout that there is no bread, simply to create excitement, along with workers who prevent others from working. If the weather were very cold they would all probably stay at home. But all this will pass and become calm, if only the Duma will behave itself."

But it was not only the tsarina who failed to see the impending storm. The Socialist Revolutionary Zenzinov declared: "The Revolution was a great and joyous surprise for us, revolutionaries, who had worked for it for years and had always expected it." The Menshevik Internationalist Sukhanov observes: "Not one party was prepared for the great overturn." The Bolshevik worker Kaourov, who took an active part in the revolution, testifies that on March 8 "no one thought of such an imminent possibility of revolution." As for the leaders of the Duma, they might whisper among each other about the possibility of a palace coup d'état; but the last thing they desired was an uncontrolled movement from below.[1]

Wartime circumstances alone made any effective guidance of a mass uprising impossible. The men who afterwards distinguished themselves in the Bolshevik Revolution were either living abroad, like Lenin and Trotzky and Zinoviev, or in prison or in Siberian exile, like Stalin, Kamenev and Dzerzhinsky. The more prominent leaders of other revolutionary parties were also absent from Petrograd in the decisive days. The Bolshevik members of the Duma had been exiled to Siberia in the first months of the war, and the Menshevik members of the War Industries Committee were arrested by the zealous minister of the interior, Protopopov, early in the year. There was a skeleton underground Bolshevik organization in Russia; but its activities were narrowly circumscribed by lack of experienced professional revolutionaries, lack of funds, and the all-pervading espionage. Indeed most of the members of the Bolshevik Petrograd Party Committee were arrested at a critical moment in the development of the movement, on the morning of March 11.

So the police measures for the protection of the tsarist regime were almost perfect. At first sight and on paper the military measures seemed equally imposing. Petrograd had a huge garrison of about 160,000 soldiers. To be sure the fighting quality of this garrison, as subsequent events were to prove, was in inverse ratio to its size. The original Guard regiments had been sent to the front (a grave strategic error, from the standpoint of the internal security of the old regime); and the troops quartered in Petrograd consisted mainly

---

[1] *Socialist Revolutionary:* the peasant-oriented, agrarian-socialist (non-Marxist) party of which Victor Chernov was leader. The *Mensheviks* and *Bolsheviks* were mutually hostile parties which had developed from an earlier split in the Russian Social Democratic Labor party. The Bolshevik party was characterized by a high degree of centralization and discipline under Lenin's leadership, and its political tactics were conspiratorial and aggressively revolutionary. The Mensheviks were loosely organized, less militant, and in general committed to an evolutionary interpretation of historical development which made them relatively passive after March 1917.—Ed.

of new recruits, untrained, housed in crowded barracks, often poorly fed.

But the tsarist authorities did not rely primarily on the unwieldy garrison for the suppression of any possible uprising. The minister of the interior, Protopopov, proposed to operate against insurgent throngs first with police, then with Cossack cavalry units, bringing troops into operation only in the last resort. An elaborate plan for the suppression of disorder in the capital had been submitted to the tsar in January. A combined force of 12,000 troops, gendarmes and police was created for this specific purpose; and a military commander was appointed in each of the six police districts into which the city was divided.

Military preparations, therefore, had not been neglected, even if there were serious omissions, quite consistent with the frequently slipshod character of tsarist administration, in paying little attention to the morale of the troops in the capital and in selecting as commander of the Petrograd Military District, General Khabalov, a man of little experience in commanding troops in actual military operations. The unforeseen circumstances that upset all the governmental calculations were the stubbornness of the demonstrators and the ultimate unreliability of the garrison.

The atmosphere of Petrograd was so charged with discontent in this third winter of an unsuccessful war that very slight causes were sufficient to bring about a formidable explosion. There had been intermittent strikes throughout January and February. Although there was not an absolute shortage of bread, poor transportation and faulty distribution made it necessary for the workers and their wives, in many cases, to stand in long queues for bread and other products. The poorer classes of the city were not apathetic from actual hunger; but they were angry and annoyed at the growing cost of living and the other deprivations which the war brought with it. Something of a sense of crowd psychology, of a sense of massed power must have developed also, from the noteworthy growth in the number of industrial workers up to approximately 400,000 as a result of the presence of many war industry plants in the capital.

The movement that was to end in the overthrow of the Romanov dynasty started on March 8, which is observed by Socialist parties as Women's Day. After speeches in the factories crowds of women poured out on the streets, especially in the working-class Viborg section of the city, clamoring for bread. Here and there red flags appeared with inscriptions: "Down with Autocracy." There were occasional clashes with the police; but the day passed off without serious conflicts. Almost ninety thousand workers struck and fifty factories were closed. A circumstance that enhanced the militant mood of the demonstrators was a lockout at the large Putilov metal works. The workers of this plant were proverbially turbulent, with a long record of strikes; and when a wage dispute had come up in one department the management on March 7 declared a general lockout. So a coincidence of three factors—the dissatisfaction with the food situation, the celebration of Women's Day and the Putilov labor dispute, which let loose over twenty thousand workers for active participation in the demonstration—combined to give the first impetus to the revolution.

The movement gained in scope and intensity on March 9, when the number of strikers was estimated at 197,000. There was a concerted drive by the workers to reach the central part of the city. Although the police guarded the bridges over the Neva, which was to some extent a boundary between the working-class and the governmental parts of the city, it was relatively easy to cross the river on the ice, and meetings and demonstrations were held in the center of the capital. An ominous symptom for the government appeared: the Cossacks showed little energy in breaking up the crowds. So a Cossack squadron rode off, amid loud cheers, leaving undisturbed a revolutionary gathering on the Nevsky Prospect, the main boulevard of Petrograd; and the police reports of the day note an incident on Znamenskaya Square, when the Cossacks responded with bows to the applause of a throng which they did not disperse.

Attacks on the police became more common on this second day of the movement, the mobs using as weapons lumps of ice, cobblestones, heavy sticks. However, firearms were not used in suppressing the disorder and there was still no general conviction of an impending crisis. The British ambassador, Sir George Buchanan, telegraphed to Foreign Minister Balfour: "Some disorders occurred today, but nothing serious."

The 10th witnessed to a large extent a repetition of the events of the 9th, but on a larger scale. The strike became general; newspapers ceased to appear; the students in the universities abandoned their studies. The numbers both of the demonstrators and of the forces employed by the government increased; and there was a longer casualty list on both sides. Although there was still no mutiny, insubordination and passivity on the part of the troops, especially of the Cossacks, were more noticeable. On Znamenskaya Square a Cossack even cut down a police lieutenant, Krilov, with his saber. The instinctive strategy of the crowd adapted itself to the mood of the troops. While there were fierce attacks on the police (by this time the police in the riotous Viborg district no longer ventured to appear on the streets, but were barricaded in their stations) there was an attempt to conciliate the troops and to avoid provoking them.

So far as there was organized leadership in the movement it aimed at winning over the troops, rather than at arming the workers. So the Bolshevik Shlyapnikov, one of the three members of the Bureau of the Central Committee of the party, tells how he opposed the more hotheaded workers who continually demanded arms, or at least revolvers: "I decisively refused to search for arms at all and demanded that the soldiers should be drawn into the uprising, so as to get arms for all the workers. This was more difficult than to get a few dozen revolvers; but in this was the whole program of action."

These three days of turmoil naturally affected the national and local legislative bodies, the Duma and the Petrograd City Council; and speeches were made demanding the appointment of a ministry responsible to the Duma. The Laborite deputy and radical lawyer Alexander Kerensky, destined to play a leading part in subsequent months, attacked the government so sharply in the Duma on the 9th that the tsarina expressed a fervent desire that he should be hanged. These speeches, however, had little effect on the movement, because the war minister forbade their publication, and after the morning of March 10, newspapers ceased to appear as a result of the general strike.

General Khabalov on March 10 received a peremptory telegram from the tsar worded as follows: "I command you to suppress from tomorrow all disorders on the streets of the capital, which are impermissible at a time when the fatherland is carrying on a difficult war with Germany." This imperial order caused a sharp change in the tactics of the Petrograd authorities. Hitherto the use of firearms had been avoided. On the night of the 10th Khabalov gave his subordinate officers instructions to fire on crowds which refused to disperse after warning. This was the decisive stake of the old regime. If the troops obeyed, the revolutionary movement would be crushed. If they did not obey . . . But this alternative was apparently not considered very seriously.

As a further sign of resolute action the police on the night of the 10th arrested about a hundred persons suspected of holding seditious views, including five members of the Petrograd Committee of the Bolshevik party. On the surface the course of events on the 11th, which was a Sunday, represented a victory for the government. There was firing on the crowds in four separate places in the central part of the city; and on Znamenskaya Square the training detachment of the Volinsky regiment used machine-guns as well as rifles, with the result that about forty persons were killed and an equal number were wounded. Toward evening there was an outburst of rebellion in one company of the Pavlovsk regiment; but it was put down with the aid of other troops, and the ringleaders were imprisoned in the fortress of Peter and Paul. The government, which was headed by Prince Golitzin as premier, apparently felt in a stronger position, because in the evening it adopted a decision to dissolve the Duma, thereby breaking off the half-hearted negotiations which had hitherto been carried on with the president of the Duma, Rodzianko, about possible cooperation between the ministry and the Duma.

Rodzianko decided to try the effect of a personal appeal to the tsar and dispatched a telegram containing the following gravely warning phrases: "The situation is serious. There is anarchy in the capital. The government is paralyzed. It is necessary immediately to entrust a person who enjoys the confidence of the country with the formation of the government. Any delay is equivalent to death. I pray God that in this hour responsibility will not fall on the sovereign."

But neither this telegram, nor the still more urgent message which Rodzianko sent on the following morning, when the mutiny of the garrison was an accomplished fact, produced any impression on Nicholas II. Rodzianko's second telegram described the growing revolt and ended: "The situation is growing worse. Measures must be adopted immediately, because tomorrow will be too late. The last hour has come, when the fate of the fatherland and the dynasty is being decided."

After reading this message the tsar impatiently remarked to his minister of the court, Count Fredericks: "This fat Rodzianko has written me some nonsense, to which I will not even reply."

There is a double significance in these last urgent appeals of the president of the Duma to the tsar and especially in his instinctive employment of the phrase "The situation is growing worse," at a moment when the revolution was moving to victory. Like the great majority of the members of the Duma Rodzianko, who was himself a well-to-do landowner, desired to see the monarchy reformed, but not abolished. All Rodzianko's actions in these turbulent days were motivated by two factors: his hope, up to the last moment, that the tsar would save himself and the monarchical principle by making necessary concessions, and his fear that the revolutionary movement would get out of hand.

The decisive hour of the revolution struck on the morning of March 12, when the center of attention shifts from rebellious workers with sticks and stones and bottles to insurgent soldiers with rifles and machine-guns. The firing on the crowds on Sunday, the 11th, was the snapping point in the frail cord of discipline that held the garrison of the capital. The mutiny that was to transform the prolonged street demonstrations into a genuine revolution started in the very unit which had inflicted the heaviest losses on the demonstrating crowds: the training detachment of the Volinsky regiment. During the night the soldiers discussed their impressions of the day's shooting and agreed that they would no longer fire on the crowds. When Captain Lashkevitch appeared in the barracks of the detachment on the morning of the 12th he was greeted with shouts: "We will not shoot." He read the telegram of the tsar, demanding the suppression of the disorders; but this only aggravated the situation. Ultimately Lashkevitch either was shot by the insurgent soldiers or committed suicide; and the troops poured out into the streets under the command of Sergeant Kirpichnikov, one of the many obscure leaders of this unplanned upheaval. They soon aroused the soldiers of the Preobrazhensky and Litovsky regiments, who were quartered in nearby barracks.

Quickly brushing aside the resistance which some officers of the Moscow regiment endeavored to offer and gaining new recruits among the soldiers of the Moscow regiment for their ranks, the swollen mass of soldiers made for the Viborg district, where they quickly fraternized with the throngs of workers and joined them in hunting down the police and breaking into arsenals, where the workers quickly secured the desired arms.

Khabalov, a weak and incompetent man at best, was thunderstruck as the news of one mutiny after another poured in on him. He formed a supposedly loyal force of six companies under the command of Colonel Kutepov, but it simply melted away as soon as it came into contact with the revolutionary mobs. This largely psychological process of "melting away" recurred, incidentally, whenever there was an attempt to send "reliable" troops against the revolutionary capital. It explains why a movement without organized leadership was nevertheless invincible. This breakdown of normal military discipline cannot be attributed to any single precise cause. It was a compound of many things: war-weariness, hatred of the hard and often humiliating conditions of Russian army service, responsiveness to the general mood of discontent in the country—all explosive stuff that was ignited by the stubborn demonstrations of the working-class population of Petrograd.

There are two features of the March Revolution that strike the observer again and again. There is the lack of planned leadership, and there is the action of the soldiers independently of their officers. The latter, with very few exceptions, simply disappeared during the decisive hours of the uprising. This fact inevitably exerted a profound effect on the subsequent morale and psychology of the soldiers, who followed leaders from their own ranks, often sergeants and corporals.

Khabalov, with the rapidly thinning remnant of his loyal troops, took refuge in the Winter Palace, where his forces on the afternoon of the 12th were reduced to "fifteen hundred or two thousand men, with a very small reserve of bullets." At the insistence of the Grand Duke Michael, the tsar's brother, the Winter Palace was evacuated and the last defenders of the old regime took refuge in the neighboring Admiralty, whence they quietly dispersed on the following morning.

So the city passed completely into the hands of the revolutionaries. The accounts of many eyewitnesses of the upheaval are pervaded with a spirit of chaotic exaltation. The monarchy had fallen; and in the masses of the population there were few who mourned it. Vast throngs gathered to watch the burning of the large District Court building and adjoining prison; and the Tauride Palace, where the Duma held its sessions, was a magnet for endless throngs of soldiers, workers, students and curious spectators of all classes. Red bands and ribbons appeared as if by magic; and trucks filled with soldiers raced through the city, with their guns levelled against nonexistent enemies. Except for the police, who were given short shrift when they were discovered hiding in garrets or firing from roofs on the crowds, the revolution, although tumultuous, was, in the main, good-natured. There were relatively few excesses, surprisingly few, if one considers that common criminals were released indiscriminately with political offenders in the prisons which were stormed by the mobs. Class lines had not begun to assume their subsequent sharpness. An atmosphere of vague, formless good-fellowship was prevalent; and the nationalist speeches of Shulgin or Rodzianko evoked the same hearty "Hurrah" as the exhortations of the revolutionary orators. The great mass of the mutinous soldiers scarcely realized what they were doing and were uncertain whether in the end they would be treated as heroes or as criminals.

The anonymous host of workers in collarless blouses and soldiers in grey uniforms overthrew the Romanov dynasty, with its three centuries of absolute rule behind it. But the rebellious mass had nothing concrete to put in the place of the old order. The efforts to form a new government inevitably revolved around the Duma, which, despite its lack of representative character and the timidity which it displayed in its dealings with the monarchy, was the sole national assembly in existence at the time of the revolution.

Leon Trotsky

BOLSHEVIK WORKINGMEN LED THE REVOLT

Leon Trotsky, born near Odessa in 1879, early became a professional revolutionary and remained in this profession until his assassination in Mexico in 1940. During an almost feverishly busy life he was a leading Marxian theoretician, a gifted and prolific journalist, a successful revolutionary, organizer of the Red Armies, and a high Soviet government official. A leader of the 1905 Revolution, he joined the Bolshevik Party in 1917 and was one of the chief organizers of the Bolshevik seizure—second in importance only to Lenin. During all his mature years, no matter what other great events gripped his attention, Trotsky wrote—speeches and orders, articles, books, and scholarly studies—all of them highly argumentative, all of them brilliant. In the History of the Russian Revolution, *from which a chapter is printed below, Trotsky describes with inimitable verve and detail his views on the leadership of the March Revolution.*

Lawyers and journalists belonging to the classes damaged by the revolution wasted a good deal of ink subsequently trying to prove that what happened in February was essentially a petticoat rebellion, backed up afterwards by a soldiers' mutiny and given out for a revolution. Louis XVI in his day also tried to think that the capture of the Bastille was a rebellion, but they respectfully explained to him that it was a revolution. Those who lose by a revolution are rarely inclined to call it by its real name. For that name, in spite of the efforts of spiteful reactionaries, is surrounded in the historic memory of mankind with a halo of liberation from all shackles and all prejudices. The privileged classes of every age, as also their lackeys, have always tried to declare the revolution which overthrew them, in contrast to past revolutions, a mutiny, a riot, a revolt of the rabble. Classes which have outlived themselves are not distinguished by originality.

Soon after the 27th of February attempts were also made to liken the revolution to the military coup d'état of the Young Turks, of which, as we know, they had been dreaming not a little in the upper circles of the Russian bourgeoisie. This comparison was so hopeless,

From Leon Trotsky, *The History of the Russian Revolution,* translated by Max Eastman, 3 vols. (New York: Simon & Schuster, 1936) Reprinted by permission of Max Shachtman.

however, that it was seriously opposed even in one of the bourgeois papers. Tugan-Baranovsky, an economist who had studied Marx in his youth, a Russian variety of Sombart, wrote on March 10 in the *Birzhevoe Vedomosti:*

> *The Turkish revolution consisted in a victorious uprising of the army, prepared and carried out by the leaders of the army; the soldiers were merely obedient executives of the plans of their officers. But the regiments of the Guard which on February 27 overthrew the Russian throne, came without their officers . . . Not the army but the workers began the insurrection; not the generals but the soldiers came to the State Duma. The soldiers supported the workers not because they were obediently fulfilling the commands of their officers, but because . . . they felt themselves blood brothers of the workers as a class composed of toilers like themselves. The peasants and the workers—those are the two social classes which made the Russian revolution.*

These words require neither correction, nor supplement. The further development of the revolution sufficiently confirmed and re-enforced their meaning. In Petrograd the last day of February was the first day after the victory: a day of raptures, embraces, joyful tears, voluble outpourings; but at the same time a day of final blows at the enemy. Shots were still crackling in the streets. It was said that Protopopov's Pharaohs, not informed of the people's victory, were still shooting from the roofs. From below they were firing into attics, false windows and belfries where the armed phantoms of tzarism might still be lurking. About four o'clock they occupied the Admiralty where the last remnants of what was formerly the state power had taken refuge. Revolutionary organizations and improvised groups were making arrests throughout the town. The Schlüsselburg hard-labor prison was taken without a shot. More and more regiments were joining the revolution, both in the capital and in the environs.

The overturn in Moscow was only an echo of the insurrection in Petrograd. The same moods among the workers and soldiers, but less clearly expressed. A slightly more leftward tendency among the bourgeoisie. A still greater weakness among the revolutionary organizations than in Petrograd. When the events began on the Neva, the Moscow radical intelligentsia called a conference on the question what to do, and came to no conclusion. Only on the 27th of February strikes began in the shops and factories of Moscow, and then demonstrations. The officers told the soldiers in the barracks that a rabble was rioting in the streets and they must be put down. "But by this time," relates the soldier Shishilin, "the soldiers understood the word rabble in the opposite sense." Toward two o'clock there arrived at the building of the City Duma many soldiers of various regiments inquiring how to join the revolution. On the next day the strikes increased. Crowds flowed toward the Duma with flags. A soldier of an automobile company, Muralov, an old Bolshevik, an agriculturist, a good-natured and courageous giant, brought to the Duma the first complete and disciplined military detachment, which occupied the wireless station and other points. Eight months later Muralov will be in command of the troops of the Moscow military district.

The prisons were opened. The same Muralov was driving an automobile truck filled with freed political prisoners: a police officer with his hand at his vizor asked the revolutionist whether it was advisable to let out the Jews also. Dzerzhinsky, just liberated from a hard labor prison and without changing his prison dress, spoke in the Duma building where a soviet of deputies was already formed. The artillerist Dorofeev relates how on March 1 workers from the Siou candy factory came with banners to the barracks of an artillery brigade to fraternize with the soldiers, and how many could not contain their joy, and wept. There were cases of sniping in the town, but in general neither armed encounters nor casualties: Petrograd answered for Moscow.

In a series of provincial cities the movement began only on March 1, after the revolution was already achieved even in Moscow. In Tver the workers went from their work to the barracks in a procession and having mixed with the soldiers marched through the streets of the city. At that time they were still singing the "Marseillaise," not the "International." In Nizhni-Novgorod thousands of workers gathered round the City Duma building, which in a majority of the cities played the role of the Tauride Palace. After a speech from the mayor the workers marched off with red banners to free the politicals from the jails. By evening, eighteen out of the twenty-one military divisions of the garrison had voluntarily come over to the revolution. In Samara and Saratov meetings were held, soviets of workers' deputies organized. In Kharkov the chief of police, having gone to the railroad station and got news of the revolution, stood up in his carriage before an excited crowd and, lifting his hat, shouted at the top of his lungs: "Long live the revolution. Hurrah!" The news came to Ekaterinoslav from Kharkov. At the head of the demonstration strode the assistant chief of police carrying in his hand a long saber as in the grand parades on saints' days. When it became finally clear that the monarchy could not rise, they began cautiously to remove the tzar's portraits from the government institutions and hide them in the attics. Anecdotes about this, both authentic and imaginary, were much passed around in liberal circles, where they had not yet lost a taste for the jocular tone when speaking of the revolution. The workers, and the soldier barracks as well, took the events in a very different way. As to a series of other provincial cities (Pskov, Orel, Rybinsk, Penza, Kazan, Tzaritsyn, and others), the *Chronicle* remarks under date of March 2: "News came of the uprising and the population joined the revolution." This description, notwithstanding its summary character, tells with fundamental truth what happened.

News of the revolution trickled into the villages from the near-by cities, partly through the authorities, but chiefly through the markets, the workers, the soldiers on furlough. The villages accepted the revolution more slowly and less enthusiastically than the cities, but felt it no less deeply. For them it was bound up with the question of war and land.

It would be no exaggeration to say that Petrograd achieved the February Revolution. The rest of the country adhered to it. There was no struggle anywhere except in Petrograd. There were not to be found anywhere in the country any groups of the population, any parties, institutions, or military units which were ready to put up a fight for the old regime. This shows how ill-founded was the belated talk of the reactionaries to the effect that if there had been cavalry of the Guard in the Petersburg garrison, or if Ivanov had brought a reliable brigade from the front, the fate of the monarchy would have been different. Neither at the front nor at the rear was there a brigade or regiment to be found which was prepared to do battle for Nicholas II.

The revolution was carried out upon the initiative and by the strength of one city, constituting approximately about 1/75 of the population of the country. You may say, if you will, that this most gigantic democratic act was achieved in a most undemocratic manner. The whole country was placed before a fait accompli. The fact that a Constituent Assembly was in prospect does not alter the matter, for the dates and methods of convoking this national representation were determined by institutions which issued from the victorious insurrection of Petrograd. This casts a sharp light on the question of the function of democratic forms in general, and in a revolutionary epoch in particular. Revolutions have always struck such blows at the judicial fetishism of the popular will, and the blows have been more ruthless the deeper, bolder, and more democratic the revolutions. It is often said, especially in regard to the great French Revolution, that the extreme centralization of a monarchy subsequently permits the revolutionary capital to think and act for the whole country. That explanation is superficial. If revolutions reveal a centralizing tendency, this is not in imitation of overthrown monarchies, but in consequence of irresistible demands of the new society, which cannot reconcile itself to particularism. If the capital plays as dominating a role in a revolution as though it concentrated in itself the will of the nation, that is simply because the capital expresses most clearly and thoroughly the fundamental tendencies of the new society. The provinces accept the steps taken by the capital as their own intentions already materialized. In the initiatory role of the centers there is no violation of democracy, but rather its dynamic realization. However, the rhythm of this dynamic has never in great revolutions coincided with the rhythm of formal representative democracy. The provinces adhere to the activity of the center, but belatedly. With the swift development of events characteristic of a revolution this produces sharp crises in revolutionary parliamentarism, which cannot be resolved by the methods of democracy. In all genuine revolutions the national representation has invariably come into conflict with the dynamic force of the revolution, whose principal seat has been the capital. It was so in the seventeenth century in England, in the eighteenth in France, in the twentieth in Russia. The role of the capital is determined not by the tradition of a bureaucratic centralism, but by the situation of the leading revolutionary class, whose vanguard is naturally concentrated in the chief city: this is equally true for the bourgeoisie and the proletariat.

When the February victory was fully confirmed, they began to count up the victims. In Petrograd they counted 1443 killed and wounded, 869 of them soldiers, and 60 of these officers. By compari-

son with the victims of any battle in the Great Slaughter these figures
are suggestively tiny. The liberal press declared the February Revolution bloodless. In the days of general salubrity and mutual amnesty
of the patriotic parties, nobody took the trouble to establish the truth.
Albert Thomas,[1] a friend of everything victorious, even a victorious
insurrection, wrote at that time about the "sunniest, most holiday-
like, most bloodless Russian revolution." To be sure, he was hopeful
that this revolution would remain at the disposal of the French
Bourse. But after all Thomas did not invent this habit. On the 27th of
June 1789, Mirabeau exclaimed: "How fortunate that this great revolution will succeed without evil-doing and without tears! . . . History
has too long been telling us only of the actions of beasts of prey. . . .
We may well hope that we are beginning the history of human be-
ings." When all the three estates were united in the National Assembly the ancestors of Albert Thomas wrote: "The revolution is ended.
It has not cost a drop of blood." We must acknowledge, however,
that at that period blood had really not yet flowed. Not so in the February days. Nevertheless the legend of a bloodless revolution stubbornly persisted, answering the need of the liberal bourgeois to make
things look as though the power had come to him of its own accord.

Although the February Revolution was far from bloodless, still one
cannot but be amazed at the insignificant number of victims, not
only at the moment of revolution but still more in the first period
after it. This revolution, we must remember, was a paying-back for
oppression, persecution, taunts, vile blows, suffered by the masses
of the Russian people throughout the ages! The sailors and soldiers
did in some places, to be sure, take summary revenge upon the most
contemptible torturers in the person of their officers, but the number
of these acts of settlement was at first insignificant in comparison
with the number of the old bloody insults. The masses shook off their
good-naturedness only a good while later, when they were convinced
that the ruling classes wanted to drag everything back and appropri-
ate to themselves a revolution not achieved by them, just as they had
always appropriated the good things of life not produced by themselves.

*   *

[1] French Socialist.—Ed.

Tugan-Baranovsky is right when he says that the February Revolution was accomplished by workers and peasants—the latter in the person of the soldiers. But there still remains the great question: Who led the revolution? Who raised the workers to their feet? Who brought the soldiers into the streets? After the victory these questions became a subject of party conflict. They were solved most simply by the universal formula: Nobody led the revolution, it happened of itself. The theory of "spontaneousness" fell in most opportunely with the minds not only of all those gentlemen who had yesterday been peacefully governing, judging, convicting, defending, trading, or commanding, and today were hastening to make up to the revolution, but also of many professional politicians and former revolutionists, who having slept through the revolution wished to think that in this they were not different from all the rest.

In his curious *History of the Russian Disorders*, General Denikin, former commander of the White Army, says of the 27th of February: "On that decisive day there were no leaders, there were only the elements. In their threatening current there were then visible neither aims, nor plans, nor slogans." The learned historian Miliukov delves no deeper than this general with a passion for letters. Before the revolution the liberal leader had declared every thought of revolution a suggestion of the German Staff. But the situation was more complicated after a revolution which had brought the liberals to power. Miliukov's task was now not to dishonor the revolution with a Hohenzollern origin, but on the contrary to withhold the honor of its initiation from revolutionists. Liberalism therefore has wholeheartedly fathered the theory of a spontaneous and impersonal revolution. Miliukov sympathetically cites the semi-liberal, semi-socialist Stankevich, a university instructor who became political commissar at the headquarters of the Supreme Command: "The masses moved of themselves, obeying some unaccountable inner summons . . ." writes Stankevich of the February days. "With what slogans did the soldiers come out? Who led them when they conquered Petrograd, when they burned the District Court? Not a political idea, not a revolutionary slogan, not a conspiracy, and not a revolt, but a spontaneous movement suddenly consuming the entire old power to the last remnant." Spontaneousness here acquires an almost mystic character.

This same Stankevich offers a piece of testimony in the highest degree valuable: "At the end of January, I happened in a very intimate circle to meet with Kerensky. . . . To the possibility of a popular uprising they all took a definitely negative position, fearing lest a popular mass movement once aroused might get into an extreme leftward channel and this would create vast difficulties in the conduct of the war." The views of Kerensky's circle in nowise essentially differed from those of the Cadets. The initiative certainly did not come from there.

"The revolution fell like thunder out of the sky," says the president of the Social Revolutionary party, Zenzinov. "Let us be frank: it arrived joyfully unexpected for us too, revolutionists who had worked for it through long years and waited for it always."

It was not much better with the Mensheviks. One of the journalists of the bourgeois emigration tells about his meeting in a tramcar on February 21 with Skobelev, a future minister of the revolutionary government: "This Social Democrat, one of the leaders of the movement, told me that the disorders had the character of plundering which it was necessary to put down. This did not prevent Skobelev from asserting a month later that he and his friends had made the revolution." The colors here are probably laid on a little thick, but fundamentally the position of the legal Social Democrats, the Mensheviks, is conveyed accurately enough.

Finally, one of the most recent leaders of the left wing of the Social Revolutionaries, Mstislavsky, who subsequently went over to the Bolsheviks, says of the February uprising: "The revolution caught us, the party people of those days, like the foolish virgins of the Bible, napping." It does not matter how much they resembled virgins, but it is true they were all fast asleep.

How was it with the Bolsheviks? This we have in part already seen. The principal leaders of the underground Bolshevik organization were at that time three men: the former workers Shliapnikov and Zalutsky, and the former student Molotov. Shliapnikov, having lived for some time abroad and in close association with Lenin, was in a political sense the most mature and active of these three who constituted the Bureau of the Central Committee. However, Shliapnikov's own memoirs best of all confirm the fact that the events were too much for the trio. Up to the very last hour these leaders thought that it was a question of a revolutionary manifestation, one among many, and not at all of an armed insurrection. Our friend Kayurov, one of the leaders of the Vyborg section, asserts categorically: "Absolutely no guiding initiative from the party centers was felt . . . the Petrograd Committee had been arrested and the representative of the Central Committee, Comrade Shliapnikov, was unable to give any directives for the coming day."

The weakness of the underground organizations was a direct result of police raids, which had given exceptional results amid the patriotic moods at the beginning of the war. Every organization, the revolutionary included, has a tendency to fall behind its social basis. The underground organization of the Bolsheviks at the beginning of 1917 had not yet recovered from its oppressed and scattered condition, whereas in the masses the patriotic hysteria had been abruptly replaced by revolutionary indignation.

In order to get a clear conception of the situation in the sphere of revolutionary leadership it is necessary to remember that the most authoritative revolutionists, the leaders of the Left parties, were abroad and, some of them, in prison and exile. The more dangerous a party was to the old regime, the more cruelly beheaded it appeared at the moment of revolution. The narodniks had a Duma faction headed by the non-party radical Kerensky.[2] The official leader of the Social-Revolutionaries, Chernov, was abroad. The Mensheviks had a party faction in the Duma headed by Cheidze and Skobelev; Martov was abroad; Dan and Tseretelli, in exile. A considerable number of socialistic intellectuals with a revolutionary past were grouped around these Left factions—narodnik and Menshevik. This constituted a kind of political staff, but one which was capable of coming to the front only after the victory. The Bolsheviks had no Duma faction: their five worker-deputies, in whom the tzarist government had seen the organizing center of the revolution, had been arrested during the first few months of the war. Lenin was abroad, Zinoviev with

---

[2] In the late nineteenth century Russian intellectuals developed an agrarian socialist philosophy which placed great weight upon the importance of the peasant and his institutions and upon the moral duty of the intellectual to help the peasants improve their lives. This *narodnik* (populist) philosophy gave rise to a series of important revolutionary movements in the nineteenth century and served as a basis for the new party of Socialist Revolutionaries in the twentieth century. Contrary to Trotsky's assertion here, Kerensky was a member of the Socialist Revolutionary party.—Ed.

him; Kamenev was in exile; in exile also, the then little known practical leaders: Sverdlov, Rykov, Stalin. The Polish social-democrat, Dzerzhinsky, who did not yet belong to the Bolsheviks, was at hard labor. The leaders accidentally present, for the very reason that they had been accustomed to act under unconditionally authoritative supervisors, did not consider themselves and were not considered by others capable of playing a guiding role in revolutionary events.

But if the Bolshevik party could not guarantee the insurrection an authoritative leadership, there is no use talking of other organizations. This fact has strengthened the current conviction as to the spontaneous character of the February Revolution. Nevertheless the conviction is deeply mistaken, or at least meaningless.

The struggle in the capital lasted not an hour, or two hours, but five days. The leaders tried to hold it back; the masses answered with increased pressure and marched forward. They had against them the old state, behind whose traditional façade a mighty power was still assumed to exist, the liberal bourgeoisie with the State Duma, the Land and City Unions, the military-industrial organizations, academies, universities, a highly developed press, and finally the two strong socialist parties who put up a patriotic resistance to the assault from below. In the party of the Bolsheviks the insurrection had its nearest organization, but a headless organization with a scattered staff and with weak illegal nuclei. And nevertheless the revolution, which nobody in those days was expecting, unfolded, and just when it seemed from above as though the movement was already dying down, with an abrupt revival, a mighty convulsion, it seized the victory.

Whence came this unexampled force of aggression and self-restraint? It is not enough to refer to bitter feelings. Bitterness alone is little. The Petersburg workers, no matter how diluted during the war years with human raw material, had in their past a great revolutionary experience. In their aggression and self-restraint, in the absence of leadership and in the face of opposition from above, was revealed a vitally well-founded, although not always expressed, estimate of forces and a strategic calculation of their own.

On the eve of the war the revolutionary layers of the workers had been following the Bolsheviks, and leading the masses after them. With the beginning of the war the situation had sharply changed:

conservative groups lifted their heads, dragging after them a considerable part of the class. The revolutionary elements found themselves isolated, and quieted down. In the course of the war the situation began to change, at first slowly, but after the defeats faster and more radically. An active discontent seized the whole working class. To be sure, it was to an extent patriotically colored, but it had nothing in common with the calculating and cowardly patriotism of the possessing classes, who were postponing all domestic questions until after the victory. The war itself, its victims, its horror, its shame, brought not only the old, but also the new layers of workers into conflict with the tzarist regime. It did this with a new incisiveness and led them to the conclusion: we can no longer endure it. The conclusion was universal; it welded the masses together and gave them a mighty dynamic force.

The army had swollen, drawing into itself millions of workers and peasants. Every individual had his own people among the troops: a son, a husband, a brother, a relative. The army was no longer insulated, as before the war, from the people. One met with soldiers now far oftener; saw them off to the front, lived with them when they came home on leave, chatted with them on the streets and in the tramways about the front, visited them in the hospitals. The workers' districts, the barracks, the front, and to an extent the villages too, became communicating vessels. The workers would know what the soldiers were thinking and feeling. They had innumerable conversations about the war, about the people who were getting rich out of the war, about the generals, government, tzar and tzarina. The soldier would say about the war: "To hell with it!" And the worker would answer about the government: "To hell with it!" The soldier would say: "Why then do you sit still here in the center?" The worker would answer: "We can't do anything with bare hands; we stubbed our toe against the army in 1905." The soldier would reflect: "What if we should all start at once!" The worker: "That's it, all at once!" Conversations of this kind before the war were conspirative and carried on by two's; now they were going on everywhere, on every occasion, and almost openly, at least in the workers' districts.

The tzar's intelligence service every once in a while took its soundings very successfully. Two weeks before the revolution a spy, who signed himself with the name Krestianinov, reported a conversation in a tramcar traversing the workers' suburb. The soldier was telling how in his regiment eight men were under hard labor because last autumn they refused to shoot at the workers of the Nobel factory, but shot at the police instead. The conversation went on quite openly, since in the workers' districts the police and the spies preferred to remain unnoticed. "'We'll get even with them,' the soldier concluded." The report reads further: "A skilled worker answered him: 'For that it is necessary to organize so that all will be like one.' The soldier answered: 'Don't you worry, we've been organized a long time. . . . They've drunk enough blood. Men are suffering in the trenches and here they are fattening their bellies!' . . . No special disturbance occurred. February 10, 1917. Krestianinov." Incomparable spy's epic. "No special disturbance occurred." They will occur, and that soon: this tramway conversation signalizes their inexorable approach.

The spontaneousness of the insurrection Mstislavsky illustrates with a curious example: When the "Union of Officers of February 27," formed just after the revolution, tried to determine with a questionnaire who first led out the Volynsky regiment, they received seven answers naming seven initiators of this decisive action. It is very likely, we may add, that a part of the initiative really did belong to several soldiers, nor is it impossible that the chief initiator fell in the street fighting, carrying his name with him into oblivion. But that does not diminish the historic importance of his nameless initiative. Still more important is another side of the matter which will carry us beyond the walls of the barrack room. The insurrection of the battalions of the Guard, flaring up a complete surprise to the liberal and legal socialist circles, was no surprise at all to the workers. Without the insurrection of the workers the Volynsky regiment would not have gone into the street. That street encounter of the workers with the Cossacks, which a lawyer observed from his window and which he communicated by telephone to the deputy, was to them both an episode in an impersonal process: a factory locust stumbled against a locust from the barracks. But it did not seem that way to the Cossack who had dared wink to the worker, nor to the worker who instantly decided that the Cossack had "winked in a friendly manner." The molecular interpenetration of the army with the people was going on continuously. The workers watched the temperature of the army and instantly sensed its approach to the critical mark. Exactly this was what gave such inconquerable force to the assault of the masses, confident of victory.

Here we must introduce the pointed remark of a liberal official trying to summarize his February observations:

> *It is customary to say that the movement began spontaneously, the soldiers themselves went into the street. I cannot at all agree with this. After all, what does the word "spontaneously" mean? . . . Spontaneous conception is still more out of place in sociology than in natural science. Owing to the fact that none of the revolutionary leaders with a name was able to hang his label on the movement, it becomes not impersonal but merely nameless.*

This formulation of the question, incomparably more serious than Miliukov's references to German agents and Russian spontaneousness, belongs to a former procuror who met the revolution in the position of a tzarist senator. It is quite possible that his experience in the courts permitted Zavadsky to realize that a revolutionary insurrection cannot arise either at the command of foreign agents, or in the manner of an impersonal process of nature.

The same author relates two incidents which permitted him to look as through a keyhole into the laboratory of the revolutionary process. On Friday, February 24, when nobody in the upper circles as yet expected a revolution in the near future, a tramcar in which the senator was riding turned off quite unexpectedly, with such a jar that the windows rattled and one was broken, from the Liteiny into a side street, and there stopped. The conductor told everybody to get off: "The car isn't going any farther." The passengers objected, scolded, but got off. "I can still see the face of that unanswering conductor: angrily resolute, a sort of wolf look." The movement of the tramways stopped everywhere as far as the eye could see. That resolute conductor, in whom the liberal official could already catch a glimpse of the "wolf look," must have been dominated by a high sense of duty in order all by himself to stop a car containing officials on the streets of imperial Petersburg in time of war. It was just such conductors who stopped the car of the monarchy and with practically the same words—this car does not go any farther!—and who ushered out the bureaucracy, making no distinction in the rush of business between a general of gendarmes and a liberal senator. The conductor on the Liteiny Boulevard was a conscious factor of history. It had been necessary to educate him in advance.

During the burning of the District Court a liberal jurist from the circle of that same senator started to express in the street his regret that a roomful of judicial decisions and notarial archives was perishing. An elderly man of somber aspect dressed as a worker angrily objected: "We will be able to divide the houses and the lands ourselves, and without your archives." Probably the episode is rounded out in a literary manner. But there were plenty of elderly workers like that in the crowd, capable of making the necessary retort. They themselves had nothing to do with burning the District Court: why burn it? But at least you could not frighten them with "excesses" of this kind. They were arming the masses with the necessary ideas not only against the tzarist police, but against liberal jurists who feared most of all lest there should burn up in the fire of the revolution the notarial deeds of property. Those nameless, austere statesmen of the factory and streets did not fall out of the sky: they had to be educated.

In registering the events of the last days of February the Secret Service also remarked that the movement was "spontaneous," that is, had no planned leadership from above; but they immediately added: "with the generally propagandized condition of the proletariat." This appraisal hits the bull's-eye: the professionals of the struggle with the revolution, before entering the cells vacated by the revolutionists, took a much closer view of what was happening than the leaders of liberalism.

The mystic doctrine of spontaneousness explains nothing. In order correctly to appraise the situation and determine the moment for a blow at the enemy, it was necessary that the masses or their guiding layers should make their examination of historical events and have their criteria for estimating them. In other words, it was necessary that there should be not masses in the abstract, but masses of Petrograd workers and Russian workers in general, who had passed through the revolution of 1905, through the Moscow insurrection of December 1905, shattered against the Semenovsky Regiment of the Guard. It was necessary that throughout this mass should be scattered workers who had thought over the experience of 1905, criticized the constitutional illusions of the liberals and Mensheviks, assimilated the perspectives of the revolution, meditated hundreds of times about the question of the army, watched attentively what was going on in its midst—workers capable of making revolutionary inferences from what they observed and communicating them to others. And finally, it was necessary that there should be in the troops of the garrison itself progressive soldiers, seized, or at least touched, in the past by revolutionary propaganda.

In every factory, in each guild, in each company, in each tavern, in the military hospital, at the transfer stations, even in the depopulated villages, the molecular work of revolutionary thought was in progress. Everywhere were to be found the interpreters of events, chiefly from among the workers, from whom one inquired, "What's the news?" and from whom one awaited the needed words. These leaders had often been left to themselves, had nourished themselves upon fragments of revolutionary generalizations arriving in their hands by various routes, had studied out by themselves between the lines of the liberal papers what they needed. Their class instinct was refined by a political criterion, and though they did not think all their ideas through to the end, nevertheless their thought ceaselessly and stubbornly worked its way in a single direction. Elements of experience, criticism, initiative, self-sacrifice, seeped down through the mass and created, invisibly to a superficial glance but no less decisively, an inner mechanics of the revolutionary movement as a conscious process. To the smug politicians of liberalism and tamed socialism everything that happens among masses is customarily represented as an instinctive process, no matter whether they are dealing with an anthill or a beehive. In reality the thought which was drilling through the thick of the working class was far bolder, more penetrating, more conscious, than those little ideas by which the educated classes live. Moreover, this thought was more scientific: not only because it was to a considerable degree fertilized with the methods of Marxism, but still more because it was ever nourishing itself on the living experience of the masses which were soon to take their place on the revolutionary arena. Thoughts are scientific if they correspond to an objective process and make it possible to influence that process and guide it. Were these qualities possessed in the slightest degree by the ideas of those government circles who were inspired by the Apocalypse and believed in the dreams of Rasputin? Or maybe the ideas of the liberals were scientifically grounded, who hoped that a backward Russia, having joined the scrimmage of the capitalist giants, might win at one and the same time victory and parliamentarism? Or maybe the intellectual life of those circles of the intelligentsia was scientific, who slavishly adapted themselves to this liberalism, senile since childhood, protecting their imaginary independence the while with long-dead metaphors? In truth here was a kingdom of spiritual inertness, specters, superstition and fictions, a kingdom, if you will, of "spontaneousness." But have we not in that case a right to turn this liberal philosophy of the February Revolution exactly upside down? Yes, we have a right to say: At the same time that the official society, all that many-storied superstructure of ruling classes, layers, groups, parties and cliques, lived from day to day by inertia and automatism, nourishing themselves with the relics of worn-out ideas, deaf to the inexorable demands of evolution, flattering themselves with phantoms and foreseeing nothing—at the same time, in the working masses there was taking place an independent and deep process of growth, not only of hatred for the rulers, but of critical understanding of their impotence, an accumulation of experience and creative consciousness which the revolutionary insurrection and its victory only completed.

To the question, Who led the February Revolution? we can then answer definitely enough: Conscious and tempered workers educated for the most part by the party of Lenin. But we must here immediately add: This leadership proved sufficient to guarantee the victory of the insurrection, but it was not adequate to transfer immediately into the hands of the proletarian vanguard the leadership of the revolution.

II FROM MARCH TO OCTOBER: THE SEARCH FOR EVER MORE RADICAL SOLUTIONS

Adam B. Ulam

DEMOCRACY FAILED TO SOLVE RUSSIA'S PROBLEMS

As a professor of government at Harvard University and research fellow at the Russian Research Center at Harvard, Adam Ulam's whole career has been centered on the analysis of Communist thought and Soviet affairs. He has particularly emphasized the complex interrelationship of ideas and events that must be fathomed if the course of history is to be explained. In addition to The Bolsheviks, *from which the selection printed herein is taken, his most important published works are:* The New Face of Totalitarianism; The Unfinished Revolution; Patterns of Government; *and* Expansion and Coexistence: The History of Soviet Foreign Policy, 1917–1967. *In the following passage Professor Ulam traces the first months of the Provisional Government and the Petrograd Soviet as they tried fecklessly to cope with internal chaos, war, and Lenin's political opposition.*

"All power to the soviets." This was the key to Lenin's proposals and to their eventual popularity. In 1905 he had made a grave tactical error; he had at first underestimated the popularity and appeal of the soviets. They were an invention of the Mensheviks and reflected the despised "spontaneity" of the masses. Now he saw that the soviets were dear to the heart of the common worker and soldier: they were *his* government, not a distant conniving parliament of the Western type. To plead for them was a masterful psychological stroke. How could anybody accuse the Bolsheviks of lusting after power? They were after all still a small minority within the soviets. Then why are the Mensheviks and the Socialist Revolutionaries afraid of the slogan? Isn't it because they are afraid of responsibility, plotting with the capitalists from the Provisional Government? "It is you gentlemen who have a majority in the [Petrograd] Soviet, not we. Why are you afraid? Why do you lie?" he wrote.

Another dimension of the slogan of which Lenin was not unaware was that to call for "all power to the soviets" was to call for practical dissolution of political authority, a situation in which a determined minority *could* seize power. How could one soberly believe that the

Petrograd Soviet, this body of two to three thousand milling members, could in any effective sense rule Russia? Or its Executive Committee of eighty or ninety? Or that the Petrograd Soviet could be infused with authority and determination, that it could dictate to its sister organizations in Moscow, Irkutsk, or on the western front? When incredibly enough the Soviet gathered its resolution and began to act like a government in June and July Lenin was hastily to abandon his slogan and not to revert to it until the Bolsheviks secured majorities within the major soviets. It was not conscious Machiavellianism that made him adopt this powerful and perverse slogan, but the sure instinct of the revolutionary: what remained of central political authority in Russia—the Provisional Government—had to be destroyed. The Bolsheviks could come to power only as heirs to anarchy.

To the effects of anarchy on his unhappy country Lenin gave but little thought. He was still a *world* revolutionary. Another installment of revolution in Russia would ignite a flame in Germany which would then spread to the rest of Europe. Then there would be time enough to restore authority in Russia and to guide it through an orderly Marxist economic and social transformation, helped and protected by the comrades from the more developed countries. But even at this, the most anarchistic phase of Lenin's career, the scientific Socialist, the Lenin of 1921, occasionally spoke out. In his theses he was emphatic that Russia was not ripe for an immediate introduction of socialism. The proletarian government would only *control,* not yet own, the means of production. While throwing out an incitement to anarchy and lawlessness in the countryside, "all land to the peasants" and right away, Lenin incongruously kept repeating that large estates should be taken over by the state (this "state," which kept vanishing more and more every day) and run as scientific model farms. But this was the small Marxist print in an otherwise anarchistic manifesto, and there is no wonder that the worker or the poor peasant could not read it. To them it was clear that Lenin wanted workers to have factories, and the poor peasants their own plots.

Confronted by this challenge, the two "half governments" were almost helpless. A more united, resolute, and unscrupulous authority would surely have exploited the initial wave of indignation that greeted the public announcement of Lenin's position. Even the sailors of the Baltic fleet, the most unruly revolutionary element, were out-raged. A Bolshevik agitator among them in those April days received an admiral's treatment: he was thrown overboard. Members of the guard that had greeted Lenin addressed the following public letter, its tortuous prose a sure sign that it came from the rank and file: "Having learned that Mister [this probably hurt him most] Lenin came to us in Russia by permission of His Majesty the German Emperor and the King of Prussia, we express our deep regret that we par-ticipated in his solemn welcome to Petrograd . . . [had we known we would have shouted] . . . instead of 'Hurrah,' 'Down with you, go back to the country through which you came to us.' "[1] On April 17 more than fifty thousand wounded and mutilated veterans passed through the streets of the capital with signs denouncing the defeatists and disorganizers of the army. There were shouts demanding Lenin's arrest.

But the "Menshevik scoundrels" from the Soviet interposed them-selves between the wrath of the masses and their enemy. Citizen Lenin was defended before the indignant crowd of the veterans not only by two Mensheviks, but also by that "arch reactionary," presi-dent of the almost defunct Duma, Rodzianko. The revolution was not to be soiled by lynchings and mob violence! The revolutionary democracy, that is, the non-Bolshevik Socialists, persisted in their heroically suicidal course. Thus the Soldiers' Section of the Soviet denounced Lenin and the Bolsheviks' subversive campaign among the front-line troops. But they added that as long as the Bolsheviks limited themselves just (!) to propaganda, no repression should be used against them. Lenin quoted this resolution with approval.[2] Yes, his party was in favor of peaceful persuasion. They did not mean to disorganize the army, they only urged soldiers to fraternize with the Germans. No, the Bolsheviks did not want a separate peace. This was a capitalist slander. So who was really threatening violence and undermining the army? Why the minister of war, capitalist Guchkov! It was he who was threatening and reprimanding those patriotic military units that fired their old officers and elected new ones!

Following its overthrow, the Provisional Government did not lack

[1] Sukhanov, op. cit., vol. 3, p. 109.
[2] *Works,* vol. 24, p. 109.

excellent advice as to what steps it might have taken to preserve democracy in Russia. The usual criticism concerns its failure to make peace and thus to remove the most persuasive element of the Bolsheviks' propaganda. But to argue this is to misunderstand the situation of Russia right after the February Revolution. As was natural in a country that had suffered so many casualties, Russia longed for peace. To an overwhelming majority of politicians and, as we have seen, to the masses of population and soldiers as well, the only way to a speedy peace was defeat of Germany. From the perspective of two world wars such resolution looks foolish and suicidal. But to the average Russian of 1917 a separate peace with Germany and Austria meant only one thing: a victory of the Central Powers and Europe's domination by Imperial Germany. Russia undoubtedly could have gotten a better peace *then* than subsequently at Brest Litovsk. But who could conceive of the Western Allies, then barely holding out, being capable of withstanding the assault of *all* Germany's armies? And in a German-dominated Europe would Russia be allowed to preserve her territorial integrity, or her newly won republican and democratic freedoms? Thus it was not only the notions of honor and of loyalty to the Allies that made the generals and politicians believe that a victorious prosecution of war was a matter of life and death for Russia, and especially democratic Russia.

But the criticism overlooks an even more basic fact. Had it believed it necessary and beneficial, the Provisional Government and the General Staff still could not have concluded a separate peace. Its severest critics, the "internationalist Mensheviks" and the Bolsheviks, all pleaded for peace, but one to be concluded with the "German workers and soldiers" after they had overthrown their emperor and generals. Had the Provisional Government at any point shown the slightest inclination to do what the Bolsheviks subsequently did at Brest Litovsk, it immediately would have been denounced for selling out to the kaiser, for betraying the revolution and the international proletariat. And Lenin's voice would have been the most insistent in this denunciation.[3]

[3] The Manifesto of the Soviet of March 14, the work of its left wing, called upon the nations of the world: "Throw out your autocracy, just as the Russian nation has thrown off its Tsar, refuse to serve as the tool of robbery and force in the hands of the kings, landowners, and bankers—with our friendly joint efforts we shall end

Equally unrealistic is the argument that the opponents of the Bolsheviks should have beaten them to the punch and introduced *immediately* an agrarian reform giving the peasant what remained of the gentry's land. The peasant masses, the argument runs, would not have been won over or at least neutralized by the Bolsheviks' demagoguery. Any tampering with the ownership of land in wartime, as Lenin's experience subsequently shows, was bound to make worse the already desperate food situation. And Russia's was a peasant army. How many soldiers would stay with their units if they were told that back in their village the landlord's estate was being partitioned among the peasant households?

Lenin's own slogan, "All power to the soviets," provided ironically the only clue as to the formula through which Russian democracy could break out of the vicious circle. If the soviets, or rather their Menshevik and Socialist Revolutionary leaders, who had behind them the vast majority of the nation, could be persuaded to assume full power, Russia might have had an effective government. But as has been pointed out the soviets were utterly incapable of governing. As to the Socialist Revolutionaries and the Mensheviks, neither party had a Lenin capable of knocking heads together and leading a unified phalanx. The non-Bolshevik Socialists were split into at least three groups. There were those who believed that the war must be prosecuted to a victorious end; the central or "internationalist" group which urged an immediate peace but only with "the German workers and soldiers"; and the left wing, which more and more followed the Bolsheviks in their disruptive tactics.

There were moments when the Soviet appeared *almost* on the point of rising to its responsibilities. A certain stiffening in its attitude followed the return from exile of Menshevik Irakli Tseretelli, a great revolutionary orator and one of the few who had no illusions as to where the Bolsheviks would lead Russia. He soon became the leading spirit of the Executive Committee though its nominal chairman remained his indecisive countryman Chheidze. Tseretelli undertook to tell some facts of life to the Soviet: "We should not consider the defense of the country as something which does not concern us, something we don't talk about. It should be for us one of the basic

this terrible war. . . ." But it also said: "The Russian Revolution will not let itself be conquered by force from the outside."

tasks of the Revolution, without which we should not be able to conclude a democratic peace and preserve the achievements of the Revolution."[4] But such frank talk shocked even some of the "defensists." To speak about war, defense, in brief about fighting anybody except the reactionaries was thought to be somewhat indecent for a Socialist. It was up to "them"—the bourgeois Provisional Government. The representatives of the revolutionary democracy, the Soviet, even if they tolerated the defense of their country, should confine themselves to the issuance of manifestos and stern vigilance over the revolution.

The majority chafed under this tyranny of revolutionary phraseology. The epithet "Socialist patriot" intimidated the most courageous. Their irritation would, however, assume indirect and petty forms. To Tseretelli and the "defensist" majority of the Soviet one of the most loathsome opponents was Steklov. He was the editor of *Izvestia,* the official news organ of the Soviet, the closest approximation revolutionary Russia had to an official gazette, and as such was sabotaging the policy of the majority. Yet it would have been "undemocratic," a violation of the minority rights, simply to fire Steklov. Hence his opponents dug out a "scandal." Steklov, whose real name was Nahamkis, had petitioned first the tsarist and then the Provisional Government authorities to have it *legally* changed to his party pseudonym. This was a shameful, un-Socialist attempt to conceal one's Jewish origin! Steklov was discredited as a revolutionary statesman, but continued editing *Izvestia.* Such were the concerns and issues that agitated the Soviet.

In the face of the growing confusion Lenin's tactics were bound to gain him adherents. Some military units in Petrograd which in April had wanted to lift him up on their bayonets were already by May under the Bolshevik influence. In the same month he had to restrain his more impatient followers. The masses were not ready yet for a civil war, hence the Bolsheviks should refrain from an overhasty insurrection.[5] "We are now in a minority. The masses as yet don't believe us. We shall know how to wait." He carefully readjusted his propaganda. Attacks upon the Mensheviks and the

---

[4] I. G. Tseretelli, *Reminiscences About the February Revolution* (in Russian) (Paris-Hague, 1963), p. 47.
[5] *Works,* vol. 24, p. 206.

Socialist Revolutionaries became less abusive. About Alexander Kerensky, still the most popular man in Russia, Lenin kept almost silent. Again hopes were to rise in the camp of his enemies that their erstwhile comrade was becoming reasonable, that perhaps, maybe, unity of socialism in Russia might yet be achieved. Martov, who finally reached Russia (also through Germany) raised his voice on the "internationalist" side, thus partly offsetting the influence of Tseretelli, and rendering the Mensheviks even more divided and impotent as a political force. No wonder the Bolsheviks were gaining in the elections to the soviets. Their members could be elected and recalled practically at any time and Lenin denounced as undemocratic the proposal that the delegates should be elected not more often than once every two or three months.

In May there returned another political exile, Leon Trotsky. He came through the good offices of the Provisional Government, which under pressure of the Soviet had to request from the British his release from Canadian internment. With his arrival the tempo of Bolshevik activity quickened. Officially, of course, Trotsky was not yet a member of Lenin's party. He headed a group of the so-called "interfaction" Socialists. This was a veritable party of revolutionary generals with no soldiers, many of them veterans of the prewar splits from bolshevism. They had become estranged from menshevism because of its democratic superstitions, from bolshevism because of their inability to accept Lenin's dictatorial ways. But now people such as Trotsky, Lunacharsky, Uritsky, and others became almost undistinguishable from Lenin's Bolshevik followers. Many of them were of the revolutionary adventurer type and it was Lenin who promised a new and exciting adventure. From the beginning, Trotsky, his old quarrel with Lenin laid aside, supplied the previously missing element in bolshevism. He was unmatched as a revolutionary orator and agitator. Lenin, despite the subsequent legend, was as Sukhanov phrased it, somewhat "aristocratic" in his political technique: he disliked giving frequent speeches before the crowds, and was at his best in closed party gatherings. Most of the old-line Bolsheviks would when it came to addressing crowds simply repeat what their leader had just written; perhaps with the exception of Zinoviev they lacked entirely this fiery individualism and the ability to establish *rapport* with the listeners that shone from

every Trotsky speech. For all his previous hostility to the man and
despite his temperamental dislike of Trotsky which, being rooted in
his own personality, never quite left him, Lenin quickly recognized
that he was indispensable for his own task, for the revolution. What
brought Trotsky to the side of the man who had so cruelly abused
him in the past, and in whom he had seen, before anybody else,
the future dictator? It was partly the recognition of Lenin as the
international revolutionary, the man who was going to make a world
revolution while the others were talking about it. Then there was the
realization that Lenin had won the intermittent political struggle in
which they had been engaged since 1903: he now loomed as the
giant of Russian Marxism, dwarfing the Plekhanovs, Martovs, and
Dans. It was better to fight and if need be to fall on the side of a
man like this, rather than to resume in the midst of a revolution the
existence of a cafe politician and journalist. Lenin's acceptance of
Trotsky was always qualified; after the revolution and the Civil War
he was careful to limit his brilliant partner's political influence. But
Trotsky's conquest by Lenin was complete. Until his death at the
hands of the assassin in Mexico Trotsky was to retain unbounded
admiration and worship for Lenin.

May also brought a ministerial crisis. Some members of the Provisional Government were growing weary of their position of being
as it were on public display in a cage labeled "the bourgeois democratic half government," subject to abuse and reprimand by their
Siamese twin "half government" of the Soviet. The Foreign Minister
Miliukov had just committed an unpardonable sin: he published a
note about Russia's foreign policy which emphasized the resolve to
continue fighting on the Allies' side and did not have a word about
those aims dear to the heart of the "revolutionary democracy": the
abjuration of annexations and contributions and the overthrow of the
kings and capitalists. It was in especially bad taste since it was published on the International Workers' Solidarity Day.[6] The government's resignation was complicated by a legal difficulty: nobody
knew who was empowered to accept it.

Having overcome this obstacle Prince Lvov (he had by now become such a shadowy figure that he was not even mentioned in the

[6] Which in Russia was celebrated on April 18 to coincide with May 1 in the West.

usual attacks upon the "capitalist ministers") thought to overcome the fury of the revolutionary democracy by discharging Miliukov and Guchkov (whose health broke down under his impossible job) and including the Socialists in his cabinet. Skobelev became minister of labor, Tseretelli minister of posts and telegraphs, Chernov (the head of the Socialist Revolutionary party, the spokesman for the vast majority of the peasants) became the minister of agriculture. And Kerensky, now more clearly than before the key man in the government, became minister of war.

On paper the new cabinet represented an impressive show of national unity. It should have stilled the shouts of "All power to the soviets." After all, the most prominent members of the Soviet now were in the government. Confronted with this unpalatable fact, the Bolsheviks immediately raised a new slogan: "Down with the ten capitalist ministers." It was explained to the masses that essentially the government still remained that of the plutocracy, and those Socialists by entering it forfeited their claim to represent the people.

If anything, the "betrayal" of the Socialist ministers bewailed by Martov and Sukhanov increased Lenin's good humor and confidence in the future. He attacked the capitalist ministers so violently, largely because he still had a lingering respect for their political and administrative abilities. For the Mensheviks' and the Socialist Revolutionaries' talents in those spheres he had nothing but contempt. The Menshevik minister, Skobelev, declared that he proposed to tax the "heavy capitalists" 100 per cent (*sic*!). Lenin undertook publicly to teach him some common sense and Marxian economics. The Bolsheviks, he wrote, repudiate all such wild and visionary schemes bound to ruin the national economy. They demand for the state just the *control* of industry and commerce. Under the Bolsheviks most of the capitalists would be able to work both profitably and honorably.[7] Though probably few of his readers believed that he was serious he meant every word. It was just like some empty-headed Menshevik phrasemonger to think that the Socialist state could dispense with the vast experience and technical skills represented by the capitalists. Lenin knew better.

The revolution was turning a corner. A wave of peasant disorders

[7] *Works*, vol. 24, p. 392.

reminiscent of but soon to surpass the events of 1905 had seized Russia. The structure of the state was dissolving. The autonomous movement in the Ukraine was turning toward a demand for independence. There was rapid erosion of all authority. On May 13 the sailors at Kronstadt declared that the only government they recognized was that of the Petrograd Soviet and that the revivified Provisional Government, for all of its six Socialist ministers, was not for them. Though "the Kronstadt republic" was soon persuaded to modify its position, it was a proof that the Bolsheviks' "All power to the soviets" was finding a ready response. Their propaganda among the front-line troops was now bearing fruit. The special organ *Pravda of the Trenches* was freely circulated with its appeals for fraternization, denunciation of the Provisional Government, and hints of a dark intrigue between the capitalists and the generals. Any attempt to reimpose strictly military discipline was by now hopeless. The new War Minister Kerensky issued on May 9 a declaration of the rights of the soldiers and sailors, which sanctioned all forms of political propaganda and activity within the army. Every soldier had the right to belong to any political or professional group he chose. When not on actual duty he was given full freedom to participate in politics (it was assumed, of course, that the soldiers could exert this right even in the trenches when not in actual combat); "the right of internal self-government, imposition of penalties and control under the given circumstances" were to belong to the soldiers' elected committees. Thus the declaration sanctified and extended, on behalf of the government this time, the principles of *Order Number 1*. The commanding officers pleaded in vain with the government not to issue or at least to soften the declaration. They were met with the rejoinder, probably realistic, that the declaration merely ratified the status quo and that to try to undo it meant risking even greater trouble. A Menshevik minister observed with tragic prescience: "When we are told to bring the Revolution to an end we must answer that a revolution cannot be begun or ended by a decree."[8] Even the "defensist" Mensheviks believed that an army, just like a government, can be run by persuasion. Tseretelli told the generals: "The soldier will trust you if he understands that you are not enemies

8 General Anton Deniken, *The Story of Russia's Time of Troubles* (in Russian) (Paris, 1921), vol. 1, part 2, p. 61.

of democracy. That is the only way by which the Soviet has firmly established its authority." It is superfluous to describe the effect of such pronouncements upon military men. They go very far in explaining why many officers came eventually to hate the democratic Socialists much more than the Bolsheviks.

Though warned by a general that if the Germans attack "the Russian army will tumble like a house of cards," the Provisional Government now announced its intention of launching a *Russian* offensive. With February fighting had practically stopped on the vast front, the Austro-Germans waiting confidently for the inevitable breakup of Russia's armies. The foolhardy decision to attack could with great difficulty be justified on the grounds that inactivity was the greatest enemy of the soldiers' morale, that the Germans were shifting divisions to the western front to deal a mortal blow to the Allies, and so on. But the major reason was, as with so many policies of the "revolutionary democracy," a fantastic belief in the power of phraseology and badly drawn parallels with the French Revolution. Then the armies of the free people dealt crushing blows to the combined forces of the European despots. Now the "freest army in the world" was going to demonstrate its superiority over the armed slaves of Prussian militarism. The contagion of revolutionary bathos was universal. It would be unfair to forget that the Bolsheviks were also at the moment under its sway. In his blueprint for a Socialist state Lenin envisaged the abolition of the standing army and its replacement by a militia with elective officers.

The embodiment of this revolutionary bathos was Alexander Kerensky. In his order to the army he called on the soldiers "to carry on the points of their bayonets peace, truth, and justice," to go forward in the name of their "boundless love for their country and the Revolution." To the superficial observer he appeared to have worked a miracle in reviving the morale of the army. Everywhere along the front lines his speeches aroused wild enthusiasm of the troops, pledges to die for the revolution. Sukhanov, whose greatest fear was that a victorious offensive might profit the *bourgeoisie,* pays him this venomous tribute: "At the feet of Kerensky calling on them to go to their death [the soldiers] threw their decorations; women would take their jewels and in the name of Kerensky were offering them for this longed-for (nobody knows why) victory." In his soldier's

tunic with an arm in a sling (he suffered from bursitis, but this gave
him the appearance of a wounded hero) the minister of war sym-
bolized the determination of Russian democracy to crush the enemy.

The danger of a military victory was not absent from Lenin's mind.
He had not altered his low opinion of Kerensky's abilities and had a
realistic view about the possibilities of a sustained victorious advance. But even a temporary success might arrest or reverse the
trend toward bolshevism among the soldiers and workers. In June,
Lenin, who a few weeks before had said "we shall know how to
wait," was ready to toy with an insurrection. Both in that month and
in July his behavior was close to what he himself described and
attacked as "adventurism." He must have been haunted by the
memories of 1905. For all the talk about careful preparation and
the need to conquer the masses before attempting to seize power,
Lenin was aware that there is a moment in every revolution which
if not grasped and exploited may never recur.

The chosen time coincided with the All-Russian Congress of the
Workers' and Soldiers' Soviets. In that assembly out of 777 delegates with party affiliations the Bolsheviks had over 100 and their
allies, the "interfaction" group, about thirty. This was a dazzling
accession of strength since February. Still, the Mensheviks and the
Socialist Revolutionaries had a substantial majority. Lenin emerged,
for the meeting, from the editorial offices of *Pravda* and delivered
a more than usually demagogic speech. What created amazement
and even some laughter was his statement that there was a party
ready to take power by itself: namely, the Bolsheviks. As to his
formula for governing, it consisted in the immediate necessity of
arresting one hundred of the most substantial capitalists and forcing
them to reveal their intrigues that kept the Russian people in war
and misery. "Are we Socialists or bullies?" was the rejoinder of
Kerensky. The revolution was still humane and it aroused distaste
even among the extreme radicals that a former inmate of the
tsarist jails should call for arbitrary imprisonment. But Lenin was
not really talking to his sophisticated audience: his words would be
reprinted in thousands of copies of *Pravda*; they would strengthen
the suspicions and class bitterness of the proletariat.

On the ninth of June an even more violent proclamation by the
Bolsheviks called upon the soldiers and people of Petrograd to take

FIGURE 2. Alexander Kerensky in 1917. (*United Press International Photo*)

to the streets. The proclamation described the government as a tool of capitalists and landlords. Kerensky's declaration of the soldiers' rights was declared a violation of their civic freedom (!). Immediate peace was demanded, but no separate treaty with Emperor Wilhelm, no secret agreements with the French and English capitalists. It was a call for rebellion and violence barely concealed by the statement that demonstrations should be peaceful: "State your demands calmly and convincingly as behooves the strong." Under prevailing conditions and with passions rising it was unthinkable that violence could be avoided during a demonstration in which thousands of armed soldiers would be participating.

It is equally clear that the Bolsheviks had as yet no concrete plan of seizing power. As the French revolutionary device had it, *On s'engage, puis on voit*—one begins action, then one can see what happens next. The aim was to overthrow the Provisional Government in order to frustrate the decision to launch an offensive, and then . . . Power might come to the Bolsheviks and their allies. They could count on the sympathy of some regiments of the Petrograd garrison where the news of the offensive aroused the natural apprehension that they might be sent to the front. They also had a more reliable force at their disposal in their own armed militia, the Red Guards.

Faced with the danger, the Congress of Soviets unexpectedly rose to the occasion. On the night of June 9 it banned all demonstrations for the next few days. Members of the highest organ of the "revolutionary democracy" were dispatched to the barracks and factories to explain the Bolshevik game to the soldiers and workers. The anti-Bolshevik units of the garrison were put on the alert. Lenin and his lieutenants were put in an unenviable and dangerous situation. The ostensible purpose of the demonstration was to bring power to the soviets. Here the highest organ of the soviets banned this "peaceful" intercession by the people on their behalf. What is more, the military units on the Bolsheviks' side were in a lamentable state of discipline and military readiness. They could be counted on to demonstrate and perhaps to rough up unarmed opponents, but what if it came to actual fighting? Even in October this question was to weigh heavily on the minds of the actual organizers of the Bolshevik military insurrection. The soldiers' willingness to follow the Bolsheviks was directly related to their unwillingness to fight. The statement that the demonstration should be peaceful was not entirely hypocritical; it also contained the assurance that violence should be limited to pushing around some capitalists and "betrayers of the proletariat." On second thought the Bolshevik Central Committee called off the demonstration.

Never backward in making a virtue out of necessity, the Bolsheviks now paraded their exemplary democratic behavior. *They* submitted to the will of the majority, even though that majority had grievously misjudged and slandered their intentions. *They* had to plead with the masses to desist from demonstrating and expressing their wrath with the "capitalist ministers" and the "defensists." And again many non-Bolshevik Socialists found this pleading convincing. Tseretelli's demand before the Congress of the Soviets that measures be taken to prevent the recurrence of the threat of the tenth of June, the calls for disarming of the Bolsheviks' private army—the Red Guards— were met with distaste and opposition by the Martovs and Sukhanovs. How can the revolution disarm the proletariat? Would it not lead to a bourgeois dictatorship, to a tsarist restoration? And the Executive Committee of the Congress contented itself with a pious resolution.

Lenin's own reaction to the failure of June 10 was characteristic. He began to wonder aloud whether the slogan "All power to the soviets" still corresponded to the needs of the hour. The soviets, with the Bolsheviks in them still in a minority, appeared suddenly to take this slogan seriously. "Even if the soviets took all power . . . we would not submit to their dictation to narrow down the freedom of our agitation; or to the prohibition of demonstrations in the capital and at the front. . . . We would prefer then to become an illegal officially persecuted party."[9] But his faith in the soviets was soon re-established. They limited themselves to a resolution and were as far as ever from attempting to exert any power, not to speak of "all" power. In three weeks the Bolsheviks were ready to try again.

With June ended the good-natured period of the revolution. It was born amidst universal democratic and patriotic enthusiasm with the belief that government could be a matter of meetings and resolutions and that peoples and not their rulers should conclude a just and lasting peace. By now the reality was shown to be quite different. From June on, those who hoped for a democratic conclusion and peace had to work with increasing bitterness and despair in their hearts. There was no longer even an appearance of national unity or of "revolutionary democracy." The extreme Left was openly committed to the use of force. Among the Right there was a growing longing for a military coup that should save Russia from the "Jews and anarchists." The legend of the invincibility of the "most democratic army in the world" was shattered when the June offensive, after some initial success, ended in a disastrous defeat.

The revolution had run out of its original impetus. There are mirage-like interludes of resolution and authority of the democratic

---

[9] *Works,* vol. 25, p. 60.

forces. The Congress of the Soviets set up a permanent Executive Committee, thus giving Russia at least nominally a centralized authority. In July this committee and the Provisional Government would still appear as saviors of democracy. The promise of the "real" parliament, the Constituent Assembly, would until the last moment keep alive the hope for a democratic conclusion of the revolution. But no such interludes could change the fact that among the people enthusiasm had been exhausted and patience was drawing to an end. The early revolution was generous and hopeful. But these sentiments could not survive exasperation with the war, food shortages, and the fumbling and impotent government. It was the setting for a dictatorship.

Nicholas N. Golovine

A DEMORALIZED ARMY SPREAD DISSATISFACTION AMONG THE PEOPLE

Before the revolution Lieutenant General Nicholas N. Golovine was a professor in the Russian Imperial General Staff College and Chief of Staff of the Russian armies on the Rumanian front. He is recognized as the best Russian authority on the history of World War I. His studies on the Russian army, pursued diligently for many years after his emigration from Russia, are deeply affected by a strong interest in the sociological impact of the war and the revolution upon Russia's soldiers. In the section presented here, the relationship between the army and the people of the nation is drawn very clearly.

As one studies the attitude of the bulk of the troops in the first days of the revolution, it becomes obvious that the degree of revolutionary feeling, and the tendency to yield to demoralizing influences increased proportionately with the distance from the front. This was observable throughout the entire year. The fact that every new wave of disintegration came from the rear was based on that; and the

From Nicholas N. Golovine, *The Russian Army in the World War* (New Haven, 1931). Reprinted by permission of the Yale University Press.

process of collapse in the army illustrated a kind of general psycho-logical law. General Serrigny . . . noticed the same thing in the French theater of war. He writes:

> *This development made itself clear during the defeatist propaganda of 1917. Regiments which had been relieved from service at the front, and were resting in the rear, were the first to yield to such propaganda; and they were infected with the poison by reinforcement units and by men who had been on home leave. Germany experienced the same thing in October 1918. She was in a state of complete disintegration. Her rear units and depot regiments were hoisting red flags and tearing the shoulder-straps from their officers, while troops in the firing line continued to fight gal-lantly. The latter, after the signing of the armistice, retreated across the Rhine in perfect order, and helped to restore it at home, for they had had no time to be infected. . . .*

In Russia, the process of the spread of military disintegration from the rear to the front showed itself in another way. For in the northern front, behind which was the chief center of revolution, Petrograd, it developed more rapidly than elsewhere. Next came the western front, behind which lay the second focus of revolution, Moscow. The southwestern front, in the rear of which was Kiev, was in a more healthy state; and the waves of dissolution reached it only later on. . . . As for the armies on the Rumanian front, they made the best showing. They were on foreign soil, and that delayed the revolu-tionary process.

The Petrograd garrison, consisting of depot units, turned out to be the revolution's driving force. Indeed it was its revolt that gave the revolution its instant victory. The Baltic fleet and the fortress troops of Kronstadt, which were nearest to Petrograd, proved to be no less demoralized.

*   *   *

Reports of the Members of the Duma

At least some approximate idea of the attitude of the soldiers in the first month of the revolution can be given by a report made by N. O. Yanushkevich, a member of the Duma, who, with other mem-bers, visited various sections of the front. His report was read before the Provisional Committee of the Duma, which in the first month of the revolution sought to maintain control over the Provisional Government headed by Prince Lvov.

This report by Yanushkevich is typical. It is almost identical with the reports of other members of the Duma, who, in March 1917, had been sent by the Provisional Government to visit the army. Undoubtedly, their common mission accounted for the similarity of their reports; and the mission they had been given was that of strengthening the army's faith in the Provisional Government. In their desire to win the confidence of the rank and file they risked seeming to play the part of demagogues. In Yanushkevich's report this may be seen in his tendency to find an explanation for all rank and file disorders in the "tactlessness" of officers not in sympathy with the revolution. The following detail is characteristic: the committees are called in the report "soldiers' and officers' committees," the word "soldiers' " being placed before the word "officers'." Similar details, written with intent to please the soldier in general, may be found in many other places. But, broadly speaking, one must admit that all such envoys of the Provisional Government were filled with a profound, patriotic, and sincere desire to help the army through the impending crisis.

The Yanushkevich report offers added evidence of the social and psychological law already spoken of, namely, that the disintegration of an army begins in its rear. Yanushkevich states that the spirit of the troops grew better as one neared the front, and that the attitude of the men in the firing line was "so cheerful, joyous, and good that one felt reassured." "The soldiers," he said "are waiting for something. . . ." That "waiting attitude" of the bulk of the troops in the first days following the collapse of the old regime has been noted by all observers. It is very significant from the psychological standpoint. Up to then the great majority of people had been wont to look passively upon all high questions of national importance; there everything was decided by the tsar and his government: and such an attitude was the product of centuries of habit. Now, and suddenly, everything was overturned. The newspapers, in which the soldiers now were greatly interested, the speakers to whom they now listened for hours, exhorted freedom; and, they said, the people were henceforward to decide everything for themselves. Most soldiers were still bewildered and did not know what to do. From somewhere deep down in their inner consciousness selfish desires would often arise: to take away the land from the landlords, to rob the bourgeois, to abandon the front, and go home. . . . But the fact that a lawful government, although its authority was shaken, was still in existence tended to restrain such anarchistic tendencies, and, for a while, they remained subconscious. Under such conditions, the sounder elements at the front were inclined to rely upon the Duma and the Provisional Government. The ovations to the member of the Duma which Yanushkevich describes in his report were sincere. Few knew as yet that the Provisional Government had already been out-trumped by the Petrograd Soviet of Workers' and Soldiers' Deputies. However, the extreme revolutionary elements in the army already suspected it. This may be seen from this sentence in the Yanushkevich report: "We were also requested to let them send their representatives to Petrograd to learn what was going on there." Later on, such representatives were sent by every army. In this way those who advocated making the Revolution more radical were able to establish contact with the Petrograd Soviet, which aspired at the leadership of the whole revolutionary movement.

This, however, Yanushkevich failed to see. Strongly impressed by the outward side of his reception, he forgot completely that all crowd manifestations are always highly emotional and subject to change, and that mere appearances could not serve as a guaranty that the same crowd, within the shortest time, would not acclaim with equal enthusiasm something entirely different. Nor did he realize that the underlying causes of the split between the officers and their men were of a more serious nature than the alleged "tactlessness" of the former. That split marked the beginning of the hostility which eventually led to civil war. He likewise failed to understand that what was said about leaves of absence and the requests of the older soldiers to be sent home were ways of showing their unwillingness to go on fighting. That "refusal to wage war" was still confined to the subconscious in the case of most of the men; though they did not dare as yet to express it openly, it existed as a potential factor.

To show that our analysis is correct we shall cite the report of two members of the Duma, M. Maslennikov and M. Shmakov, who visited the southwestern front one month later in April. Heretofore, what had been taking place in the army at the time of Yanushkevich's visit appeared only in symptoms that were sporadic and barely perceptible, but everything had now become very plain. Moreover, it should be borne in mind that the disintegration of the southwestern front, visited by Maslennikov, proceeded at a slower pace than the northern, with Petrograd in its immediate rear.

As we consider the report of Maslennikov and Shmakov, the following fact must not be left out of sight: during the first month of the revolution, the soldiers' soviets were being formed in every section of the front. The commanding officers, anxious to get control over that elemental movement in the rank and file, decided to create committees of men and to place representatives of the officers on those committees. They hoped that in that way the soldier's confidence in his officers might be restored, and the gap between them bridged anew. Instructions to take such action were given by General Alexeev, who, as we have said, had replaced the grand duke as commander-in-chief.

By the time Maslennikov and Shmakov arrived at the front, committees in every regiment, division, and army corps had already been formed. Therefore, the task of the two members of the Duma, in so far as their being able to arrive at the attitude of the soldiers was concerned, was easier than that of Yanushkevich, who had visited the front when the committees were in process of formation and soldiers' meetings differed but little from casual gatherings apt to be carried away by the appeal of an eloquent speaker.

During their first visit to two regiments, described by Maslennikov and Shmakov as quite capable of fighting, they heard the formula "peace without annexations and contributions," which was the first slogan used by the defeatist propaganda of the Bolsheviks. The peculiar way in which the soldiers interpreted it may be judged from the many cases where they refused to dig new trenches, even at short distances in advance of their lines, and when trenches were needed to strengthen the positions they were holding.

A frank explanation of the meaning of "without annexations and contributions," as understood by the soldiers, was given to the members of the Duma by the chairman of a conference of the committees of the Second Army, a war-time lieutenant, whose manner of speech "was clearly Bolshevik." After he had described the Duma as representing the interests of the *bourgeois* classes and the capitalists,

> he declared that the army would fight to the end only on the condition that the actual intentions of the Allies were made known, and Russia given a guaranty that the war was not being waged for their capitalistic aims. Taken as a whole, the speech gave the impression of being made to undermine the prestige of the Duma and the Provisional Government, as well as confidence in the Allies. It was with this situation that the Duma's representatives were, for the first time, confronted. The speech of the chairman had an enormous success. . . .

Further confirmation came when they visited the engineers of the Guard.

> The political views of the presiding body of the committee [says the report] proved to be very radical, and Bolshevik in their nature. At this meeting the question of peace was taken up for the first time in our tour of the front. A member of the presiding body, the editor of a Lettish paper, suggested a peace conference as the quickest way to liquidate the war. Other speakers demanded that our agreements with the Allies be published, to show that we were not fighting for their imperialistic and capitalistic aims. A lack of confidence in our Allies was clearly felt. Not a single word was said that was hostile to Germany. Nevertheless, the meeting ended with cheers.

But, later on, Maslennikov and Shmakov encountered frank displays of defeatism:

> Soldiers of infantry regiments have often cut the telephone wires from artillery "observers" to the batteries. They have threatened to lift the artillery men on their bayonets if the latter opened fire on the enemy. The same threat to use the bayonet prevents all machine-gun fire. Fraternizing is in progress, though not to the same extent as at Easter when it took a monstrous form. . . . We were told that in our trenches, some thirty yards from those of the Germans, the machine-guns were kept in their covers. . . .

*　　　*　　　*

The Role of Kerensky

The great majority of the soldiers, as we have said, had been bewildered, in the first days of the revolution, by the rapidity and ease of the overthrow of the imperial regime. Correspondingly and with bursts of excitement then, they acclaimed the new authority represented by the Provisional Government. But very soon news began to reach them that the actual power was not with that government, but in the hands of the Petrograd Soviet of Workers' and Soldiers' Deputies. While the soldiers did not wish to break with the Provisional Government, carried to the top by the first wave of the revolution, their sympathies were with the Soviet organization. Highly significant is that part of the report which says that the views of the committees of those army units whose readiness to fight had been least impaired, were identical with the political views of the right wing of the Petrograd Soviet of Workers' and Soldiers' Deputies. That was true everywhere. M. Yakovlev proves it when he states that "in the first days of the Revolution these [military] committees were headed by Social-Revolutionist and Menshevist elements which tried to stretch the Revolution on the Procrustean bed of bourgeois half-reforms." Such forces were responsible for that tremendous popularity which Kerensky enjoyed among the soldiers at the front, from the beginning of the revolution. Due to that popularity, in July he was made head of the government, despite the fact that he no longer satisfied the revolutionary aims of the Petrograd Soviet. In this lay the tragedy in the role played by Kerensky. All his power depended on the support of soldiers at the front. And, while their attitude was being changed more slowly than was the mood of the Petrograd Soviet, that chief center of the revolution, every further intensification of it tended to undermine Kerensky's strength and increase that of the Soviet. Under such circumstances the army, at the front, became an arena for the struggle between two tendencies. One aimed to keep the revolution to politics alone, the other sought to change it, most speedily, into a social revolution. There is no doubt, however, that the representatives of the former, including Kerensky, were involuntarily pushing it on to transformation to the social phase. At the soldiers' meetings, Kerensky used to cry out, "Comrades, let us intensify the Revolution." Yet in that, as in similar cases, his words were dictated purely by demagoguery; and by means of it, he and his political sympathizers were seeking to gain power over the masses. The same foolish demagoguery also accounts for the orders given by Kerensky which led to the decline of the prestige of army leaders, to the destruction of discipline, and to further disintegration of the army. Kerensky did not understand what had been at work in the army from the beginning of the revolution. There was another important factor in the situation. Though suffering from a psychosis, the troops had to go on fighting. It is only natural that the burden of the war—so little understood by them—which had weighed upon them for three years, had stirred in them a spirit of ever growing discontent and unwillingness. Consequently, from the beginning of the revolution a desire to end the war, along with the political, economic, and social stimuli at work in every revolution, spread rapidly in both the army and the people.

Deserters

The vast increase in the number of cases of desertion and evasion of military service, which followed upon the outbreak of the revolution, bears testimony to the urgent desire of the bulk of our soldiers to end the war. Let us go back to a few figures given in earlier chapters. The average monthly total of the sick increased 120 per cent, although the army suffered from no epidemic diseases and the sanitary conditions were no worse than before. The monthly record of deserters increased 400 per cent. Furthermore, beginning with March 1917, there was a great "leakage" of soldiers from the front; and, in the rear, it became increasingly frequent for men to refuse, under varying pretexts, to join their regiments.

In the memoirs of General Polovtsev, who commanded the troops of the Petrograd military district, we find a description of one of the methods of desertion, and one practiced under the very nose of the Provisional Government.

> A rumor [he says] to the effect that all soldiers over forty were to be discharged had got abroad, and an agitation began to make this rumor a reality. As a result, soldiers of forty commenced to desert, and to arrive in the capital with requests for legal discharges. They camped on the Semenovsky drill grounds, formed companies, founded their own republic, and sent deputations everywhere. Having no success, they commenced to parade the city, sometimes more than fifty companies at once. Chernov had encouraged them. Kerensky became enraged and had them driven out. I decided to starve them, and ordered their rations to be stopped. But it turned out that their republic could subsist independently,

that they could live on what they made from the sale of cigarettes, from carrying baggage at the railroad stations, and the like.

. . . More than 2 million men left the army in 1917 wilfully, and under various pretexts, since the revolution began. It was a stupendous flow of men to the rear, that could only be called a spontaneous [de]mobilization.

The above figures fully justify the statement that "the refusal to wage war" became, soon after the revolution had begun, a part of its fundamental character. The political leaders, placed at the helm by the first changes, leaders who for the most part belonged to the progressive bourgeoisie, failed to understand it. Nor was it understood by Kerensky, who in July had succeeded Prince Lvov, and, assisted by the Social-Revolutionists of the Right, had become the master of Russia's destiny. They all continued to exhort the people to go on with the war until final victory was won.

Only one small group, the Bolsheviks headed by Lenin, staked their success by going to the army and calling for the immediate ending of the war.

*   *   *

The Offensive of June, 1917

The main attack in the summer campaign of 1917 was to be launched by the southwestern front in the direction of Lemberg. The attacks on the northern, western, and Rumanian fronts were to be only of a subsidiary nature. On June 18, the Eleventh and the Seventh Armies began the offensive. An excellent plan had been worked out. Artillery and technical equipment in quantities previously unknown to Russia's forces were concentrated to prepare the infantry assault. All enemy works were literally leveled with the ground. Then and only then did the infantry advance in the zone of the enemy's fire; for the most part the picked shock units headed the advance. But the rest of the infantry followed with reluctance. Some regiments, having reached the enemy's lines, turned back on the pretext that the trenches had been so completely destroyed that it would be impossible to occupy them overnight. Nevertheless, thanks to the excellent artillery preparation and the heroic action of the picked units, the enemy positions were taken in the first two days. After that the Eleventh and Seventh Armies only marked time, inasmuch as the infantry was unwilling to advance further.

> I feel in duty bound to report [wrote the commander of the Eleventh Army] that, despite the victory won on June 18 and 19 which should have strengthened the spirit and increased the zeal of the troops, no such effect could be seen in most regiments, while in some the conviction prevails that they have done their work and must go no further.

In the meantime, on June 23, the Eighth Army, on the left flank of the southwestern front, went into action. General Kornilov, commanding, had concentrated all his best units for a break through. But the same thing happened. The attack was successful, and even more so than in the center; for the Austro-Hungarian divisions facing the Eighth Army were of inferior quality. On the first day 7,000 prisoners and 48 guns were taken, and the Russian troops penetrated far into the enemy zone. But, as the advance progressed, the picked units, having suffered heavy losses, melted away, while the remaining infantry in their rear became so disorganized that a slight center attack from the enemy caused the entire army to fall back in the greatest confusion.

By July 2 this offensive on the southwestern front was at an end. The losses in the three armies amounted to 1,222 officers and 37,500 men. Such figures, compared with the losses before the revolution, were small. But they were suffered solely by the picked units and the few regiments not yet in disintegration. Thus they were heavy indeed, for they meant the loss of all elements imbued with a sense of duty, and available for preserving some sort of order among the troops. As they no longer existed, the three armies became nothing but tumultuous crowds, which any first pressure by the enemy could put to flight. Such pressure was brought to bear on the left flank of the Eleventh Army where at that time there had been concentrated 7 army corps or 20 divisions—a total of 240 battalions, 40 squadrons, 100 heavy and 475 field guns and howitzers. The opposing enemy had only 9 divisions, or some 83 battalions, with about 60 heavy and 400 field guns and howitzers. Despite such enormous numerical superiority, the detachments of the Eleventh Army began to retreat of their own accord. Soon the whole army was following in a panic.

And the rest of the story may show how completely unfit it was to fight. On July 9 it reached the line of the Seret. An attack by three German companies put to flight the One Hundred and Twenty-sixth and the Second Finnish Divisions. Resistance to the advancing enemy was offered only by cavalry and infantry officers and non-commissioned officers supported by single soldiers. The rest of the infantry was fleeing, while crowds of deserters blocked every road. To tell how many there were it is enough to say that 12,000 were arrested in the neighborhood of Volochisk by a single battalion of picked men, who had been posted in the rear. And these fleeing mobs committed every act of violence. They murdered officers, robbed the people, and assaulted women and children.

On July 9 the committees and commissars of the Eleventh Army sent the Provisional Government the following telegram:

The German offensive, which began on our front on July 6, is turning into an immense catastrophe which perhaps threatens revolutionary Russia with ruin. A sudden and disastrous change occurred in the attitude of the troops, who had recently advanced under the heroic leadership of a few units. Their zeal soon spent itself. The majority are in a state of growing disintegration. Authority and obedience exist no longer. Persuasion and admonition produce no effect. Threats and sometimes shots are the answer. . . . For hundreds of miles one can see lines of deserters, armed and unarmed, in good health and in high spirits, certain they will not be punished. The situation calls for strong measures. . . . An order to fire upon them was issued today by the Commander-in-Chief, with the approval of the commissars and committees. And all Russia should be told the truth. . . . Though she shudder at it, it will give her the necessary determination to deal with those who by their cowardice are ruining and betraying both their country and the Revolution.

David Mitrany

A PRIMITIVE PEASANTS' WAR
GAINED MOMENTUM

*David Mitrany was born in Bucharest in 1888 and completed his advanced
studies at London. He was once a member of the editorial staff of the*
Manchester Guardian, *and has held teaching positions at London, Harvard,
Yale, and Smith College. He has also been associated with the Royal Institute of International Affairs and is Permanent Member of the Institute for
Advanced Study at Princeton. Mitrany has long been interested in the special characteristics of the peasant in revolution. In particular he has explored
the strange process by which peasant revolutions have given power to
Marxists, whose theory of revolution is founded upon the urban proletariat.*

It is unlikely that anyone could have forecast the way in which the
revolution worked itself out, or indeed that anyone can as yet
analyze soundly why and how things happened as they did. What is
plain, and relevant to our subject, is that it was a double revolution
—a peasant revolution and a political one; and while the peasant
revolution at first took more or less its natural course, the other
was given an accidental twist through the sudden injection of the
Bolshevik element into the process of revolutionary gestation.
Peasantism and Marxism were thus brought sharply face to face,
not as before in a theoretical disputation but in a direct and purpose-
ful issue of power. Trotsky has pointed out frankly in his brilliant
History of the Russian Revolution all that divided the two categories
in the stream of social evolution. In Russia, he wrote, the "chronic
lag of ideas and relations behind new objective conditions," which
creates "in a period of revolution that leaping movement of ideas
and passions," was of a double kind. Russia's agrarian problem was
still unsolved; the bourgeois revolution that had so profoundly
affected France and England had had but small effect in Russia.

*In order to realize the Soviet State there was required a drawing together
and mutual penetration of two factors belonging to completely different*

From David Mitrany, *Marx Against the Peasant: A Study in Social Dogmatism* (Chapel
Hill, 1951). Reprinted by permission of The University of North Carolina Press and
George Weidenfeld & Nicolson, Ltd.

*historic species: a peasant war—that is, a movement characteristic of the
dawn of bourgeois development—and a proletarian insurrection, the
movement signaling its decline. That is the essence of 1917.*

Herein lay the root of the many turns in Soviet agrarian policy,
and in no small degree indeed of the Soviet system's whole dictatorial destiny. From the moment that Marxism, that is, analytical
theory based on English conditions, gave place to Leninism, that is,
revolutionary strategy based on the "objective situation" in eastern
Europe, the issue of rent, which presupposes the existence of
capitalist farming, was thrust into the background by the peasants'
demand for land. Trotsky's historical distinction was in fact reflected
strikingly in the attitude of the two revolutions on this issue. It was
characteristic of Kerensky's "provisional" regime, with its bourgeois-
liberal tendency, that it proposed to postpone agrarian reform till
the convening of a national assembly. The government which took
over after the October Revolution, however, at once handed over the
land by decree to the peasants. Lenin had included the Left Social
Revolutionaries in his government and had taken over their agrarian
program, nationalization of all the land and its equal distribution
among the peasants, though the Social Revolutionary group left it
after only a few months.

There was indeed not much else that Lenin could do. The peasant
revolution was well under way by the time the Bolsheviks staged
their "proletarian" attack. From an admirable first-hand study of
reports of local authorities Professor Robinson has shown that the
rural revolution had spread quickly and effectively to all the provinces. The collapse of the old regime had been like a break in a
dam, through which first a small trickle and then a rushing stream
of spontaneous revolutionary action poured. The peasants began at
once to take over forcibly large estates and forests, the number
rising with every month—from 17 in March, 204 in April, 259 in May,
577 in June, to 1,122 in July. It was estimated that in the first two
years the peasants in thirty-six departments had taken over 86 per
cent of the large estates and 80 per cent of their farm equipment;
this increased their holding from 80 to 96.8 per cent of all usable
land.

But Yakovlev's description of the way in which the peasants dealt with the landlords also brought out clearly the nonpolitical character of their revolt. The Bolsheviks, however, had reasons of their own not only for accepting the accomplished fact but for speeding the process. They had before then adopted the view that the simplest way to break the back of "feudal-bourgeois regimes" in the eastern countries was to let the peasants take over the land. At the particular moment, and in opposition to the Kerensky regime and its supporters, it was also a matter of policy with them to stop the "imperalist" war so as to let the revolutions which they implicitly expected in Germany and elsewhere get under way; and this fitted in with their urgent local need to prevent the army under its tsarist officers from being turned against them. Though passive, the Russian armies were still holding the front, but they quickly disintegrated when the peasant soldiers heard that the land was theirs for the taking. One might perhaps sum it all up in this way, that 1917 was a diffused peasant revolution which the Bolsheviks took in hand and organized. They would indeed not have got very far had they not literally released and spurred the pent-up restlessness of the peasant masses. Evidence for this view is to be found in the political war of maneuver which for many years after they had to wage, and in the drastic means they finally had to use before they could bring to a head their own Bolshevik Revolution.

Launcelot A. Owen

THE PEASANT BECAME "AUTOCRAT OF RUSSIA"

Launcelot A. Owen, now Senior Lecturer in History and Social Sciences at the Sydney Teachers' College, New South Wales, Australia, carried out his doctoral work at the London University School of Slavonic and East European Studies, where he worked with the late Sir Bernard Pares. His principal published work, The Russian Peasant Movement, 1906–1917, *is a*

From L. A. Owen, "The Russian Agrarian Revolution of 1917," *The Slavonic and East European Review* 12 (July 1933): 156–166. Reprinted by permission of Launcelot A. Owen and *The Slavonic and East European Review.*

major contribution to knowledge about the peasant in revolution. His article here is a carefully documented study of the changing tenor of life in Russia's rural communities during 1917.

By 3 April a new note of anxiety appeared in official documents. It was little more than a month since Nicholas II's abdication. The planting of seed for the harvest was imminent. Army and people depended upon that as on no other single economic factor. The Provisional Government issued an "appeal to citizens." That appeal received the support of the Soviet of Workers' and Soldiers' Deputies —which was symptomatic of the dyarchy which ruled in Petrograd until October. From the contents of the Minister's Circular one might assume that interference with estates in the vicinity of villages had already occurred, even if information upon that subject were not obtainable elsewhere.

The "tenor of village life" was deemed worthy of inquiry by the Central Government on 11 April. The suggested systemization of reports itself conclusively reveals by internal evidence the various types of disorder that menaced authority over the length and breadth of the decaying empire. An "agrarian movement" was now definitely recognized. Its phases were now catalogued—infringement of land laws; unauthorized acts affecting owners, landowners and land leaseholders; unauthorized plowing of land; incendiarism; illicit timber-cutting; removal of farm implements; "cattle-lifting"; destruction of boundary marks; and, finally, trespassing.

To such qualitative analysis of the Russian agrarian situation, a quantitative survey is a useful supplement. Statistics which illuminate the period are to be extracted from *Information on the number and nature of violations of the law based on the sources of the Chief Administration of affairs of the Militia for March-September, 1917.* In March one finds only seventeen cases of infringement of land laws, whether implying attempted seizure of estates, interference with timber rights or the removal of labor from estates. Other general acts of criminal intent—involving burglary, robbery, deaths during disturbances, unauthorized arrests and searches, not to mention liberation of convicted prisoners—amounted to fifty-six cases. (The second figure is inclusive of urban disturbances.)

The month of April showed a considerable loosening of social discipline. Landed property rights were infringed in 204 cases. Yet cases of violence leading to fatal results or implying robbery or incitement of the populace to riot, amounted to 32 cases only. The figures for March and April cannot be directly compared, since some instances of violence were placed under the heading of landed-property infringements. Despite this minor reservation, the totals for March and April (73 and 236 cases, respectively) need little comment. A great change had evidently occurred in the countryside.

Numerous telegrams from private individuals told later of arrests and of the unauthorized activities of village communities. Cantonal committees, even before 13 April, were depriving landowners, both large and small, of "the possibility of executing their duty to the State." Undefined control over rural affairs was already exercised by the village communities themselves. A "land question" now appeared. An "unauthorized settlement" of this problem "in the interests of the population itself concerned in the matter"—a "fortuitous arrangement" governed solely by a "narrowly local point of view"—was a prospect upon which the administration of Prince Lvov could not but frown. The liberty of the individual, it appeared, no longer rested upon the sanctions of the old legal system. The consolidation of the new regime was menaced by unauthorized decrees—presumably of cantonal and village communities. It is abundantly clear that Provincial Commissaries had an unenviable task, suspended as they were in mid-air between a weakening authority above and the seething multitudes below. Dualism of government was not an unshared peculiarity of Petrograd.

As early as 6 May a fuel crisis had arisen—menacing both army and town. Local village committees were asserting a right as old as serfdom to the produce of forested areas in their neighborhood. Yet it must not be imagined that peasant aggrandizement was the predominant factor in this crisis. Transport, of necessity, played an important part, as did the decreasing supplies of mineral fuel. It was the old Transport Regulations of 1916 that were now, in May 1917, invoked to cure a serious disease.

On 8 May the Provincial Commissaries were reminded that they must see "that the Central Government was always in touch with events." The first "All-Russian Peasant Congress" met in Petrograd in May. It must have been a matter of concern to Prince Lvov's administration to know how far any potential radicalism among the delegates was likely to be supported in the villages. Lenin, too, was present, trying his ground and seeing what assistance his party might derive from the "radical bourgeois peasant who had not yet territorialized himself." The Bolshevik leader's reception at the Congress must have caused relief in the first post-revolutionary cabinet. When Lenin advocated direct seizure of power, the assembled delegates are reported to have laughed. Strange how soon, in a revolutionary crisis, what seems ridiculous in spring will seem practicable in autumn!

Spirit depots[1] were causing disquiet before 9 May—riotous behavior inevitably becoming even more dangerous in their vicinity. Yet the First Provisional Government was not inclined to allow the preventive destruction of such commercially valuable stores.

What directly affected the army was the shortage, during March and April, of fodder. Brusilov, commander-in-chief of the southwest front, had already complained of its insufficiency.

If the picture presented in the Official Circular of 12 May is not exaggerated—and evidence from other sources does not lead one to suppose it can be—social dissolution was already not a potential but an actual phenomenon. Illegal arrests and searches, expulsion of estate staffs, destruction of estates, robberies and violence were the order of the day. "Respected officials" were no longer treated with respect. Various organizations were assuming governmental powers. Levies were being imposed by local authorities. Mobs were being incited to attack government representatives. Cleavages were appearing based on class, racial or religious distinctions.

Still more definite proof of Russia's dangerous position was the announcement that "wholesale desertions were rendering the army impotent as a fighting force." That army, one must not forget, was a peasant army. Desertions on such a scale were bound to increase the more militant elements of the villages that were soon to demand "Peace and Land."

Could Guchkov's successor, Kerensky, keep the army on a military footing? Could Shingarev's successor, Chernov, assuage rural passions and hold in leash the peasant mastiff?

---

[1] Government alcohol storage centers.—Ed.

It is not often understood what a revolution was implied in the resignation of Prince Lvov (7 July). To have a Socialist prime minister gave Russia a unique position in the political world of Europe. To have a "narodnik" minister of agriculture was also an innovation, at which the worshippers of the popular communal land tenure in the sixties and seventies of the nineteenth century would have marveled no less than their opponents. The more conservative elements of the First Provisional Government were willing to step aside if only the avowed representatives of (peasant) socialism could control the village—now almost uncontrollable. Could Russia be kept on a war-footing regardless of the disasters of the previous years? Or would 1917 prove to be the epilogue to the drama whose prologue had been 1905? Still more sand had to run through the glass before one could tell.

The head of the First Provisional Government publicly explained on 9 July the position which led to his resignation. His words are of import as indicating the failure of that government's attempt to base itself upon personalities emanating from the last and Fourth Duma of Nicholas II. It is certain that, in Prince Lvov's administration, Milyukov and Guchkov had played, or had intended to play, more prominent parts. Yet it was the increasing impotence of the government in agrarian affairs that drove Prince Lvov from office and indirectly at least, gave the "trudovik"[2] Social Revolutionary, Kerensky, the reversion of the leadership.

"Although I believe" (wrote the retiring prime minister in the *Novoe Vremya* of 9 July)

> that land ought to be handed over to the peasants, I cannot agree either with the content or the spirit of the land laws submitted by the minister of agriculture (i.e. Chernov) to the Provisional Government for ratification. The Provisional Government has declared that the occupation of the land should be organized in the interests of the working classes and of national welfare, but the minister seems to me to depart from this principle and introduce laws which undermine the people's conception of justice. Far from combating aggressive tendencies or bringing order into agrarian relations, he appears to justify the disastrous seizures of property that are taking place throughout Russia and aims at confronting the Constituent Assembly with a fait accompli. To my mind, the laws proposed by

[2] Trudovik: laborite.—Ed.

him are part of a party program and not measures necessary for the good of the country. I consider the Minister of Agriculture's land program disastrous for the country, for it will ruin and undermine it both morally and materially, and I very much fear that it will create throughout Russia the state of things against which the Provisional Government has been, during the last few days, energetically struggling in Petrograd.

One is left in no doubt from the above letter that it was firstly the agrarian agitation and secondly the Social Revolutionary party's increasing influence that caused Prince Lvov's withdrawal from office. Until July the advocates of a modernized "cherny peredel" (general redivision of all lands) stood behind the self-determination of the various cantonal and village assemblies of Russia. The views of Chernov, one of the principal theoreticians of the party and the object of the retiring prime minister's attack, naturally form a subject of interest in the study of the period. At a lecture delivered on 30 April 1917, in the Shanyavsky University, Moscow ("Agrarny vopros i sovremenny moment," reproduced in *Zemlya i Volya,* No. 44, Moscow), Chernov had reemphasized a fact that everyone knew—that the Russian army was a "peasant"—a "village army." Upon the village fell the burden of the bloodshed. It was this "peasant army" that was especially interested in the land question. Rumors of land redistributions had even in the first two months after the revolution caused disquiet and desertions—desertions that threatened to impair the fighting-machine, already lacking in "morale" after the defeats of 1915 and the collapse of Rumania in the previous autumn. The emphasis of Chernov's remarks lay in his assertion that the agrarian question had a vital significance for the army. The land question (he asserted) naturally stood in the center of all the organized tasks of the moment. He considered that the prospective strength of labor democracy in the future Constituent Assembly would lead to another page in Russia's chronicle which should reproduce "the glorious history of the First and Second Dumas." He advised the slogan, "Land through the Constituent Assembly," while envisaging an elastic form of the oft-discussed "general redivision" based upon the labor capacity or actual size of the peasant family. His concluding declaration that "the peasantry itself was the real autocrat of Russia" ("Sam narod eto istinny Samoderzhets Rossii") was a statement the truth of which was never more evident than in the succeeding October, when he himself was hurled from power by those who utilized the forces that had placed his party in office.

If this article were not meant simply to summarize the main features of the peasant risings of 1917, it would be instructive to pursue the implications of the opposition of Lvov to Chernov—an opposition which showed that the forces of agrarian discontent were no longer latent. In fact, a new 1905 had dawned, this time considerably magnified.

The quantitative significance of the peasant aggrandizement in May and June certainly gave the First Provisional Government little cause for optimism. Compared with the 204 cases in April, May provided 259 cases of law-breaking in landed property relationships. In contrast with the 32 cases recorded in April of violence or destruction involving person or property, there were 152 cases in May. The month of June certainly showed no decrease in the first type of offense, of which there were 577 instances. Of the second type, however, a decrease is recorded, there being 112 instances.

It was in July, however, the month when the more conservative elements were in retreat, leaving the agrarian socialists and moderate Social Democrats masters of the field, that the alarming total of 1,122 cases was registered as the number of infringements of landed property rights in the Russian dominions. Of this amount, 1,100 instances occurred in European Russia alone. Seizure of property or assault upon the person represented 387 cases, of which the majority (342) were again in Europe.

It may be pertinent to note here that the "organized" or "inspired" nature of the peasant movements had now reached its acme. The more moderate Social Revolutionaries, as champions of peasant rights, were necessarily no longer interested in stirring up the peasantry against a government whose leader, Kerensky, was their own man and in which their ideas were admittedly predominant. Yet later months, from August to October, were to make it questionable whether the nominally triumphant party had in fact led the agrarian offensive. One might be forgiven for supposing that they had simply walked in front of spontaneously advancing hosts. It was certainly no easy task to control the peasant rear when the efforts of the new head of the Provisional Government had so signally failed to galvanize the front into a patriotic offensive.

On 18 July, H. G. Tsereteli,[3] not long returned from his Siberian exile to which he had been despatched with other socialist members of the Second Duma ten years before, issued an appeal for order in rural areas. The conditions reported to him from the countryside menaced "the army, the country and the existence of the State itself." Proceeding, he declared that "Revolutionary Russia must be secured from hostile action without and cold and hunger within." He deprecated illegal redivisions of land which, he stated, threatened the food and fuel supplies. But despite the ability of Kerensky and Tsereteli to control the capital, the thousands of village communities were a different proposition.

July witnessed the culmination of peasant self-determination as far as it was encouraged by parties, such as that of the Social Revolutionaries, or by persons speaking in that party's name. For every hundred cases of peasant infringement of the old legal arrangements, March had reported only six to be inspired. In April, 33 cases were supposed to be of organized character. May announced 67 instances of that type; June, 86; July, 120.

The Social Revolutionary party, together with its Social Democratic allies (or the representatives of these parties in power), considered the prosecution of the war of greater moment than the drastic rearrangement of the social and economic relations of the village. The government now relied upon "the fulness of its revolutionary authority to preserve the whole land fund unimpaired until the convocation of the All-Russian Constituent Assembly which will transfer the land into the hands of those working it." If one recalls the pre-revolutionary decade and the stormy debates of the First Duma, one understands fully the social implications of the above announcement. To quell peasant disturbances and to persuade the war-weary army to resume the conflict at the front, the government categorically adopted the program of the "Trudoviki" (Labor Group) of Russia's first modern parliament. Certainly the prospective redistribution rested with the so far unconvened legislature. The cantonal and village assemblies were offered a promissory note to be honored later. The value received was to be renewed peasant support of the war-aims of the Second Provisional Government.

---

[3] Then minister of the interior.—Ed.

Simultaneously the government challenged the authority of the multiplicity of "executive committees" that had sprung mushroom-like from the soil of Russia at Nicholas II's abdication. Of these spontaneously acting bodies the Soviet in Petrograd was but one. Cantonal committees were now ubiquitous. Provincial and District Commissaries were becoming either figure-heads or puppets in their hands. The Food and Land Committees, responsible to their central bodies in the capital, were, indeed, recognized by the government. It was in fact A. I. Shingarev, a Constitutional Democrat (Liberal), who had promulgated the decree that instituted them. Chernov, his successor, followed in his footsteps. These Food and Land Committees found little support locally, save where their personnel either coincided with, or was controlled by, the cantonal or village executive committees. The inability of the central government to guide these local committees led to the ultimate elimination of Kerensky and Chernov in October.

The ensuing months witnessed a series of attempts to restore the authority of Petrograd over Russia by the application of military force. General Kornilov now (on 31 July) made generally applicable to the whole war zone a "Compulsory Decree" (No. 737) which had originally been declared, on 8 July, to cover only the southwestern front. Railway transport, the commander-in-chief asserted, was in ruins. Food for the troops and forage for the animals was still deficient. "The agrarian question can in no wise be decided in unauthorized fashion with the use of violence."

Whether the cause lay in the increased firmness of the central government's handling of affairs, as witnessed by the above decree, or whether the requirements of harvesting turned village minds to their usual economic labors, there did occur a decrease in the number of reported cases of rural illegalities. Whereas July had shown 1,122 breaches of land laws, August reported only 691. On the contrary, acts of seizure accompanied by violence increased from 387 in July to 440 in August.

The question of the gathering of the harvest now (by 2 September) caused anxiety in Petrograd. The minister of agriculture, Chernov, required Provincial and District Commissaries to prevent any interference in that operation by cantonal committees. On 26 August, General Kornilov made his premature attempt to seize Petrograd and

stay the progress of revolutionary events. His action and the subsequent loss of prestige which Kerensky experienced actually helped
to "deepen" the revolution and make certain future events almost
inevitable. The army continued to disintegrate. The garrisons in the
rear showed less and less inclination to act against their village
compatriots.

On 8 September, Kerensky, in his capacity of prime minister and
commander-in-chief, reiterated what the now deposed Kornilov had
earlier decreed. There was clearly increasing anarchy in every
sphere of rural life. A food and fuel crisis threatened both front and
rear. Local Commissaries were definitely instructed to apply for
military assistance if necessary.

If account is taken of the numerical value of the breaches of land
laws in September, it is found that the previously-mentioned decline
in August continued in the succeeding month. The August total of
691 cases sank to 629 in September. Harvesting, as before, probably
affected the figures. Yet the number of cases of seizure accompanied
by violence—certainly a truer reflex of the government's weakness
and of the loosening of social bonds—rose from 440 in August to
958 in the next month.

October presented a catastrophic appearance. A state of civil
war virtually existed. The Ministry of the Interior, at this date under
N. D. Avksentyev, recognized that "the internal position of the
country is continually growing weaker" (7 October). Commissaries
were asked to endeavor "to unite the well-disposed elements of the
population in the fight against increasing anarchy." The "active
support of the population" was essential. Certainly that was the one
factor that the government had failed to secure. "The foreign enemy
(it was proclaimed) was penetrating further and further into the heart
of the country." The government was convinced that "all must experience immediate alarm over the disorders which were happening
everywhere in the wildest forms." The Russian people "did not show
any signs of a protective instinct (spasitelnovo podema) which love
of country, dread for its fate and a sense of self-preservation should
inspire." Inertia among the villagers menaced the authority of the
Provisional Government. Every social organization should be asked
to cooperate with the Provincial Commissaries in restoring order.
The new cantonal *zemstva* were one of the expedients on which

Petrograd counted to retain peasant loyalty. But that new institution —despite its basis of universal suffrage—could not withstand the village executive committees.

As a last despairing hope it was announced that "selected and trustworthy military men, released from service or given leave to join," were to supplement the notoriously feeble militia. The peasantry sank into a political coma from which the prospective loss of its gains during the year under review alone could awaken it almost twelve months later.

Even parish churches were exposed to attack. Monastic and church land had not escaped expropriation during the period of the supremacy of local executive committees. So alarming had the situation become that the Militia Department now (on 7 October) instructed the Commissaries that the provisions of the "General Act Governing the Peasant Estate," as set forth in the Collection of Laws (Svod Zakonov), should be utilized "to compel village communities to maintain guards over local churches and monasteries." Had the old and oft-quoted peasant esteem for the religion of his fathers failed to survive in the general chaos? One can draw no other conclusion.

Upon the question of the danger to the public peace owing to the riotous destruction of spirit stores it appears that even on the eve of the fatal 25 October the government hesitated to sanction their official demolition in view of the consequent financial loss to the treasury.

Even more disquieting was the food situation. The "consuming" provinces (not to mention Petrograd and Moscow) feared starvation. The provinces of the south and east that produced a grain surplus were unable to secure adequate manufactured articles to warrant a continuance of internal trade. The quid pro quo was absent. This breakdown of economic relations menaced what little chance there was of maintaining the active army at the front. Military assistance was offered to the local commissaries, who were to employ troops at double the usual rates. The result resembled that which met Canute when he rebuked the waves. Even reinforcements in the form of reserve regiments failed to stem the tide of rural rebellion.

The month of October provided 42.1 per cent of the total number

of cases of destructive activity registered since Nicholas II's fall
from power. The number of estates affected by the agrarian movement increased in September by 30.2 per cent over August, and, in
October, by 43.2 per cent over September. The period of pseudo-
legality, of ostensibly legal sequestration of private estates, gave
place in the last two months of Kerensky's administration to one of
real peasant war.

Richard Pipes

NATIONAL MINORITIES SOUGHT
AUTONOMY AND INDEPENDENCE

*Born in Poland in 1923, Richard Pipes completed his formal studies at
Harvard University, where he is now a professor of history and director of
the Russian Research Center. The political aspects of the nationality movements in the Soviet Union have been his special interest for two decades,
and the work from which the selection here is taken is a brilliant contribution to our knowledge of developments in this field during and immediately
after the revolution. In recent years Professor Pipes has published several
new and valuable studies, among which are* Karamzin's Memoir on Ancient
and Modern Russia *and* Social Democracy and the St. Petersburg Labor
Movement.

The Russian Empire, as it appeared in 1917, was the product of
nearly four centuries of continuous expansion. Unlike other European
nations, Russia was situated on the edge of the vast Asiatic mainland
and knew relatively few geographic deterrents to aggrandizement.
This geographically favorable situation was made even more advantageous by the political weakness of Russia's neighbors, who were
especially ineffective on the eastern and southern frontiers. Here vast
and potentially rich territories were either under the dominion of

internally unstable and technologically backward Moslem principalities, or else sparsely populated by nomadic and semi-nomadic groups without any permanent political institutions whatsoever—forces incapable of long range resistance to the pressures of a large and dynamic state. Hence Russia, somewhat like the United States, found outlets for expansive tendencies along its own borders instead of overseas. The process of external growth had been rapid, beginning with the inception of the modern Russian state and developing in close connection with it. It has been estimated that the growth of the Russian Empire between the end of the fifteenth and the end of the nineteenth century proceeded at the rate of 130 square kilometers or fifty square miles a day.

Almost from its very inception the Moscow state had acquired dominion over non-Russian peoples. Ivan the Terrible conquered Kazan and Astrakhan and brought the state a large number of Turks (Volga Tatars, Bashkirs) and Finns (Chuvashes, Mordvinians) from the region of the Volga River and its tributaries. In the seventeenth century, the tsars added Siberia, populated by Turkic, Mongol, and Finnish tribes. The left-bank regions of the Dnieper River, with their Cossack population—the forerunners of modern Ukrainians—came under a Russian protectorate in 1654. During the eighteenth century, moving west, Peter the Great conquered from Sweden the eastern shores of the Baltic Sea (today's Estonia and Latvia), while Catherine the Great, as a result of agreements with Austria and Prussia, seized the eastern provinces of the Polish-Lithuanian Commonwealth. Catherine's successful wars with Turkey brought Russia possession of the northern shores of the Black Sea, including the Crimean peninsula. The Transcaucasian Kingdom of Eastern Georgia was incorporated in 1801, Finland in 1809, and the central regions of Poland in 1815. The remainder of Transcaucasia and the Northern Caucasus were acquired in the first half of the century, and Alexander II added most of Turkestan.

The first systematic census, undertaken in 1897, revealed that the majority (55.7 per cent) of the population of the empire, exclusive of the Grand Duchy of Finland, consisted of non-Russians. The total population of the empire was 122,666,500. The principal groups were divided, by native language, as follows (the figures are in per cent):

Slavs	
Great Russians	44.32
Ukrainians	17.81
Poles	6.31
Belorussians	4.68
Turkic peoples	10.82
Jews	4.03
Finnish peoples	2.78
Lithuanians and Latvians	2.46
Germans	1.42
Caucasian Mountain peoples *(gortsy)*	1.34
Georgians	1.07
Armenians	0.93
Iranian peoples	0.62
Mongolians	0.38
Others	1.03

One of the anomalies of pre-1917 Russia was the fact that although, to quote one observer, "the Russian Empire, Great Russian in its origin, ceased being such in its ethnic composition," the state, with some exceptions, continued to be treated constitutionally and administratively as a nationally homogeneous unit. The principle of autocracy, preserved in all its essentials until the Revolution of 1905, did not permit—at least in theory—the recognition of separate historic or national territories within the state in which the monarch's authority would be less absolute or rest on a legally different basis from that which he exercised at home. In practice, however, this principle was not always consistently applied. At various times in history Russian tsars did grant considerable autonomy to newly conquered territories, partly in recognition of their special status, partly in anticipation of political reforms in Russia, and in some cases they even entered into contractual relations with subject peoples, thus limiting their own power.

Poland from 1815 to 1831 and Finland from 1809 to 1899 were in theory as well as in practice constitutional monarchies. Other regions, such as the Ukraine from 1654 to 1764, Livonia and Estonia from 1710 to 1783 and from 1795 to the 1880s, enjoyed extensive self-rule. But those exceptions were incompatible with the maintenance of the principle of autocracy in Russia itself. Sooner or later, for one reason or another, the privileges granted to conquered peoples were retracted, contracts were unilaterally abrogated, and the subjects, together with their territories, were incorporated into the regular administration of the empire.

At the close of the nineteenth century, Finland alone still retained a broad measure of self-rule. Indeed, in some respects, it possessed greater democratic rights than Russia proper; Finland under the tsars presented the paradox of a subject nation possessing more political freedom than the people who ruled over it. It was a separate principality, which the Russian monarch governed in his capacity as grand duke *(Velikii kniaz').* The tsar was the chief executive; he controlled the grand duchy's foreign affairs; he decided on questions of war and peace; he approved laws and the appointments of judges. The tsar also named the resident governor general of the grand duchy, who headed the Finnish and Russian armies and the police on its territory, and who was responsible for the appointments of local governors. A state secretary served as the intermediary between the Russian monarch and the Finnish organs of self-rule. The Finns had complete control over the legislative institutions of the state. They possessed a bicameral legislative body, composed of a Senate and a Seim (Diet). The Senate considered legislative projects and performed the function of the supreme court of the state. The Seim was the highest legislative organ in the country. Called every five years on the basis of nation-wide elections, it initiated and voted on legislation pertaining to its domain. No law could become effective without its approval. Finnish citizens in addition enjoyed other privileges. Every Finnish subject, while in Russia proper, could claim all the rights of Russian citizens, although Russian citizens in Finland were considered foreigners. In every respect, therefore, Finland had a uniquely privileged position in the Russian Empire, which resembled more closely the dominion relationship in existence in the British Empire than the customary colonial relationship prevalent in other parts of Russia. The Finns had originally acquired these privileges from the Swedes, who had ruled their country before the Russian conquest. The tsars preserved them because Finland was acquired by Alexander I, a monarch of relatively liberal views, who, for a time, had thought of introducing a constitutional regime into Russia proper.

Prior to 1917, the Russian Empire also possessed two protectorates, the Central Asian principalities of Bukhara and Khiva. In 1868 and 1873 respectively, these states recognized the sovereignty of the Russian tsar and ceded to him the right to represent them in relations with other powers. They also granted Russians exclusive commercial privileges and were compelled to abolish slavery in their domains. Otherwise, they enjoyed self-rule.

The remaining borderlands of the Empire were administered, in the last decades of the *ancien régime,* in a manner which did not differ essentially—though it differed in some particulars—from that in effect in the territories of Russia proper. Whatever special powers the imperial government deemed necessary to grant to the authorities administering these territories were derived not so much from a recognition of the multinational character of the state or from a desire to adapt political institutions to the needs of the inhabitants, as from the impracticability of extending the administrative system of the Great Russian provinces in its entirety to the borderland.

Whereas, for example, Russia was divided into provinces *(gubernie),* administered by governors, most of the borderland areas were grouped into general gubernie, which included anywhere from a few to a dozen regular provinces, and were headed by governors general, usually high army officers. The distance of the borderlands from the center, the sparsity of population in some and the existence of strong nationalist traditions in others, required that the persons administering such areas be granted greater powers than was necessary in the central provinces of the empire. The governor general was a viceroy, with extraordinary powers to maintain order and to suppress revolutionary activity. He had a right to employ any means necessary to the performance of his duty, including arrests or expulsions without recourse to courts. In some regions, the governor general also received additional powers, required by local conditions. There were ten such governors general: in Warsaw (with jurisdiction over ten Polish provinces), in Kiev (with jurisdiction over the Ukraine, or Little Russia, including the provinces of Kiev, Volhynia, and Podolia), in Vilna (today's Lithuania and Belorussia, with the provinces of Vilna, Grodno, and Kovno), two in Central Asia (Turkestan and Steppe), and two in Siberia (the so-called Irkutskoe, and Priamurskoe). The governor general of Finland, although bearing the title, had in effect very little authority, and could not be classed in the same category as the other governors general. The official heading the administration of the Caucasus, on the other hand, while formally called a viceroy, was for all practical purposes a full-fledged governor general. The city of Moscow, because of its importance and central location, also formed a general guberniya.

Under the governor general were the provincial governors who had to communicate with the central political institutions of the empire through him, but who, as a rule, were called "military governors" *(voennye gubernatory)*, and had both civil and military jurisdiction. The military governors of Turkestan were directly appointed by the Russian Ministry of War.

The gubernie, or provinces, were—as elsewhere in Russia—further subdivided into districts *(okruga,* or less commonly *uezdy),* but in the eastern borderlands such circumscriptions generally embraced much larger territories and had a simpler structure. On the lowest administrative level there existed considerable variety. In some regions, the population was divided into villages or *auly;* in others, where the inhabitants were nomadic, they were organized into tribes; in yet others, they were administered together with the local Russian population.

Russian law also made special provisions for certain groups of non-Russian subjects. Russia, prior to 1917, retained the system of legally recognized classes and class privileges, long since defunct in Western Europe. Within this system there was a social category of so-called *inorodtsy,* a term which has no exact equivalent in English and can best be rendered by the French *peuples allogènes.* The inorodtsy comprised the Jews and most of the nomadic peoples of the empire, who were subject to special laws rather than to the general laws promulgated in the territories which they inhabited. For the nomadic inorodtsy, this meant in effect that they possessed the right to self-rule, with their native courts and tribal organization. Their relations with the Russian authorities were limited to the payment of a fixed tribute or tax, usually to an agent of the Ministry of Interior or of State Properties. By settling on land and abandoning nomadic habits, an inorodets changed from his status to that of a regular Russian citizen, with all the duties and privileges of the class which he had joined; as long as he retained his inorodets status, he gave nothing to the government and received nothing in return. Russian treatment of the nomads was, on the whole, characterized by tolerance and respect for native traditions. Much of the credit for this must be given to the great liberal statesman, M. M. Speranskii, who, at the beginning of the nineteenth century, had laid down the basic principles for their administration.

For the other subgroup of inorodtsy, the Jews, membership in this class entailed stringent restrictions (most of them stemming from eighteenth-century legislation). These forbade them to move out of a strictly defined area in the southwestern and northwestern parts of the empire, the so-called Pale of Settlement, to purchase landed property, or to settle outside the towns. Such disabilities brought severe social and economic suffering, for the Jews were crowded into towns where they had no adequate basis for livelihood and had to rely heavily on primitive handicraftsmanship and petty trade to survive. By creating abnormal economic conditions in the Jewish communities and preventing them from taking their place in the life of society, the restrictive legislation contributed to the large number of Jews found in radical movements at the beginning of the twentieth century. The Jew could alter his status only by adopting Christianity.

At no point in its history did tsarist Russia formulate a consistent policy toward the minorities. In the early period of the empire, approximately from the middle of the sixteenth until the middle of the eighteenth century, the attitude of the government toward its non-Russian subjects was influenced strongly by religion. Where discrimination existed, the principal reason was the desire of the regime to convert Moslems, Jews, and other non-Christians to the Orthodox faith. Toward the end of the eighteenth century, with the secularization of the Russian monarchy, this religious element lost its force, and political considerations loomed ever larger. Thereafter, the treatment of the minorities, as of the Great Russians themselves, was largely determined by the desire on the part of the monarchs to maintain and enforce the principle of autocracy; minority groups which challenged this effort in the name of national rights were treated as harshly as were Russian groups which challenged it in the name of democracy or freedom in general.

The period from the accession of Alexander III (1881) to the outbreak of the 1905 Revolution was that in which persecution of the minorities culminated. The Russian government perhaps for the first time in its entire history adopted a systematic policy of Russification and minority repression, largely in an endeavor to utilize Great Russian national sentiments as a weapon against growing social unrest in the country. During this period, Finnish privileges were violated through a suspension of the legislative powers of the Seim (1899), the introduction of the compulsory study of Russian in Finnish secondary schools, the subordination of the Finnish Ministry of Post and Telegraphs to the corresponding Russian institution, and other restrictive measures. Polish cultural activity was severely limited; the Jewish population was subjected to pogroms inspired or tolerated by the government, and to further economic restrictions (for instance, the revocation of the right to distill alcohol); the Ukrainian cultural movement was virtually brought to a standstill as a result of the prohibitions imposed on printing in the Ukrainian language (initiated in the 1870s); the properties of the Armenian church were confiscated by the viceroy of the Caucasus (1903). It was, however, not accidental that this era of Russification coincided with the period of greatest governmental reaction, during which the Great Russian population itself lost many of the rights which it had acquired in the Great Reforms of Alexander II (1856–1881).

The outbreak of the Revolution of 1905 and the subsequent establishment of a constitutional monarchy brought to a halt the period of national persecution but it did not repair all the damage done in the previous quarter-century. The Dumas, especially the First, in which the minorities were well represented, gave only slight attention to the national question, though they provided an open rostrum of discussions on that topic. In 1907, the government regained supremacy over the liberal elements; it changed the electoral laws in favor of the Russian upper classes, among whom supporters of the autocracy were strong, depriving the remainder of the population of a proportionate voice in the legislative institutions of the state. The borderlands, where liberal and socialist parties enjoyed a particularly strong following, were hardest hit by the change, and some (Turkestan, for instance) lost entirely the right to representation.

National Movements in Russia

The paradox—and tragedy—of Russian history in the last century of the *ancien régime* was the fact that while the government clung to the anachronistic notion of absolutism, the country itself was undergoing an extremely rapid economic, social, and intellectual evolution, which required new, more flexible forms of administration. The nineteenth century was a period when capitalism and the industrial revolution penetrated Russia, stimulating the development of some social classes which had previously been weak (a middle class, an industrial proletariat, and a prosperous, land-owning peasantry), and undermining others (e.g., the landed aristocracy). Western ideas, such as liberalism, socialism, nationalism, utilitarianism, now found a wide audience in Russia. The Russian monarchy, which until the nineteenth century had been the principal exponent of Western ideas in Russia, now lagged behind. The second half of the reign of Alexander I (1815–1825) marked the beginning of that rift between the monarchy and the articulate elements in Russian society which, widening continuously, led to conspiratorial movements, terrorist activity, and revolution, and finally, in 1917, to the demise of monarchy itself.

The national movement among the minorities of the Russian state, which also began in the nineteenth century, represented one of the many forms which this intellectual and social ferment assumed. Because the traditions and socio-economic interests of the various groups of subjects, including the minorities, were highly diversified, their cultural and political development tended to take on a local, and in some cases, a national coloring. Romantic philosophy, which first affected Russia in the 1820s, stimulated among the minority intellectuals an interest in their own languages and past traditions, and led directly to the evolution of cultural nationalism, the first manifestation of the national movement in the Russian borderlands.

Next, in the 1860s and 1870s, the spread of Russian Populism, with its emphasis on the customs and institutions of the peasantry, provided the minority intellectuals with a social ideology and induced them to establish contact with the broad masses of their own, predominantly rural, population. Finally, the development of modern political parties in Russia, which took place about 1900, led to the formation of national parties among the minorities, which in almost all instances adopted either liberal or socialist programs and affiliated themselves closely with their Russian counterparts. Until the breakdown of the tsarist regime, such Russian and minority parties fought side by side for parliamentary rights, local self-rule, and social and economic reforms; but while the Russian parties stressed the general needs of the whole country, the minority parties concentrated on local, regional requirements. The fact that the minorities in Russia developed a national consciousness before their fellow-nationals across the border (the Ukrainians in Austrian Galicia, Armenians in the Ottoman Empire, Azerbaijanis in Persia, and so on), was a result of the more rapid intellectual and economic growth of the Russian Empire.

The refusal of the tsarist regime to recognize the strivings of the minorities was part of the larger phenomenon of its failure to respond to the growing clamor on the part of all its citizens for fundamental reforms, and had equally dire results.

*   *   *

The outbreak of the Russian Revolution had, as its initial consequence, the abolition of the tsarist regime and, as its ultimate result, the complete breakdown of all forms of organized life throughout Russia. One of the aspects of this breakdown was the disintegration of the empire and the worsening of relations between its various ethnic groups. In less than a year after the tsar had abdicated, the national question had become an outstanding issue in Russian politics.

Immediately after resuming power, the Provisional Government issued decrees which abolished all restrictive legislation imposed on the minorities by the tsarist regime, and established full equality of all citizens regardless of religion, race, or national origin. The government also introduced the beginnings of national self-rule by placing the administration of the borderlands in the hands of prominent local figures. Transcaucasia and Turkestan were put under the jurisdiction of special committees, composed largely of Duma deputies of native nationalities, to replace the governors general of the tsarist administration. The southwestern provinces were put in charge of Ukrainians, though the government refused to recognize the existence of the entire Ukraine as an administrative unit until forced to do so under Ukrainian pressure in the summer of 1917. Those were pioneering steps in the direction of adapting the governmental machinery to the multinational character of the empire and giving the minorities a voice in the administration of their territories, but unfortunately the local committees to which the Provisional Government had relegated authority possessed very little real power, and after the summer of 1917 functioned only nominally.

The Provisional Government considered itself a temporary trustee of state sovereignty, and viewed its main task as that of preserving unity and order until the people should have an opportunity to express its own will in the Constituent Assembly. Throughout its existence the government resisted as well as it could all pressures to enact legislation which might affect the constitution of the state. Any such measures it regarded as an infringement on popular sovereignty. This attitude, sound from the moral and constitutional points of view, proved fatal as political practice. The February Revolution had set into motion forces which would not wait. The procrastinating policies of the Provisional Government led to growing anarchy which Lenin and his followers, concentrating on the seizure of power and unhampered by any moral scruples or constitutional considerations, utilized to accomplish a successful coup d'etat.

The growth of the national movements in Russia during 1917, and especially the unexpectedly rapid development of political aspirations on the part of the minorities, were caused to a large extent by the same factors which in Russia proper made possible the triumph of bolshevism: popular restlessness, the demand for land and peace, and the inability of the democratic government to provide firm authority.

The growing impatience of the rural population with delays in the apportionment of land which caused the peasantry of the ethnically Great Russian provinces to turn against the government and to attack large estates, had different effects in the eastern borderlands. There the dissatisfaction of the native population was not so much directed against the landlord as against the Russian colonist; it was he who had deprived the native nomad of his grazing grounds and with the aid of Cossack or Russian garrisons had kept the native from the land which he considered his own by inheritance. When the February Revolution broke out, the native population of the Northern Caucasus, the Ural region and much of the steppe districts of Central Asia expected that the new democracy would at once remedy the injustices of the past by returning to them the properties of which they had been deprived. When this did not happen, they took matters into their own hands, and tried to seize land by force. But in doing so they encountered the resistance of Russian and Cossack villages. Thus, in the second half of the year, while a class struggle was taking place in Russia proper, an equally savage national conflict developed in the vast eastern borderlands of the empire: Chechen and Ingush against Russian and Cossack; Kazakh-Kirghiz against the Russian and Ukrainian colonist; Bashkir against the Russian and Tatar.

In the Ukraine, too, the agricultural question assumed a national form although for quite different reasons. The Ukrainian peasants, especially the rural middle class, found it advantageous, as will be seen, in view of the superiority of the soil in their provinces, to solve the land question independently of Russia proper.

War-weariness was another factor which tended to increase nationalist emotions. Non-Russian soldiers, like their Russian comrades, desired to terminate the fighting and to return home. Uncertain how to go about it, they organized their own military formations and military councils, hoping in this manner to be repatriated sooner, and to obtain by common action a better response to their demands. By the end of the year the formation of such national units had increased to the point where non-Russian troops, abandoning the front, frequently returned to their homes as a body. Once on their native soil, they augmented native political organizations and provided them with military power. The national movement in 1917 had perhaps its most rapid development in the army.

The Bolsheviks, inciting Russian peasants and soldiers against the government, were persuasive in contending that the government did not grant their demands because it had become a captive of the "bourgeoisie." The non-Russian, on the other hand, could be led to believe that the trouble lay not so much in the class-character of the Provisional Government, as in its ethnic composition. Nationalistic parties in some areas began to foster the idea that all Russian governments, autocratic as well as democratic, were inspired by the same hostility toward the minorities and should be equally mistrusted.

Immediately after the fall of the *ancien régime* the minorities, like the Russians, established local organs of internal self-rule. The original purpose of these institutions was to serve as centers of public discussion for the forthcoming Constituent Assembly and to attend

to nonpolitical affairs connected with the problems of local administration. Whether called Soviet, Rada (in the Ukraine and Belorussia),
Shura (among the Turkic peoples), or their equivalents in other native
languages, they were originally not intended to infringe upon the authority of the Provisional Government. In time, however, as the
authority of the Provisional Government declined, these organs
acquired a correspondingly greater voice in local affairs. At first they
only assumed responsibility over supply and communication, the
maintenance of public order, and, in some cases, the defense of their
territories from external enemies—services which Petrograd could
not provide. But at the end of 1917, when, as a result of the Bolshevik
coup, a political vacuum was created in the country, they appropriated sovereignty itself. While the soviets, largely under the influence
of the Bolsheviks and Left SR's, proclaimed the overthrow of the
Provisional Government and the establishment of rule of the Congress of Soviets, the minority organizations took over the responsibilities of government for their own peoples and the territories which
they inhabited. These local organs of administration which arose in
the borderlands during the October Revolution and succeeding
months were based on the principle of national self-rule and functioned alone or in condominium with the soviets.

For a time it seemed possible that these national organs would
cooperate with the new Russian government. In the initial period of
Communist rule no one knew how the new regime would treat the
minorities. But before long it became apparent that the Soviet government had no intention of respecting the principle of national self-
determination and that in spreading its authority it was inclined to
utilize social forces hostile to minority interests. In the Ukraine, it
favored that part of the industrial proletariat which was, by ethnic
origin and sympathy, oriented toward Russia and inimical to the
striving of the local peasantry; in the Moslem areas, the colonizing
elements and the urban population composed largely of Russian
newcomers; in Transcaucasia and Belorussia, the deserting Russian
troops. The triumph of bolshevism was interpreted in many borderland areas as the victory of the city over the village, the worker over
the peasant, the Russian colonist over the native.

It was under such circumstances that the national councils, bol-
stered by sentiments which had matured in the course of the year,

proclaimed their self-rule, and in some instances, their complete independence.

Isaac Deutscher

BOLSHEVIKS LED WORKERS TOWARD RADICAL REVOLUTION

Isaac Deutscher was born in Poland and educated at Cracow. He engaged in journalistic work in Poland from 1924 until 1939, and was a member of the Polish Communist party until 1932, when he was expelled for anti-Stalinist opposition. He continued his journalistic activities in London after 1939 and wrote many excellent studies on Russian affairs. Among his best-known books in this field are: Soviet Trade Unions; a trilogy on Trotsky, of which the first volume, The Prophet Armed, Trotsky, 1879–1921, *is most useful on the revolution; and the justly famous* Stalin, *from which the following selection is taken. The latter is undoubtedly the most exhaustive and balanced study of Stalin yet written.*

During May and June the revolutionary fever in Petersburg continually mounted. Municipal elections in the capital exposed the weakness of Miliukov's Constitutional Democrats (Cadets), the party that predominated in the government. Half the vote went to the moderate Socialists, leaving the two extreme parties, Cadets and Bolsheviks, as influential minorities. The predominantly Cadet government gave way to a coalition of Cadets, Mensheviks, and Social Revolutionaries. But the new government as it tried to ride the storm showed few signs of real strength. The Bolsheviks were becoming the masters in the working-class suburbs of Petersburg. From the army came the ever louder clamor for peace, while Russia's western allies were pressing the Russian Supreme Command to start an all-out offensive against the Germans. The Bolsheviks met the new coalition with grim hostility; but in opposing it they displayed a tactical imagination and subtlety which could not fail to yield massive and quick rewards. They did not simply shout down the whole government, for they knew that the working class was still favorably impressed by the fact that Socialist parties were now in office, for the first time in Russian history. But the working classes were also suspicious of the middle-class Cadets, the senior partners in the coalition. Lenin therefore pressed the moderate Socialists to break up the coalition and form a government of their own, based on the soviets. In the Red suburbs of the capital hosts of Bolshevik agitators raised two plain slogans: "Down with the Ten Capitalist Ministers!" and "All Power to the Soviets!" The first slogan stirred the widespread suspicion of the Cadets common to the Menshevik and Bolshevik rank and file. The demand that all power be transferred to the soviets was equivalent to the demand that the moderate Socialists should take power alone, since they wielded a majority in the soviets; and so that slogan, too, had its appeal to the ordinary Menshevik worker. Throughout May and June, legions of Menshevik workers were converted to bolshevism. On 18 June half a million workers and soldiers marched in the streets of the capital in a procession which was nominally called by the Menshevik leaders of the soviets. The vast mass of demonstrators carried placards and banners with almost exclusively Bolshevik slogans. The first All-Russian Congress of Soviets was just then in session; and the delegates from the provinces, among whom the Bolsheviks were still a minority of one-sixth, could not help being impressed by this demonstration of Bolshevik influence in the capital.

At the Congress of the Soviets there occurred a significant incident. When one of the Socialist ministers was apologetically explaining the need for a broadly based government and arguing that no party could cope singlehanded with the disintegration and chaos engendered by the war, Lenin, from the floor, interrupted the speaker with a curt statement that his party was ready to assume the whole power. Lenin's words were received with loud, derisive laughter; but the mass processions in the streets of the capital imparted to them a deadly earnestness.

In fact, the Bolsheviks were not yet ready to take power. They continued to regard the soviets as the legitimate source of revolutionary authority; and, as long as his party was in a minority in the soviets, Lenin ruled out any attempt on its part at seizing power. But he had to work hard to keep on a leash the impatient, semi-anarchist groups of workers, soldiers, and sailors who fretted at his prudent tactics. He saw that his scheme of action was imperiled by the uneven rhythm and impetus of the revolution. While his policies were still too extreme for the provincial working class, a large section of the garrison and the proletariat in the capital was already beginning to suspect the Bolsheviks, too, of excessive moderation or of insufficient revolutionary pluck. In *Pravda* Stalin was compelled to warn the Red suburbs against the anarchist and semi-anarchist agitators who urged the workers to "come out" prematurely. In the next few months bolshevism uneasily balanced between the hazards of delaying the revolution and the risks of premature action.

The hazards and risks were increased by the fact that the counter-revolution, too, was preparing for a showdown. Monarchist generals, leagues of patriotic officers, associations of ex-service men and the Cadet middle class, all took notice of the meaning of the June demonstration and made up their minds to throw back the mounting tide of bolshevism by a violent coup. The moderate Socialist leaders were intimidated and vaguely played with the idea that such a showdown would rid them of their rivals on the left, against whom they themselves were more and more helpless. Lenin and his colleagues were determined not to allow themselves to be driven into premature insurrection. They were fairly confident that, basing themselves on the proletarian masses of the capital alone, they could seize power immediately; but they were equally convinced that they could not hold it against the opposition of the rest of the country. They were also aware that every major demonstration in the streets of Petersburg was now more likely than not to degenerate into street fighting. The workers were armed. Soldiers were reluctant to march in any demonstration without their rifles. Each unarmed procession offered a shooting target to the bands of the counter-revolution. The Central Committee of the Bolshevik party therefore banned all demonstrations. It was, however, unable to enforce the ban—the revolutionary temper in the suburbs and barracks had grown beyond its control. This was the background to the grave crisis of the "July days," in which Stalin played a curious role, and which ended in a severe though temporary setback for bolshevism.

A vivid and apparently truthful account of the events was given by Stalin himself in a report to the Sixth Congress of the party which

met a couple of weeks after the "July days." On 3 July, in the afternoon, a delegation from one of the regiments burst into the city
conference of the party and declared that their regiment and others
had decided to "come out" that same evening, that they had already
sent messengers to other regiments and factories calling everybody
to join in the revolt. Volodarsky, the leader of the Petersburg Committee, sternly reminded the soldiers that the party expected them, as
its members, to observe the ban on demonstrations. The Central
Committee, the Petersburg Committee, and the Bolshevik Military
Organization then met, once again confirmed the ban, and sent agitators to the factories and barracks to enforce it there. At the same
time the Central Committee delegated Stalin to inform the Executive
of the Soviets, which was controlled by the Mensheviks, about the
new development. Two hours after these events had begun to unfold,
Stalin was carrying out his mission. But the avalanche was already on
the move. Toward evening, crowds of workers and a number of
regiments, fully armed and flying their colors, assembled in front
of the offices of the Petersburg Committee of the party. Bolshevik
speakers urged the crowd to disperse peacefully, but they were interrupted by hoots and catcalls. The raging element of revolution struck
over their heads. They then proposed that the demonstrators march
towards the Tauride Palace, the seat of the Soviet, and submit their
demands to the Soviet Executive. To the tune of the *Marseillaise* the
procession moved on. All through the night the crowd virtually be-
sieged the Tauride Palace, waiting in vain for an answer to their main
demand that the Soviet leaders disown the Provisional Government
and themselves assume power.

Mensheviks and Social Revolutionaries were biding their time,
meanwhile, in the expectation that they would soon be rescued by
"loyal" government troops. So far the meetings and processions were
peaceful, but with every hour the excitement was boiling up to an
explosion. The minister of agriculture, Chernov, was recognized by
the crowd and "placed under arrest" by a group of thugs—only
thanks to Trotsky's presence of mind and his courageous intervention
was the minister, himself an old revolutionary, saved from violence
and released. Long after midnight, from the balcony of the Tauride
Palace, Zinoviev tirelessly argued in his high-pitched voice with the
crowd, trying to achieve the impossible: to persuade the multitude

to go home and yet not to damp its revolutionary temper but, on the contrary, to keep it hot. The Bolshevik Central Committee was in permanent session, struggling with the awkward dilemma. In the end it decided that the party should take part in the demonstration in order to lead and direct it into peaceful channels. The risk was that they would not succeed in doing so; that a battle would not be avoided; and that it might end in a major defeat that would swing the scales in favor of the counter-revolution. Defeat in such a show-down was the more probable as the Bolsheviks pulled their punches all the time. The other course of action open to them was to dissociate themselves from the demonstrators and let events run their own way. The party of the revolution, however, could not show such equanimity. The masses, left to themselves, to their own passion and impatience, were sure to walk into the trap of civil war. They would never have forgiven the Bolsheviks what would have amounted to a desertion at a time of crisis. The Bolsheviks could not afford to discredit themselves in the eyes of those very people on whose confidence and support their ultimate victory depended.

In the next few days the demonstrations, growing in size and turbulence, led to sporadic clashes and bloodshed. But the worst fears of the Bolsheviks did not materialize—the clashes did not lead to regular civil war. The whole movement spent its impetus and petered out. Almost simultaneously a counter-movement was gathering momentum. To the relief of the upper and middle classes armed groups of the right wing came into action. The Bolsheviks headquarters and the offices of *Pravda* were wrecked. In the middle of all this turbulence came the news of the collapse of the Russian offensive on the front. The Bolsheviks were blamed; and a cry of vengeance went up. Agitators of the right branded Lenin and his followers as German spies. A popular newspaper published faked documents purporting to prove the charge. Government troops were engaged in punitive expeditions in the Red suburbs.

Throughout the "July days" Stalin, on behalf of the Central Committee, parleyed with the Executive of the Soviets and did his best to bring unwieldy elements under control. At the outset he brought the Bolshevik decision against the demonstration to the knowledge of the Executive, only to learn later on that the decision had been reversed. He then presumably had to report the change to the Soviet leaders and explain its reasons. In the ruling circles of the soviets, Stalin's good faith was apparently taken for granted, for later on when the government issued writs for the arrest of most Bolshevik leaders, he, though a member of the Central Committee, was not molested. It also fell to him to carry out the final act in the winding up of this semi-insurrection, the surrender by the rebels of the powerful Peter and Paul fortress. Accompanied by a Menshevik member of the Soviet Executive, Stalin went to the fortress, which was situated on an island opposite the Bolshevik headquarters, just at the moment when those headquarters were being occupied by government troops. The garrison of the fortress consisted of fiery Kronstadt sailors, the machine-gunners who had initiated the revolt, and civilian Red Guards, all refusing to surrender and preparing for a long and bloody siege. It is easy to imagine how difficult and delicate was Stalin's mission. He was helped by official assurances that the rebels would not be penalized; but they still persistently refused to surrender. In the end Stalin shrewdly persuaded them to capitulate to the Executive of the soviets, which sounded more honorable than a surrender to the government. A blood-bath was avoided.

The Bolshevik setback was superficial, as events would prove. Immediately after the "July days," however, the setback was exaggerated by all parties. Most Bolshevik leaders, including Lenin, thought themselves more thoroughly defeated than they actually were. The baiting of Bolsheviks grew. Lenin and Zinoviev were indicted as spies in German pay. The moderate Socialists knew the accusation was false, but their grudge against the Bolsheviks was strong enough to prevent them from defending Lenin and his colleagues against it. Many of them suspected Lenin of having made a serious attempt, in the "July days," to seize power.

The Central Committee now discussed whether Lenin and Zinoviev should hand themselves over to the authorities or whether they should go into hiding. Lenin and Zinoviev were hestitant: they feared that to avoid trial would confirm, in the eyes of uninformed opinion, the charges leveled against them. This was at first also the view of Lunacharsky and Kamenev. Stalin, on the contrary, advised them to go into hiding. It would be folly, he said, to trust the justice of the Provisional Government. An anti-Bolshevik hysteria was being so unscrupulously whipped up that any young officer or ensign escorting the "German spies" into prison, or from prison to court, would think it an act of patriotic heroism to assassinate them on the way. Lenin still hestitated to follow Stalin's advice. Stalin then approached the Executive of the Soviets and told them that Lenin was prepared to face trial if the Executive guaranteed his life and personal safety from lawless violence. As the Mensheviks and Social Revolutionaries refused to shoulder any such responsibility, Lenin and Zinoviev finally made up their minds to go into hiding.

On 8 July Lenin disappeared, no doubt remembering the example of Robespierre who, shortly before his rise to power, was similarly hunted and found refuge with a Jacobin carpenter. Lenin's "carpenter" was the workman Alliluyev, Stalin's old friend. In his house Lenin lived for a few days. On 11 July Stalin and Alliluyev escorted Lenin through the darkening streets of the city to the Maritime Station where Lenin left to hide first in the villages near the capital and then in Finland. From now on until the October Revolution he remained underground, inspiring the strategy, if not the tactics, of his party through the pamphlets, articles, and letters which he showered on the Central Committee. Together with Lenin departed Zinoviev. A few days later Kamenev was imprisoned. So were Trotsky—after he had openly declared his solidarity with Lenin—Lunacharsky, and others. The great leaders and tribunes were dispersed. At that critical moment Stalin once again stepped to the fore to lead the party. His relative anonymity stood him in good stead; for his name did not arouse the anger and the hatred inspired by the others.

Soon after Lenin's departure he published under his full signature ("K. Stalin, member of the Central Committee," &c.) an appeal "Close the ranks," addressed to the defeated but not routed party. He repeated that in the "July days" the hands of the Bolsheviks were forced by events, that the counter-revolution had gone over to the attack, and that the "conciliators" burdened themselves with a heavy responsibility. The offensive of the counter-revolution was not yet over—"from the attack on the Bolsheviks they are now passing to an attack on all Soviet parties and the soviets themselves." He forecast a new political crisis: "Be ready for the coming battles. . . . Our first warning is: do not lend yourselves to counter-revolutionary provocation, arm yourselves with endurance and self-control, save forces. . . . Our second warning is: draw closer around our party . . . encourage

the weak, rally those who lag behind." He repeated the same instructions to the city conference of the Bolsheviks, which had begun before
the "July days" and was now half-secretly resumed. The conference
adopted a manifesto written by Stalin in a style that was a peculiar
mixture of the revolutionary and the oriental, sacerdotal idiom:

> *Those gentlemen evidently hope to confound our ranks, to sow doubt
> and confusion amid us and to make us distrust our leaders. The wretches!
> They do not know that never have the names of our leaders [i.e. the
> names of Lenin, Trotsky, Zinoviev, Kamenev] been as dear and near to
> the working class as they are now when the impudent bourgeois rabble
> is slinging mud at them. The venal traitors! They do not even guess that
> the heavier the slander of bourgeois hirelings the deeper the love of the
> workers for their leaders. . . . The shameful stigma of slanderers . . . take
> that stigma from the hands of 32 thousand organized workers of Peters-
> burg and carry it to your grave. . . . And you, gentlemen capitalists and
> landlords, bankers and profiteers, priests and agents of the counter-
> espionage . . . you are celebrating your victory too early. You have taken
> too early to burying the great Russian Revolution. The Revolution is alive,
> and will yet let you feel it, Messieurs the grave-diggers.*

The Bolsheviks, indeed, quickly recovered from the blow. By the
end of July they were able to hold half-secretly a national congress
at which 240,000 members, three times as many as in April, were
represented. Stalin and Bukharin were the chief spokesmen for the
Central Committee. A highlight of the congress was a debate between Stalin, Bukharin, and Preobrazhensky on the character of the
approaching revolution. In part the debate was an echo of the controversy over Lenin's April Theses; in part it was an anticipatory flash
of a more dramatic controversy in years to come. Stalin tabled a motion to the effect that the victorious Russian Revolution would direct
its power "in alliance with the revolutionary proletariat of the advanced countries toward peace and the Socialist reconstruction of
society." Preobrazhensky, a young Marxist economist, tabled an
amendment saying that the revolutionary government should "direct
its power towards peace and—if proletarian revolution materializes
in the west—towards socialism." In both versions the "alliance" between the Russian Revolution and the western European proletariat
was taken for granted. In Preobrazhensky's view, however, Russia
could not embark upon Socialist construction unless western Europe,

FIGURE 3. V. I. Lenin in Disguise, August 1917.

too, was revolutionized. Failing this, the revolution could only achieve peace (and presumably the consolidation of the democratic order). Bukharin defined the objectives of the revolution in much the same way. Stalin saw no reason why Russia could not start building socialism, regardless of whether there was a revolution in the west or not:

> *"You cannot rule out the possibility," so he argued against Preobrazhensky, "that precisely Russia will be the country that paves the way to Socialism. . . . The base of the revolution is broader in Russia than in western Europe, where the proletariat stands alone against the bourgeoisie. With us the working class is supported by the poor peasantry. . . . In Germany the apparatus of state power works with incomparably greater*

efficiency. . . . We ought to discard the obsolete idea that only Europe can show us the way. There exists a dogmatic Marxism and a creative one. I am opting for the latter."

Paradoxically enough, at that stage, Stalin's view appeared to be identical with Trotsky's; for Trotsky, too, argued that Russia would *begin* the Socialist revolution before Europe. Stalin did not yet expound the idea of socialism in one country, the view that Russia by herself, in isolation from the rest of the world, could build to the end the edifice of socialism. Only seven or eight years later would he formulate that view jointly with Bukharin and against Trotsky. But already now there was a stronger emphasis in his words on Russia's peculiar Socialist mission than either in Trotsky's or in Lenin's. In Trotsky's and Lenin's writings of those days that emphasis could also be found but it was offset by their equally categorical insistence on the *ultimate* dependence of the fate of socialism in Russia on proletarian revolution in the West. Russia could and would begin the building of socialism before the other more advanced countries, but she could not carry it far all by herself—argued Lenin and Trotsky. Stalin tended to repeat the first half of the thesis but not the second. His words did in fact breathe an implicit, only half-conscious faith in Russia's revolutionary self-sufficiency. In July and August 1917 nobody was aware of these meaningful hints at future schism.

There is a touch of irony in the circumstance that at a congress run by Stalin, Trotsky's group formally merged with the Bolshevik party and that the still-imprisoned Trotsky was elected to its new Central Committee. The other members were Lenin, Stalin, Kamenev, Zinoviev, Sverdlov, Rykov, Bukharin, Nogin, Uritsky, Miliutin, Kollontai, Artem, Krestinsky, Dzerzhinsky, Yoffe, Sokolnikov, Smilga, Bubnov, Muralov, Shaumian, Berzin. The congress paid its homage to the persecuted leaders by electing Lenin, Trotsky, Zinoviev, Lunacharsky, Kamenev, and Kollontai to the "honorary presidium."

Meanwhile, the man who directed the party in the absence of the great ones produced no great ideas. There was no sweep of original thought in his speech. His words were dry and lacked fire. But he had the confidence of a man who had in the middle of battle stepped wittingly into a breach. His steadfastness and reliability were enough to quell any incipient panic in the ranks. While he was making his report to the congress news was received of punitive expeditions against the Bolsheviks in various towns, including Tsaritsyn (the future Stalingrad) and of virtual martial law in various parts of the country. The congress did not stir. Like the Koba of the old Baku days, during the ebb of the First Revolution, the Stalin of these was still able calmly to weather the storm.

After the congress, when the imprisoned leaders, first Kamenev and then Trotsky, Lunacharsky, and others were gradually released, Stalin again withdrew into the twilight of the *coulisse.*

At the end of August the capital was alarmed by the revolt of General Kornilov, the commander-in-chief, against the Provisional Government, a revolt that confirmed the persistent Bolshevik warnings of an imminent counter-revolution. The origin of the coup was obscure. The Prime Minister Kerensky had contemplated a final show-down with the Bolsheviks and had asked General Kornilov to send reliable forces to the capital. The general was not content with the plan to suppress bolshevism—he wanted to rid the country of the soviets, the moderate Socialists, and Kerensky himself as well. In-flated with self-confidence and the sense of his own mission as "savior of society," he made no bones about his intentions, withdrew allegiance from the government, and, having surrendered Riga to the Germans, ordered his troops to march on Petersburg.

The government, the soviets, the Menshevik and Social Revolu-tionary Committees and Executives were now in a panic. They were not in a position to defeat Kornilov's coup without help from the Bolsheviks, without arming the workers who followed Lenin, without reviving the soviets and calling back to life the Red Guards sup-pressed in the "July days." Kerensky himself asked the Bolsheviks to induce the sailors of Kronstadt, who had been so active in the July mutiny, to "protect the revolution." Keeping their own grievances and resentments under control, the Bolsheviks responded to the ap-peal and fought "in the first ranks" against Kornilov. The counter-revolution overreached itself and drove all Socialist factions to form a "united front," which spelt its doom. The Bolsheviks, on the other hand, were careful not to commit a similar mistake. When the sailors of Krondstadt visited Trotsky in his prison and asked him whether they should not "deal" with Kornilov and Kerensky at one stroke, Trotsky advised them to tackle their adversaries one by one. After a few days the Kornilov coup collapsed.

The abortive counter-revolution gave bolshevism the impetus it needed for the last lap on its road to power. The Bolsheviks emerged from the crisis with the halo of the most determined, if not the only, defenders of the revolution. When, after the suppression of Kornilov's revolt, Lenin openly called upon the Mensheviks and Social Revolutionaries to break up their partnership with the Cadets, Kornilov's accomplices, to take the reins of government into their own hands, and to base it exclusively on the soviets, promising that if his advice was followed the Bolsheviks would play the role of a legal, constitutional opposition within the framework of the soviets; and when the Mensheviks and Social Revolutionaries rejected that advice, they irretrievably discredited themselves in the eyes of the working classes. The popularity of the Bolsheviks grew in the army together with their ever louder clamor for peace and for land for the peasants. . . .

A few days after the arrest of General Kornilov, an important event occurred in the Petersburg Soviet. As a result of recent by-elections, the Bolsheviks became the majority party. Similar shifts occurred in the soviets of Moscow and other towns. Soon Trotsky, released on bail, was elected president of the Petersburg Soviet, the post he had held in 1905. Under his guidance the Soviet demanded from the Central Executive, still dominated by the moderate Socialists, that the second All-Russian Congress of Soviets should be called and all power transferred to it. Logically, this resolution was the prelude to insurrection. As long as Mensheviks and Social Revolutionaries were in a majority, the Bolsheviks clamor "all power to the soviets" could have no immediate practical consequences. What that slogan meant was that the Soviet majority, Mensheviks and Social Revolutionaries, should take full power. It was up to that majority to follow or not to follow that course of action. But presently "all power to the soviets" implied power for the Bolsheviks, the new majority party. And what—the question inevitably arose—if the Provisional Government refused to yield to that demand and efface itself in favor of the soviets? Then, the soviets would be under the political obligation to assert their claims against the Provisional Government, to overthrow it, and to put an end to the existing dualism of power. This could be achieved only through insurrection.

III THE BOLSHEVIK VICTORY: WHY THE PROVISIONAL GOVERNMENT FELL AND WHY THE BOLSHEVIKS WERE SUCCESSFUL

Alexander Kerensky

BOTH LEFT AND RIGHT BETRAYED THE PROVISIONAL GOVERNMENT

Alexander Kerensky, who was born in 1881, studied at St. Petersburg University and became a lawyer. He was a member of the Fourth Duma, and during the revolutionary events of 1917 he played a series of leading roles which are characterized in detail by several of the selections of this book. Mr. Kerensky spent most of the years after 1917 in the United States. Always active and articulate, he remained at the center of fierce controversies about the reasons for the Provisional Government's failures and vigorously defended himself in several books. In these works, as in the article presented here, his primary purpose was to explain his interpretation of the events.

I must here observe that that tendency to dictatorship of which I have written above, infected during the war persons who would have seemed to have been fully guaranteed against this psychosis. I quite understand the personal, human, most torturing experiences on the front, which urged Russian commanders and the officers generally into an unfortunate adventure which was hopeless from the first. But for myself even till now remain quite inexplicable the motives which induced some of the military representatives of our principal allies, both in Petersburg and at headquarters, to give active support to the general movement against that government which was directing operations important for our Allies at the front. Surely by supporting the conspiracy these foreign representatives promoted a new break of discipline in the army, exactly at the time when that army was successfully completing the execution of its principal strategical task. Even if we must admit that the failure of the March Revolution heavily compromised the military position of the Allies, part of the responsibility for that failure must fairly be accepted by some of their official representatives.

Now, considering the diplomatic side of the military policy of the Provisional Government, we shall see that the task which we set ourselves, namely, the earliest conclusion of a general peace, was

From Alexander Kerensky, "The Policy of the Provisional Government of 1917," *The Slavonic and East European Review* 11 (July 1932): 10–19. Reprinted by permission of Alexander Kerensky and *The Slavonic and East European Review*.

almost attained, and the war would not have dragged on to November 1918 if the unfortunate attempt to establish the dictatorship of General Kornilov had not opened the door to the dictatorship of Lenin.

Perhaps the unfavorable attitude towards the Provisional Government of some extremely important foreign circles of our then Allies is to be explained by those new objects of the war which Russia set herself after the March Revolution, and which were only too foreign to the psychology of the time in France and England, at least for official France and England. The formula of a democratic peace, which was later developed in the famous Fourteen Points of the declaration of President Wilson, but was then for the first time proclaimed in a condensed form in the April declaration of the Provisional Government, seemed to many in the West inadmissibly doctrinaire at the time of the war and revolution and almost as criminally Germanophil.

In its solemn manifesto on the objects of the war the Provisional Government declared that, defending its frontiers, the free and democratic Russian people did not want to seize foreign territory, would not impose contributions on its enemies, and aimed at the quickest possible general and just peace on the basis of the self-determination of peoples.

Now, in 1932, for English public opinion which so clearly understands all the imperfections of the Treaty of Versailles, it is difficult to imagine with what keen apprehension and often unconcealed irritation diplomatists in 1917 received our formula of a "democratic peace." However, for the Provisional Government the formulating of new and extremely democratic war aims was not only a demand of "revolutionary idealism," but even a practical necessity; the renunciation of "imperialist war aims," the declaration of defense of one's own country as the only cause for the continuation of military operations, was the obligatory first psychological condition of restoring the efficiency of the front.

Besides that, the new war diplomacy of the Provisional Government, resting on these new war aims, made it possible to prepare the exit from the war of some of the Allies of Germany, particularly Bulgaria and Turkey. I have already mentioned the psychological effect which the March Revolution had on the Slavonic troops and partly on the Turkish (in consequence of the renunciation of Constantinople) in the armies of the coalition of the Central Powers. A similar favorable effect for us and our Allies the March Revolution produced also on the civil population of the Slav parts of Austria, of Bulgaria and of Turkey. Therefore it is not surprising that the result of the ardent work of our foreign minister, M. I. Tereshchenko, together with the diplomatic representatives of the United States, which were not at war with Bulgaria and Turkey, was that both these states were quite ready to go out of the war even without the agreement of Berlin and Vienna. They were preparing to go out about November 1917. It will be understood of itself what really decisive importance would have resulted from the opening in wartime of the Dardanelles for Russia and for her Allies. Now—and the whole world now knows what the Provisional Government knew then, alas! on the eve of Lenin's rising of 7 November—the world now knows, that Vienna just before the Bolshevik Revolution had definitely decided to conclude peace, even a separate peace, at whatever cost.

Thus, the new international war policy of Russia after the fall of the monarchy was adapted to the circumstances and at any rate fully carried out the first requisites of a wartime diplomacy; it contributed to the success of the war, it brought its end nearer, and it did not weaken the efficiency of our own front.

I do not in the slightest doubt that the real history which will be written when the passions of contemporary political strife sink down and die with us—that this history will make the following conclusions: the world war would not have lasted so long if the natural post-revolution internal process of restoring the ties of state and of society in Russia had not been interrupted by a premature attempt to establish a personal dictatorship by civil war.

To prevent a civil war was the whole object of the internal policy of the Provisional Government.

As I have written above, after the collapse of the monarchy the Provisional Government was bound in conditions of war (i) to restore, that is, from top to bottom, the administrative apparatus of the state, and (ii) to fix the foundations of a new state and social order. Two conditions, independent of any human will, excluded the application, for the attainment of the two above-named objects of internal policy, of a dictatorial or, as they liked to say at that time, of a "strong" government. First of all, for a "strong" government, in the dictatorial sense of the word, that is, for a government which did not direct and govern, but commanded and punished, it was first necessary to have in one's hands a highly-organized and accurately functioning administration and police. Such a machinery, or even the most distant suggestion of it, the Provisional Government after the collapse of the monarchy did not possess at all. It had to be created anew with the greatest difficulties and imperfections. But till it was established, the government had to replace police compulsion by moral conviction. We see that later on Lenin, too, for his counter-revolutionary coup d'état, utilized the military and administrative apparatus established by the Provisional Government, planting everywhere, among the troops, in government institutions, in the soviets, and in the town councils, his militant cells.

The second condition which decided the internal policy of the Provisional Government was the war, which by its very nature not only in Russia, which had been so extremely weakened, but even in all the other states at war demanded the very closest and most real national unity. Such a sacred alliance of all parties and classes finally created for the needs of the war a government which by external signs was all-powerful, a kind of dictatorial government, or even a quasi-dictatorship "of a strong personality." The first of these we saw in England at the time of the War Cabinet with Lloyd George, the second in France with Clemenceau.

Finally, at the front itself there was not only a mass of more than ten million soldiers highly agitated, recognizing a certain authority only of the Left socialist parties. At the front there were also thousands of officers whose efficiency it was also necessary to maintain in conditions which were for them peculiarly tragical. The enormous majority of the officers, especially of the regular officers, and especially in the Higher Command, in the main recognized the political authority of the bourgeois parties. Of these parties, that of the Cadets or Constitutional Democrats, led by Professor Milyukov, was in a kind of monopoly. This party, which up to the fall of the monarchy had represented the liberal-radical wing of the bourgeois opposition, at the time of the March Revolution, with the disappearance of the conservative parties from the open political stage, covered the whole Right political sector.

All that has just been said fixed, I will repeat, the main lines of all the internal policy of the Provisional Government, which did not change throughout the whole time of its existence, in spite of frequent alterations in its composition. The main line of our internal policy consisted in a continuous attempt to unite all the live creative forces of the country in order (i) to reestablish the functioning of the state apparatus, (ii) to create the bases of a new post-revolutionary political and social order, and (iii) to continue the defense of the country. The only way of opposing the forces of disruption which were driving the country into the chaos of civil war, was to draw into responsible government work the leading representatives of all political parties without exception, whether bourgeois or socialist, which recognized the new order and the supreme authority of the Constituent Assembly, which had to be summoned, even in spite of the war, at the earliest possible date.

It must be said that the sudden crash of the monarchy came about so unexpectedly for the socialist parties that their leaders did not at once understand their own role in the new political conditions when suddenly the masses of the people—workers, peasants and soldiers—obtained an overwhelming weight in the life of the state. In the first days of the revolution it seemed to the leaders of the Left parties that henceforward the deciding role in the administration of the state had passed into the hands of the liberals and that the socialist parties ought to help the government, though not participating in it, in so far as it did not act to the disprofit of the interests of the working classes. However strange it may seem, the cause of the so-called dualism of government and soviets in the first two months of the March Revolution was exactly this failure of the socialist parties to appreciate their importance and the part that they would have to play after the revolution. Conscientiously executing the part of a kind of responsible opposition to the government, the soviets never measured their own pressure by the weakness of resistance both of the broken administrative machinery and of the bourgeois classes, crushed by the weight of the fall of the monarchy.

In spite of a generally-held opinion, it is precisely the strictly bourgeois original composition of the Provisional Government—where, out of eleven ministers, I was the only representative of the non-bourgeois democracy—that was in office in the period of the greatest "weakness of authority" of that government. But besides that —and here again we have a paradox—it was just this cabinet that carried out "by way of revolution" all the program of those radical political and social reforms for which afterwards, at the time of the psychological preparation of General Kornilov's coup d'état, the blame was thrown on Kerensky and his "having finally fallen under the power of the soviets."

As a matter of fact, it was just this first "capitalist" cabinet of the Provisional Government which, besides a number of decrees on freedom of speech, assembly, inviolability of person, etc., worked out the great agrarian reform (the abolition of nonlaboring land tenure and landed property), prepared the law on self-government of county and town councils on the basis of proportional, universal suffrage without distinction of sex, introduced workers' control into factories and workshops, gave wide powers to workers' trade unions, introduced the eight-hour working day in all government works, laid down the principles of cooperative legislation, gave soldiers all rights of citizens apart from their service in the ranks, laid down the principle of the transformation of the empire into a federation of free peoples, drew up the principles of the electoral law for the Constituent Assembly, and so forth. And all this vast legislative work, which transformed the whole political and social system of Russia, the Provisional Government carried out without any pressure "from the soviet democracy." Of its own free will it realized, with great enthusiasm and full class-abnegation, the social and political ideas of the whole Russian liberation movement, liberal and revolutionary, which had had the services of many generations from the time of Novikov and Radishchev.

To tell the truth, the legislative work by way of decrees was the easiest of all for us. The hardest was the administration in the narrow sense of the word, government work which in the chaos of the revolutionary explosion demanded an extremely strong administrative and police apparatus, which it was still necessary to create. We had to create the technical machinery, and we had to establish the authority of the government. For this last task, the government had to possess the confidence of those new strata of the population which, up to the revolution, were only an object and not a subject of power. The whole administrative apparatus was also restored in the first two months of the revolution, but more on paper than in reality. For the new government did not know how to give orders and the population did not wish to submit, often demanding for the dispositions of the government confirmation from this or that soviet.

Thus, not only the conditions of war, but also the public mood, shaken by the revolution, demanded the presence in the Provisional Government of representatives of all parties. After some resistance, both from the Petersburg leaders of soviets and from an insignificant minority in the Provisional Government which believed in illusions of the hegemony of the bourgeoisie, and after a brief convulsion of street fighting, representatives of the soviets and socialist parties entered the government. From the middle of May and right up to the Bolshevist counter-revolution, the Provisional Government throughout remained the government of a bourgeois-socialist coalition, including representatives of all those parties which, accepting the revolution that had taken place as final, refused all forms of dictatorship, whether personal, party, or class.

A policy of national union, of softening of class antagonisms, of averting civil war, which was always possible in the first months of the revolution, of course, excluded all that struck the chord of the need of a "strong authority." A policy of cooperation in the administration of the state by many parties with the most various programs is, of course, as is well known in Europe, a policy of compromise. But a policy of compromise, a policy of agreements and mutual concessions, is for a government the most difficult and unpopular, for parties the most unpleasant and irritating for the self-esteem of committees, and for the country, or more properly for the wide masses of the population not always clear and intelligible.

It may be said that war conditions fixed for Russia after the revolution a system of the formation of government, the coalition system, which is the most difficult of all. We know that even in time of peace in countries with a prolonged experience of parliamentarism, coalitions in the government delay and complicate the government work and soon alienate public opinion. The leading members of the Provisional Government who remained in it to the end—and there were only two such—very clearly saw the objectionable sides of coalition in the government in a period of revolution; but, apart from civil war and an immediate separate peace, we had no choice whatever.

Usually the history of the March Revolution is told as a continually growing collapse at the front and a continually increasing anarchy in the country. In actual fact the history of this revolution represents a curve of slow rise and, later, sharp fall—after the revolt of General Kornilov.

Of the essence of the war policy of the Provisional Government which rested on a coalition, I have already spoken. The essence of its internal policy was not so clear, but just as definite. This is most indisputably confirmed by the actual attempt, by way of a coup d'état, to replace the coalition authority of the Provisional Government by the personal dictatorship of a general. As we know, this attempt took place only after the Provisional Government had suppressed the July rising of the Bolsheviks. The summer months which preceded the movement of Kornilov were the time of the greatest fall of Bolshevist influence, in the soviets, in the factories, and at the front. At the front the commanders, together with the commissaries of the War Minister, from the time of the July offensive were able to employ disciplinary measures, including the application of military force, that is, including shooting. The authority of the commanders, which had fallen after the collapse of the monarchy almost to nil, towards the middle of the summer had been sufficiently reestablished for the chiefs of the military conspiracy to feel assured that the troops would execute their orders and that the breaking up of the soviets and the overthrow of the Provisional Government would not call forth any serious mutiny in the ranks of the army. As we know, these calculations proved to be extremely exaggerated; the attempted revolt of generals again smashed all discipline in the army and killed the authority not only of the High Command, but of the Provisional Government itself. But these consequences of their "patriotic exploit," which the reckless generals had not foreseen, in no way weaken my assertion: it was only when they again felt a certain authority in their hands that the adherents of a personal dictatorship at the head of the army and among the liberal and conservative politicians, decided on their unhappy adventure. And we know it was just the same in Germany. The famous attempt of Kapp and Ludendorff to repeat in 1920 Kornilov's march of 1917 also took place only after the German democracy had conquered anarchy on the Left, suppressed the Spartacists, and reestablished the military and administrative machinery of the state.

But apart from a proof drawn from the other side, namely, from the attempt at a military pronunciamento, there are also positive evidences of the correctness of the coalition policy of the Provisional Government. The anarchy which broke out in March at the works and factories and reached the greatest excesses, gradually towards autumn died down, to break out again with new force only before the actual coup d'état of the Bolsheviks. In the country districts the number of acts of violence of the peasants on the lands of the squires was falling. Transport was being reestablished. The food position of the towns was improving. The town and country self-government was reviving. Towards the end of August, in most of the towns there were already at work town councils elected by universal suffrage. Country self-government was being restored, though more slowly than in the towns. The organs of local self-government based on universal suffrage were weakening the authority of the soviets and diminishing their part in the local life. *Izvestia* itself, then the central organ of the Congress of the Soviets (which were not yet Bolshevist) wrote on 25 October:

> *The soviets of soldiers' and workmen's deputies as a whole organization of proportions all-Russian as to the ground covered and all-democratic as to their social composition, are passing through an evident crisis. The department of the central executive committee for other towns, at the time of the highest development of soviet organization, reckoned 800 local soviets. Many of them no longer exist, still more exist only on paper. The net of soviet organization has in many places been broken, in others it has weakened and in others again it has begun to decay. The soviets were an excellent organization for the fight with the old regime, but they are quite incapable of taking on themselves the building up of a new regime; they have no specialists, no experience, no understanding of business, and, finally, even no organization.*

The summons of the Constituent Assembly, fixed for the month of November, would finally have reduced to nothing the part of the soviets in the history of post-revolutionary Russia. The watchword of the Bolshevist counter-revolution, "All power to the soviets," already in October appeared simply a demagogic cover for the dictatorial plans of Lenin.

I will not here enter into a consideration of the economic and financial policy of the Provisional Government. At a time of war, and even in conditions of blockade, with profound social changes going on in the country itself, everything in this domain had a temporary and conditional character. But even then there was already felt an immediate need of a better planned direction of the whole economic life of the country, for which there was created by us a Higher Council of National Economy, such as after the war also sprang up in Germany and later in other countries, too.

In general, all that I have written on the policy of the Provisional Government, in the first place is far from exhausting the whole subject and, secondly, in no way pursues any objects of self-defense or self-justification. Up to this time I still do not see by what other road than that of cooperation of the whole nation it was possible to try to save Russia from civil war and a separate peace "at the mortal hour of her existence," to quote once more the prophetic phrase of Prince Lvov. Even now it seems to me that the main lines of military and internal policy of the Provisional Government were correctly traced. I entirely agree that in the weakness of our personal strength and ability, we were not able to carry out this policy properly. But then, the realization of our government program was interrupted by those who for some reason thought that they would know better than the Provisional Government how to govern Russia. Meanwhile, at the time when the government of the March Revolution began to be attacked from the Right in the name of dictatorship, there were absolutely no objective data for reckoning the cause of the saving of Russia and the reestablishment of her internal strength as lost. We must further bear in mind that, as opposed to dictatorships of any kind, the Provisional Government did not devise its policy out of its own head, but for the whole time of its existence accurately expressed resolutions freely adopted by all parties, except the Bolsheviks, that had any weight at all in the country.

In the course of its existence of eight months, the Provisional Government lived through four cabinet crises. Each time, all the members of the government, without exception, declared their agreement or even their wish to leave the cabinet, if this was desired by the parties that entered into the coalition. I personally, the member most responsible for the work of the Provisional Government, resigned, both before Kornilov's attempt at a coup d'état and before the November counter-revolution. Each time I proposed to those persons and parties which considered themselves as having a better claim than ourselves to the government of the state, openly to take on themselves the responsibility for the future of the country and, according to their discretion, to form a cabinet. Neither the politicians responsible for the tragic escapade of General Kornilov nor the adherents of a Bolshevist dictatorship decided to respond to this. They knew that all the organized and quite free public opinion of Russia was against any kind of dictatorship, against changes of the system of government till the summons of the Constituent Assembly. Only by way of conspiracy, only by way of a treacherous armed struggle was it possible to break up the Provisional Government and stop the establishment of a democratic system in Russia after the revolution. However, apart from the path chosen by the Provisional Government, no one had any other road but the terrible road of civil war.

In October 1917, the adherents of a personal dictatorship of some or other general, after their own disaster, immediately awaited the overthrow of the Provisional Government by Lenin. "Let the Bolsheviks only finish with them, and then we in three weeks will establish a powerful national authority." Instead of three weeks, we have the third "five years" of the dictatorship of the Bolsheviks. The experience of the Bolshevist dictatorship has lasted infinitely longer than all the dictatorships of gallant admirals and generals, whether in Siberia or in South Russia. But in both places the result for Russia was just the same.

Leonid I. Strakhovsky

KERENSKY BETRAYED RUSSIA

Leonid Strakhovsky, long a professor in the Department of Slavic Studies at the University of Toronto, had a varied and interesting career. Born in Russia, he served in the Russian armed forces from 1916 to 1920. After emigrating to the United States he taught history at Georgetown University and the University of Maryland, and lectured at Harvard, London, Oxford, and Cambridge. His several historical works include books on the Civil War in the Soviet Union and a biographical study of Tsar Alexander I. In the article presented below, Strakhovsky's strong monarchist feelings and the evidence he examined led him to make very serious charges against Alexander Kerensky and to argue that there was no Kornilov revolt. As this article and others in this section indicate, these issues are still very hotly debated.

Recently an article by Abraham Ascher in the *Russian Review* and a chapter in a new book by Robert D. Warth have discussed extensively the most crucial period of the Russian Revolution, during which the fate of Russia was decided, and the way was paved for the Bolshevik seizure of power.[1] Both authors have branded General Kornilov's action early in September 1917 as a rebellion against the Provisional Government and particularly against its prime minister, Alexander Kerensky, and have emphasized the thesis that had it not been for this incident, "the Provisional Government would have been able to weather the revolutionary storm that was raging throughout Russia" and would have prevented the Bolshevik coup d'état of November. Both authors want us to believe that Kornilov was the real villain. This is essentially the thesis first advanced by Kerensky himself in his book *Prelude to Bolshevism,* written in self-justification, and since then maintained by all supporters of the Kerensky regime. Yet from the study of the evidence it would seem that the real villain was not Kornilov, but Kerensky himself, who in deliberately betraying Kornilov also betrayed Russia into the hands of the Bolsheviks.

From Leonid I. Strakhovsky, "Was There a Kornilov Rebellion?—A Re-appraisal of the Evidence," *The Slavonic and East European Review* 33 (June 1955): 372, 378–395. Reprinted by permission of Leonid I. Strakhovsky and *The Slavonic and East European Review.*

[1] Abraham Ascher, "The Kornilov Affair," *The Russian Review* 12 (1953); Robert D. Warth, *The Allies and the Russian Revolution* (Durham, N. C., 1954).

*   *   *

. . . At midnight on 5–6 August, Kornilov finally accepted the Supreme Command and left Berdichev for Mogilyov, seat of the Supreme Headquarters. Thus for a whole week the Russian army was actually without a supreme commander, and this crisis coincided with a crisis in the Provisional Government itself when, in the heat of the struggle for power, ministers, including Kerensky, resigned their offices in turn and then took their resignations back, so that at one time there remained only Nekrasov, the deputy prime minister, to represent the Provisional Government. Finally, on 6 August, a new Provisional Government was formed, much more to the Left than the previous one, with eleven out of the eighteen portfolios held by socialists. Contrary to precedent, the new government issued no joint declaration of policy, but merely an appeal to the nation signed by Kerensky alone. And while Kerensky spoke of the necessity of "iron rule" and asserted that "freedom welded by national unity and enthusiasm cannot be defeated," he could offer no constructive program. In fact he was becoming more and more a prisoner of the soviets, to which the socialist ministers had to report twice a week every decision taken by the government, even in secret sessions. Kerensky's friend of the time, Zinaida Gippius, states plainly: "He is afraid of them." And it was with such a man that Kornilov had to work in his effort to regenerate the army and to save the nation from utter ruin.

At this juncture Ascher asks us to believe that both Kerensky and Kornilov "wanted to reestablish discipline in the army and order in the country" and that "one complemented the other"; that Kerensky was "a thoroughgoing democrat," who "merely wanted to bolster the power of the Provisional Government by gaining the adherence of a 'strong' military man." But actually from that time and until the Bolshevik overthrow of his regime, Kerensky thought of Kornilov only as a dangerous rival, because in the words of Savinkov,[2] "to him (and that is an incontestable fact) liberty, revolution were foremost and Russia only second." But Warth adds that while Kornilov "was not an outspoken reactionary, yet with a sure instinct, men of con-

---

[2] Boris Savinkov, member of the Socialist Revolutionary party and former terrorist. —Ed.

servative sentiment—industrialists, landowners, officers, Cadets
[members of the Constitutional Democratic party] and Allied diplo-
mats—scented the banner of counter-revolution long before the
object of their attentions had done so himself and flocked to his
support." But a thoughtful historian does not think that Kornilov
represented counter-revolution when he comments:

> *In the past, during the political rivalry between the Provisional Government
> and the soviets, it was possible to choose between the tactics of the
> Moderate Democrats and the Socialists, between Miliukov and Kerensky.
> But the situation had undergone a radical change. The opposing forces
> now were Lenin on the one hand and Kornilov on the other—communism
> versus military dictatorship. The country had to make a choice between
> the two.*[3]

Yet to Kerensky, the tight-rope walker who clung to power at all
costs, even at the cost of Russia's future, Kornilov was merely "a
dangerous rival." As for the latter, he considered Kerensky more
and more a tool rather than a master. And while he was willing to
cooperate with Kerensky and his handpicked ministers for the best
interests of Russia, a time was to come when he would realize that
Kerensky was a puppet, whose strings were more and more being
pulled by the soviets with their constantly growing and overwhelm-
ingly vociferous membership of Bolsheviks.

On the basis of his agreement with Commissar Filonenko before
taking up the Supreme Command, Kornilov proceeded to work out
a program of reforms in the armed forces. He was visited by Savinkov
and by Tereshchenko, the minister of foreign affairs, and on 10
August, the liberal newspaper *Rech* reported: "An agreement seems
to have been reached, and the conditions laid down by Kornilov for
taking command accepted." To this Kerensky retorted through an
official release of the Provisional Government's Press Bureau: "The
communications of some newspapers that the conditions laid down
by General Kornilov have been accepted by the Provisional Government do not conform to reality, but at any rate an understanding between the Provisional Government and General Kornilov has been
reached." Indeed, General Kornilov believed that an understanding

[3] George Vernadsky, *A History of Russia* (New Haven, 1929), p. 243.

had been reached and so he came to Petrograd on 16 August in order to present his report and to press for its acceptance. But the measures proposed by Kornilov were anathema to the soviets and hence to Kerensky, who passed the report on to Savinkov and Filonenko, for revision. Thus Kornilov reported only on the general military situation, painting a gloomy picture and warning of a possible enemy offensive on the Riga front. He concluded: "Although counter-measures have been taken, it is unlikely that, in view of the general instability of the armed forces and particularly of the army on the northwestern front, we could stop the enemy's advance."

It was during this report to the full membership of the Provisional Government that a significant incident occurred. In his later testimony before the Investigating Committee Kornilov stated:

> When I broached the subject of a possible offensive on a certain sector of the front, provided certain conditions were met, the prime minister, who sat next to me, bent over and whispered that I should be careful about what I was saying. This warning was provoked by a note handed to Kerensky by Savinkov and Tereshchenko which said: "Is the prime minister sure that the Russian and Allied state secrets being revealed by General Kornilov will not become known to the enemy through comradely channels?" I was stunned and deeply disturbed by the realization that in the Council of Ministers of the Russian State the supreme commander could not without apprehension touch upon such matters which he considers necessary to lay before the government in the interests of national defense. At the end of the meeting it became clear to me from certain remarks made by Savinkov that the warning had in view Chernov, the minister of agriculture.

Ascher, following Kerensky's own lead, treats this incident lightly, but one can imagine the shock which the stalwart soldier experienced when he realized that there were potential traitors among Kerensky's cabinet ministers. No wonder that his distrust of this Second Coalition Provisional Government grew steadily as time went on, and he found no cooperation from this government for the enactment of measures which he rightly considered not only as necessary but essential for the salvation of Russia.

Before leaving the capital at 3 a.m. on 17 August, Kornilov gave an interview to the press. *Rech* reported: "General Kornilov proposed certain measures for the improvement of conditions in the army. He is convinced, and feels that the Provisional Government is of the same mind, that without these measures, the enactment of which he expects in the next few days, it is impossible to restore the fighting ability of the army. It is very necessary that the Provisional Government should adopt these measures." But *Izvestiya,* the organ of the soviets, commented: "The demands of General Kornilov, in the form of an ultimatum, supported by the possibility of a new attack by the enemy, put the Provisional Government in a very difficult position, and the future alone knows how it will act. This, however, may be said at present: the sympathies of the democracy [i.e. the soviets] are not on the side of General Kornilov." From this moment on the leftist press, taking a cue from *Izvestiya,* started an energetic campaign against Kornilov. This in turn led to the passing of resolutions by the Council of the Union of Cossack Troops on 19 August, by the Union of Officers of the Army and Navy on 20 August, and by the Union of the Knights of St. George on 21 August, vigorously supporting the supreme commander.

Meanwhile Kerensky stubbornly refused all Savinkov's entreaties even to read the text of Kornilov's proposed measures as revised by Savinkov and Filonenko. Finally, on 21 August, he informed Savinkov bluntly that under no circumstances would he sign such a document. This was Kerensky's fatal mistake. But Ascher exonerates him: "Indeed, in the light of the existing political situation it was most difficult for him to do so. It would most probably have meant the alienation of groups whose support he desperately needed." Indeed, Kerensky needed the support of the soviets to maintain himself in power, but in relying on it he not only prepared his own downfall, but the collapse of Russia as well.

Exasperated by Kerensky's stubbornness and lack of unselfish statesmanship, Savinkov tendered his resignation as deputy minister of war. But Kerensky refused to accept it. Then Savinkov learned that Kornilov had decided not to come to Petrograd for another effort to get his proposed and revised measures enacted, as had been agreed at the end of his first visit, because of intelligence which had reached him that an attempt on his life was being prepared in the capital. In desperation Savinkov and Filonenko called Kornilov by telegraph on 22 August. "Your presence here tomorrow is absolutely essential," pleaded Savinkov; "without your help I shall not be able to defend what both you and I consider right." To this Filonenko added that he and Savinkov had planned to give "general battle" the next day in order to change the government's policy in line with Kornilov's program. Finally Kornilov yielded to the arguments of these two political friends, who were to desert him, nevertheless, at the crucial hour. But he took precautions and came to Petrograd on 23 August accompanied by a squadron of the Tekinsky Cavalry Regiment armed with machine guns.

Contrary to Mr. Ascher's statement, it was not Kornilov who was afraid of Kerensky, but Kerensky of Kornilov. Having learned of Savinkov's *démarche* in urging Kornilov's visit to Petrograd, Kerensky, without informing Savinkov, had dispatched the following telegram to the supreme commander: "The Provisional Government did not call for you, nor did it insist on your arrival and therefore does not assume any responsibility in this matter, in view of the existing strategic conditions." But this telegram reached Kornilov only when he had already arrived in the capital, and it is doubtful whether it would have stopped him.

Kornilov was met at the station by Savinkov and Filonenko, who handed to him the revised copy of his original report which they had both signed. From the station Kornilov went directly to Kerensky's apartment in the Winter Palace. It is difficult to ascertain what happened at this meeting because of the opposing evidence of Kornilov and Kerensky, but one thing is certain, namely that Kerensky won a tactical victory when he prevented Kornilov's report, modified by Savinkov and Filonenko, from being discussed by the full membership of the Provisional Government on the ground that he himself had had no time yet to study it. Nevertheless, the report, to which Kornilov had also affixed his signature, was read and discussed by Kornilov that evening at a private meeting with Kerensky, Nekrasov and Tereshchenko, at which it was strongly argued against by the latter two while Kerensky kept silent. While this meeting was taking place, Savinkov read Kornilov's report to his friends, the Merezhkovskys. Here is how Zinaida Gippius recorded it in her diary:

> Savinkov read it to us in its entirety, beginning with a most detailed and all-embracing analysis of the situation at the front (it is most shocking even on the surface!) and ending by a similarly concise exposition of those immediate measures which have to be enacted both at the front and in the rear. This very lengthy report, in which every word has been thought

out and weighed, will some time find its commentator—at any rate it will not be lost. I shall say only what is most important: it is undoubtedly that minimum which as yet might save the honor of the revolution and the life of Russia in her present unheard-of situation.

I think that, indeed, there will still be bargaining with Kerensky. But it seems that even in all its details it is a minimum, including the militarization of the railways and the death penalty in the rear. I can imagine how the "comrades" will howl! (And Kerensky is afraid of them, this must be remembered.)

They will howl, because they will discover in this a fight against the soviets—that hideous abnormally developed phenomenon, that breeding place of bolshevism, a phenomenon before which even now the democratic leaders and sub-leaders, non-Bolsheviks, reverently bow. It is some kind of immutably stupid criminality!

They will be right: it is a fight against the soviets, although openly nothing is said in the report about the destruction of the soviets. On the contrary, Boris [Savinkov] added even that "it is necessary to retain the soldiers' committees, because one cannot do without them." But no committee of any sort should be permitted to interfere in matters of command.

And still it is (at last!) a fight against the soviets.

And Kerensky must have understood that the report meant exactly what Zinaida Gippius surmised—a fight against the soviets. But he was not only afraid of them, he had to rely on their vacillating support to remain in power, which was more important to him than the fate of Russia. And Kornilov must have been aware by this time that Kerensky was too weak to head a "strong" government, because he would never dare to challenge the vicious authority of the soviets. It was then that he decided to appeal directly to the nation in an attempt to arouse the sane, vital, patriotic and honorable sentiments still alive in the country. This he was to do at the Moscow Conference, an unwieldy heterogeneous gathering of over twenty-five hundred delegates supposedly representative of the nation as a whole, which the Provisional Government had called for 25 August.

In the meantime another attempt to force Kerensky's hand was made when in the morning of 24 August Kokoshkin, a leading member of the Constitutional Democratic party, who held the office of state-comptroller in the Provisional Government, threatened to resign from the government, if Kornilov's program was not adopted forthwith. In order to appease Kokoshkin and the other members of his party who held cabinet posts, Kerensky informed the members of his government for the first time at a meeting that day of the contents of Kornilov's report, but only in its first version and revealing only the portions dealing directly with military affairs. After a heated discussion a compromise was reached, accepting Kornilov's program in principle—another fine example of Kerensky's prevarication.

"The Moscow State Conference opened in an atmosphere charged with alarm and nervous expectation," reported *Rech*. The membership was about equally divided between the socialist and non-socialist groups. And Kerensky attempted to steer a middle course, throwing threats to the Right and to the Left alike, whereas "on the Left there was the real and growing danger of bolshevism and on the Right only the spurious and problematic menace of 'counter-revolution' and military dictatorship."[4] Zinaida Gippius commented bitterly on Kerensky's behavior at the conference:

> *He is like a railway carriage that has left the rails. He sways, vacillates painfully and—without any glamour. . . . I loved him as he was before (and do not deny it); I understand his difficult position; I remember how during the first days he took an oath before the soviets always to remain with the democracy, how with one stroke of the pen he abolished the death penalty forever. . . . And now if he were to join Kornilov and Savinkov it would be a betrayal of the oath to the soviets, and the death penalty again. . . . But still there are only two honorable ways for Kerensky, only two. Either to go along with Kornilov, Savinkov and the famous program, or to declare quietly and openly: this is what is needed at this critical moment, but I cannot do it and hence I am leaving. . . . But he is seeking a third way, wants to hold back something, to put putty in the ominous crack, to prolong the lingering. . . . But there is no third way, and Kerensky will find himself without a way, he will meet an inglorious end. . . . and it is good, if it is his end alone.*

And Kerensky did exactly this. He did not heed the warning of General Kornilov, delivered at the Moscow Conference on 27 August, when the supreme commander said:

> *It is with deep sorrow that I must declare openly that I have no certainty that the Russian army would fulfill unflinchingly its duty to the fatherland. . . . The shame of the Tarnopol disaster is the direct and inevitable*

---

[4] Michael T. Florinsky, *Russia: A History and an Interpretation* (New York, 1953), 2:1434.

*consequence of that unheard-of ruin which befell our army, once glorious
and victorious, as the result of influences from outside and of careless
measures adopted for its reorganization. . . . The enemy is already pound-
ing at the gates of Riga and if the instability of our army will not give us
a possibility to hold on to the shore of the Riga Gulf, the road to Petrograd will be open to invasion. . . . I have faith that the fighting qualities
of our army and her former glory will be restored. But I declare that* there
is no time to lose, *that one should not waste* a single minute. *We need
determination and the firm unflinching carrying out of proposed measures.
. . . The army must be revived at all costs, for without a strong army there
can be no free Russia and no salvation of the country. In order to revive
the army, it is necessary to accept at once and* without delay *(Kornilov
repeated this twice) the recommendations which I have made to the Provisional Government. My report was countersigned, without any reserva-
tions whatsoever, by the deputy minister of war, Savinkov, and Commissar
Filonenko, attached to Supreme Headquarters. . . . It is inconceivable to
admit that determination should manifest itself each time only under the
pressure of defeats and loss of territory. If stern measures for the restoration of discipline at the front were introduced as the result of the Tarnopol
disaster and the loss of Galicia and Bukovina,* one should not permit that
the establishment of order in the rear *would be the consequence of our
loss of Riga or that order on the railways should be restored at the price
of ceding to the enemy Moldavia and Bessarabia.*

The impression made by Kornilov's speech was immense and
deeply depressing. This time he gave a warning and appealed not
only to the government, but to the nation at large. But the government, personified by Kerensky, who was "its head, its inspiration,
and its symbol,"[5] now saw in Kornilov not merely a dangerous rival,
but the leader of a counter-revolutionary plot. As to the nation it was
now more divided than ever. The so-called "democratic forces," i.e.
the socialists of various hues, including the Bolsheviks, were more
concerned with what they called "the gains of the revolution" than
with the future of Russia and, while ostensibly supporting Kerensky,
actually drove him further and further into the abyss. Whereas all
the sane and vital elements of the country now looked toward Kornilov
as their only hope to save Russia from oblivion. And coming events
seemed to play into the general's hand.

On 31 August the Germans started their offensive against Riga,
as Kornilov had warned, and three days later, on 3 September, not-

---

[5] Florinsky, *Russia,* p. 1434.

withstanding feverish efforts of the Supreme Command, which were nullified by the refusal of soldiers to fight, the city was captured by the enemy with little effort. And as Kornilov predicted, this new disaster stirred the government into action. It was decided to send to the front all those regiments stationed in the capital which had participated in the July uprising and to replace them by more reliable units, particularly cavalry regiments, which had already been arriving in Petrograd on their way to Finland. At the same time Savinkov, who had just been appointed also deputy minister of the navy, was sent to Supreme Headquarters on 4 September to confer with Kornilov. There, on 6 September, he informed the supreme commander that the latter's proposed measures would be enacted in a few days; that a Bolshevik uprising was expected about 9–10 September and that the publication of Kornilov's program would provide them with a new stimulus to action; that the reaction of the Socialist-Revolutionaries and of the Mensheviks was uncertain and hence the government could not rely on the garrison. "Therefore," he said, "I ask you to issue orders that the Third Cavalry Corps should be concentrated in the vicinity of Petrograd and be placed at the disposal of the Provisional Government. In case, besides the Bolsheviks, the members of the Soviet of Workers' and Soldiers' Deputies also rise against the government, we shall have to apply decisive and merciless measures against them as well." It was then also agreed that Kornilov should inform Savinkov by telegraph of the exact time when the Third Cavalry Corps would approach Petrograd so that the Provisional Government would know when to proclaim the capital under martial law. Thus the concentration of the Third Cavalry Corps in the vicinity of Petrograd, a measure which was later claimed by Kerensky and Savinkov and their apologists as the first step of the Kornilov rebellion, was carried out at the specific demand of Savinkov who, supposedly, was following Kerensky's instructions.

At this juncture an important question arises: was Kerensky straightforward in his dealings with Kornilov or was he trying to set a trap for the supreme commander and the "counter-revolutionary conspiracy," which he was ferreting out ever since the Moscow Conference? In the opinion of Milyukov, Gippius, and Florinsky all the evidence points strongly to the fact that Kerensky betrayed Kornilov. And the episode of V. N. L'vov, who took upon himself the task of reconciling the opposing attitudes of Kerensky and Kornilov by acting as go-between, of which both Ascher and Warth make a great deal, only played into Kerensky's hands. Professor Vernadsky sums up the situation very aptly in these words:

> *Kornilov's plan of reinstating discipline in the army was based upon the cooperation of the Provisional Government. If he had had to deal with the first Provisional Government, headed by Prince Lvov, it is quite likely that his plan of subjecting the government to his will would have succeeded. But unluckily for him, the head of the government was no longer Prince Lvov, but Kerensky, who was not sufficiently strong to retain power for himself, but who had enough political cunning to prevent anyone else from taking it from him so long as the Provisional Government continued to exist.*[6]

The crisis came to a head with the so-called "mission" of V. N. L'vov. A constitutional democrat, member of the last Duma and former procurator of the Holy Synod in the First Provisional Government, L'vov visited Kerensky at the Winter Palace on 4 September and urged him to reorganize his government on a broader basis to include even moderate monarchists. According to L'vov's statement to the Investigating Committee, Kerensky showed perfect willingness to follow L'vov's advice, even stating that he was ready to step down from the office of prime minister. Thus L'vov felt not only encouraged by this interview, but even that he was entrusted by Kerensky to negotiate for the formation of a new government. Actually Kerensky wanted to use L'vov in order to ferret out the "counter-revolutionary" plot which had become his obsession since the Moscow Conference.

The next day L'vov left Petrograd on his "mission." After stopping in Moscow, where he had interviews with conservative political leaders, L'vov proceeded to Mogilyov where he had two meetings with Kornilov on 6 and 7 September. He assured the supreme commander that he had been entrusted by Kerensky, "who does not cling to power and is willing to resign if he were in the way," to find out Kornilov's views on a reorganization of the government. Kornilov stated bluntly that in view of the critical situation both at the front and in the rear he could not see any way out of the dilemma except through the establishment of a dictatorship and the placing

6 Vernadsky, *A History,* p. 243.

of the entire country under military law. "I declared," he testified later, "that I have no personal aspirations to power and that I am ready to submit immediately to the one who is invested with dictatorial powers, whether it is Kerensky himself or some other person." At the same time he announced that if dictatorial powers were conferred upon him by the Provisional Government, he would not refuse to do his duty.

But when L'vov reported to Kerensky on 8 September, Kornilov's suggestions were presented as demands. Kerensky seized upon this ultimative nature of Kornilov's proposal as reported by L'vov to proclaim it to be a plot against his regime. He even went so far as to impersonate L'vov, already under arrest, in an exchange of messages by telegraph with Kornilov in order to obtain confirmation of the would-be conspiracy. Yet a careful scrutiny of the text of these messages does not reveal any plot on the part of Kornilov, who pursued the much discussed idea of the formation of a strong government either with himself or some other strong personality at the head of it, and with the participation of Kerensky. Even at this stage Kornilov trusted Kerensky.

> *Although he did not believe that Kerensky would dare to undertake an open struggle against the Soviet, he believed fully that Kerensky, like himself, was inspired not by a personal taste for power but by the welfare of the country. He did not expect that at the last minute Kerensky would stubbornly cling to power in a desire to hold to it at all costs, even at the risk of jeopardizing what, in Kornilov's opinion, was the last chance to save the Russian state.*[7]

After the exchange of messages with Kornilov, which ended with Kerensky's promise to visit Supreme Headquarters the next day, ostensibly to come to an agreement with the supreme commander, the prime minister announced to his astounded cabinet members that he had discovered Kornilov's plot against the government and demanded unlimited powers to deal with the situation as well as to reorganize the government. Whereupon all fourteen cabinet ministers handed him their resignations. From then on and until a new government was formed, there were no more cabinet meetings, and Kerensky acted dictatorially.

[7] P. N. Milyukov, *Istoriya vtoroy russkoy revolyutsii* (Sofia, 1921), 1:181–182.

Kerensky's first act was to send a telegram in his own name and without an official number dismissing Kornilov from the Supreme Command and demanding his presence in Petrograd. This came as a thunderbolt to Kornilov, who was expecting Kerensky's and Savinkov's arrival that very day. Before receiving the order of his dismissal, Kornilov, in fulfillment of his agreement with Savinkov, sent him the following telegram, dated 9 September at 2:40 p.m.—"The corps will be concentrated in the vicinity of Petrograd towards the evening of 10 September. I request proclamation of martial law in Petrograd on 11 September. No. 6394. General Kornilov. Countersigned: Lukomsky, Romanovsky." Was that the act of a plotter and would-be rebel—to inform the opponent of his plans and troop concentrations? It was natural, then, for Kornilov to assume, upon receipt of Kerensky's personal telegram announcing his dismissal that the prime minister had fallen completely under the influence of the soviets and was acting on his own and not as the head of the Provisional Government. Hence Kornilov refused to surrender his command. It was obviously an act of insubordination, but certainly not of mutiny or rebellion as Kerensky wanted it to appear.

From the beginning of the crisis Savinkov believed that it was a misunderstanding and wanted to get in touch with Kornilov the very evening of 8 September, when Kerensky informed the cabinet of the supreme commander's "rebellion," but was prevented from doing so by Kerensky. Yet the very next day, 9 September, Savinkov gave an interview to the press in which he declared that "General Kornilov enjoys the absolute confidence of the Provisional Government," that his proposals have been "accepted" and that "the measures of the supreme commander for the improvement of the front and of the rear and for the restoration of discipline in the army are supported by the Provisional Government which will not delay enacting them." But at the same time Kerensky revealed at a conference with some former members of his cabinet the text of a declaration in which, distorting the facts completely, he declared that General Kornilov had sent V. N. L'vov, member of the State Duma, to him

with a demand that the Provisional Government hand over to General Kornilov all civil and military powers so that he may, according to his own judgment, form a new government. The fact of the authorization of V. N. L'vov was confirmed by General Kornilov in a conversation with me by direct wire. Having concluded *that the presentation of these demands expresses the desire of certain circles of the Russian public to take advantage of the difficult situation in the state for* the reestablishment in the country of a regime opposed to the conquests of the revolution, *the Provisional Government has found it necessary in order to save the fatherland, liberty and the* republican *form of government to authorize me to take quick and decisive measures so as to cut at the roots all attempts to* challenge the supreme authority *in the state and* the rights of citizens won by the revolution.[8]

This was an accusation of General Kornilov as a counter-revolutionary who desired to reestablish the monarchy, which was blatantly untrue. As to the republican form of government, it was still an open question since it was up to the Constituent Assembly to decide it. As Zinaida Gippius noted in her diary: "It was obvious from the beginning that the ulcer of enmity had burst in Kerensky towards Kornilov *(not* the reverse). That the attacking party is Kerensky and not Kornilov. And that for the present the winning side will be Kerensky and not Kornilov, who did not expect this direct blow."

Among the ministers who attended the conference with Kerensky there was still a feeling that the whole thing was a misunderstanding, and they suggested that before the declaration was made public, the prime minister should contact Supreme Headquarters. This Kerensky accepted and the conference adjourned at 1 p.m. But it was Savinkov who was delegated to try to clear the misunderstanding. And Savinkov, who had been refused this opportunity by Kerensky the night before, was eager to do so, because he must have felt that his own political reputation and integrity were in jeopardy, since he knew that the movement of the Third Corps towards Petrograd was undertaken upon his order and in the name of Kerensky.

When contact was established with Kornilov by telegraph, Savinkov urged Kornilov to obey the order of the Provisional Government, to surrender his command and to leave Supreme Headquarters. After referring to new alarming news—which had to deal with the German preparations to make a landing on the shores of the Gulf of Riga; with the murder of a divisional commander and of an army commissar by soldiers; and with the appalling results of the explosion in the ammunition depot in Kazan, the work of German agents—

[8] Author's italics.

Kornilov reiterated that he had sent no ultimatums to Kerensky; that he had received V. N. L'vov as an emissary of the prime minister who came to offer to Kornilov a choice of three ways to reorganize the government, and that he had chosen the principle of a military dictatorship in the firm belief that there was no other way to save the country from imminent catastrophe; that he considered the participation of both Kerensky and Savinkov in the new government as essential, and that in view of the forthcoming Bolshevik uprising in Petrograd he had been and was still urging both Kerensky and Savinkov to come to Supreme Headquarters, because their presence in the capital was wrought with danger for both of them, while he guaranteed their safety on his word of honor. He spoke further of his great surprise in receiving the order of his dismissal at the time when he was expecting Kerensky's arrival as promised by the latter the day before. Then he concluded:

> *I am deeply convinced that the completely unexpected decision of the government was undertaken under pressure of certain definite organizations. To leave my post under the pressure of these people I consider equal to desertion in the face of the enemy. Therefore, fully conscious of my responsibility before the nation, before history and before my conscience, I firmly declare that in this terrible hour in the life of the fatherland I shall not leave my post.*

As Zinaida Gippius comments: *"There was no Kornilov rebellion."* And Savinkov and half a dozen officials who were with him during this conversation must have felt so, since even before the end of it Savinkov dispatched an aide to Kerensky with a request to hold up the issue of the prime minister's denunciation of Kornilov. But it was too late: Kerensky had broken his promise given at the conference with his former ministers and, even before the beginning of the conversation between Savinkov and Kornilov, had not only issued his declaration but had ordered resistance to the advancing Third Corps.

The fat was in the fire, and Kerensky was obviously the culprit, but he even made the pretense of stopping the publication of the government declaration, which was rather childish, since not only the text of it had been telegraphed to Supreme Headquarters but by his orders railway lines were being dismantled and fortified posts erected to stop the progress of the "rebellious" Third Corps.

Milyukov, the historian and politician, comments:

Did Kerensky understand at this moment that, by declaring himself an opponent of Kornilov, he was delivering himself and Russia into the hands of Lenin? Did he understand that this moment was the last one when the struggle against the Bolsheviks could have been won by the government? But to understand this, one had to relinquish a great deal. The tragedy of Kerensky was that, although he had by now understood a great deal, he was not willing to relinquish anything. . . . If one could pin on one chronological point Kerensky's crime against Russia, about which so much has been said, then that crime was committed at that moment.[9]

Up to 10 September the public in general was not aware of the crisis, except for rumors about it in the capital, beginning as early as 8 September, which were fanned by the socialist ministers, who were also members of the Petrograd Soviet, as recorded in Zinaida Gippius's diary. But the storm broke with the publication all over Russia of Kerensky's indictment of Kornilov as head of a mutiny against the Provisional Government, accompanied by an order to surrender his command to General Klembovsky, commander of the northern front (which defended Petrograd) and the countercharge of the supreme commander, in which he called Kerensky's statement a lie, branded the whole move as a betrayal, and appealed to the nation in the name of God and of the Holy Orthodox Church to rally to the salvation of the fatherland. Kerensky opened the arsenals to arm the workers of Petrograd, who became later the nucleus of the Bolshevik Red Guard, since they never surrendered their arms, but used them effectively against Kerensky's government on 7 November. The troops of the garrison started lustily to dismantle the rails ("it was not the Germans to face, there was no fear" as Zinaida Gippius commented), while the Soviet and its affiliated body, the Railway Union, mobilized their forces and sent trained propagandists to win the men of the Third Cavalry Corps to their side. At this moment Kornilov issued a stirring appeal to the nation and to the Provisional Government, which is worth quoting in full, since neither Kerensky nor his apologists have seen fit even to mention it:

I, General Kornilov, Supreme Commander of the Russian Armed Forces, declare, before the whole nation, that my duty as a soldier, my

---

[9] Milyukov, *Istoriya*, pp. 216–217.

feelings as a self-denying citizen of Free Russia, and my boundless love for my country, oblige me, at this critical hour of Russia's existence to disobey the orders of the Provisional Government and to retain the Supreme Command over the Army and Navy. Supported in this decision by all the Commanders-in-Chief of the Fronts, I declare to the whole of the Russian people that I prefer to die rather than give up my post as Supreme Commander. A true son of Russia remains at his post to the end and is always ready to make the greatest of all sacrifices for his country—that of his life.

In these truly terrible moments of our country's existence, when the approaches to both capitals are almost open to the victorious advance of the triumphant foe, the Provisional Government, forgetting the great and essential question of the very independence of Russia, frightens the Russian people with the phantom of counter-revolution, which it is calling forth by its inability to direct the affairs of the country, by the weakness of its authority and its indecision.

It is not for me—a son of the people—who has given myself up, heart and soul, to the services of that people, to go against the great liberties and the great future of Russia. But at the present this future is in weak and impotent hands. The arrogant foe, by using bribery, corruption and treachery, has made himself master here as if he were at home, and threatens not only the liberties, but the very existence, of the Russian nation. Come back to your senses, O sons of Russia, recover from your madness and see the abyss into which our country is rushing blindly!

Desirous to avoid all strife, to forestall all shedding of Russian blood in civil war and forgetting all insults and injuries, I, before the whole nation as witness, appeal to the Provisional Government: "Come to Supreme Headquarters, where your freedom and safety are guaranteed on my word of honor, and together we will work out and form such a government of national defense as will make secure the liberties of the people and lead Russia to a great future, worthy of a free and mighty nation."

Kerensky's answer to this was to order the arrest of General Kornilov. Meanwhile the "defense" of the capital was taken over by the Petrograd Soviet, which formed the "Committee of People's Struggle against Counter-Revolution." Although the Bolsheviks were in a minority in this committee, it is symptomatic that the report of the committee's activity to the Soviet was made by a Bolshevik deputy. It was made by Bogdanov on 13 September, and said in part:

When the Provisional Government began to waver and it was not clear how the Kornilov adventure would end, there appeared would-be intermediaries, such as Milyukov and General Alekseyev, who could have spoiled the whole business. *Then the Political Section of the Committee [of which Bogdanov was a member] came forward and with all its energy* prevented *any possible* conciliation *between the government and Kornilov. We declared that there could be no hesitation, that the government has but one way before it—that of a merciless struggle against Kornilov.* Under our influence *the government stopped all negotiations and refused to accept any of Kornilov's offers. . . . As to the defense of Petrograd, here too we had taken all necessary measures. . . .* During these three days we have committed many unlawful acts. *Since the Provisional Government could not take care of everything, it had asked us to inform it of the* evidence *in our possession. But* in order to obtain such evidence *it was often necessary to have recourse to decisive action. In this case we considered it our duty to help the government* regardless of the illegal aspect of our action. We decreed *the closing of four newspapers [guilty of having published Kornilov's appeal],* we carried out *searches and arrests . . .* we confiscated *all arms found in the possession of unauthorized persons [including the Polish National Committee!].*[10]

Need one emphasize after this that the Soviet had usurped the authority of the government? The day before this report was made Savinkov, who had been appointed governor general of Petrograd on 9 September, was dismissed from all his posts by Kerensky in an unprecedented way—by telephone. "My dismissal," Savinkov related, "was demanded by the Soviet of Workers' and Soldiers' Deputies." A few days later Savinkov was even deprived of membership in the Socialist-Revolutionary party. Obviously, the Soviet did not forgive him his earlier support of General Kornilov.

As to the troops of the Third Cavalry Corps, they stopped their bellicose advance when informed that there was no Bolshevik uprising and fraternized with the propagandists of the Soviet and the "defenders" of Petrograd. Hence there was no bloodshed. Naively Mr. Ascher comments: "Kornilov's whole plot melted away," and Mr. Warth adds: "The organization and planning of the coup was so inept as to endanger the whole enterprise." But it seems clear from the whole story that there was no "plot," no "mutiny," no "rebellion." Kornilov tried, as it proved against insurmountable odds, to save the country from the abyss into which it was being pushed by Bolsheviks, Mensheviks, and left-wing Socialist-Revolutionaries alike, not *against* Kernsky, but *with* Kerensky. He defied Kerensky's order of dismissal,

[10] Author's italics.

because it was by now an established fact that Kerensky had betrayed him and given himself into the hands of the Petrograd Soviet. "Kerensky may have thought," comments a distinguished soldier, Lord Ironside, "that a Military Dictatorship was an impossible solution to the difficulties of his government, but by destroying the Commander who might have helped him he allowed a free reign to the Bolsheviks, who were preparing a Dictatorship which was to destroy him." To this may be added even a stronger indictment from the pen of Professor Milyukov: "A taste for power took precedence of actions which were imperatively dictated by the interests of Russia." But the most devastating appraisal, yet one which is most to the point, of Kerensky's role in this fatal hour of Russia's history is given by his former friend and admirer, Zinaida Gippius, who wrote in her diary on 21 October 1917:

> When history changes its perspectives, someone will perhaps try again to place a hero's crown on Kerensky's head. Then my voice should also be taken into account. I do not speak personally. And I know how to observe a contemporary from afar, without emotion. Kerensky was what he had been at the beginning of the revolution. But Kerensky now is a cowardly and irresponsible person; and since in fact he stood on top then he alone is guilty of Russia's fall to the bottom of a bloody pit. He alone. Let people remember this.

And since concerted efforts are being made "to place a hero's crown on Kerensky's head," let the facts in this case speak out the truth, and let history pronounce its verdict of guilty in betraying Russia against the former prime minister of the Provisional Government, to whom the dubious gains of the March Revolution were dearer than the welfare, the future, and the very existence of his country and its people.

Robert Vincent Daniels

LENIN GAMBLED WILDLY AND WON

Robert Daniels, a professor of political science at the University of Vermont, is one of the most perceptive and brilliant men presently working in the field of Soviet studies. He has published many valuable works dealing with Russian and Soviet history and Marxist theory, the most important of which is probably his book, The Conscience of the Revolution. *In the book excerpted here he has closely reexamined Soviet documentary materials in an effort to get nearer the truth about Lenin's role in the events leading to the October seizure of power and the reasons for the Bolsheviks' success. His theses sharply challenge Soviet explanations, as well as those accepted by many Western scholars. With his original and penetrating analysis he has reopened the discussion of this question, provoking new controversy about what happened in October and why the events culminated as they did.*

Three o'clock in the morning, October 24. The lights were still burning in the cabinet room, the resplendent Malachite Hall on the river side of the Winter Palace. Prime Minister Kerensky, meeting with his cabinet, had finally decided that the time had come to settle with the Bolsheviks. Since no reply to General Bagratuni's ultimatum had come in, the cabinet authorized the arrest of the leaders of the Military Revolutionary Committee. Now the ministers had gone home, leaving Kerensky with General Bagratuni and Colonel Polkovnikov to set in motion the forces they hoped would decapitate the Bolshevik movement.

A messenger brought a note in. It was the news that no one had expected, nor scarcely desired—the Bolsheviks had, after all, accepted the ultimatum. At this late hour, Kerensky was in no mood to suspend his preparations for a preemptive attack. Taking satisfaction in the implication that "the organizers of the uprising were compelled to announce officially that they had committed an unlawful act which they now wished to retract," Kerensky nonetheless reasoned that "this was but another case of the usual delaying tactics and a deliberate deception." General Bagratuni continued to send out telephone and telegraph messages to call reliable troops into Petrograd. Colonel Polkovnikov ordered all the commissars appointed by the MRC removed from their units and prosecuted for any "illegal actions" they had committed. A detachment of Cadets was ordered to close down the Bolshevik newspapers *Rabochi Put* and *Soldat,* on the ground that they were inciting insurrection. To preserve political balance, the government simultaneously ordered two right-wing papers shut down.

At five thirty in the morning the Cadets arrived at the printing plant where *Rabochi Put* and *Soldat* were rolling off the presses, near the river on Konnogvardeiskaya Street, less than half a mile from Smolny. They stopped the presses, broke up the plates, confiscated the papers already printed, closed the shop and left it under seal, with a few policemen on guard. Ironically, the feature item in the suspended edition of *Rabochi Put* was an editorial by Stalin assuring the masses that everything they wanted would be delivered by the Congress of Soviets the next day, and that the Provisional Government would give way peacefully if the populace showed their firmness. Along with Stalin's article, and perhaps more pertinent, were reports "on the eve of the second Kornilov movement" of government troop movements and the machinations of headquarters. The MRC's defiant proclamation of the 22nd was included, having apparently missed publication on the 23rd. Otherwise, save by considerable stretch of the historical imagination, there was nothing in *Rabochi Put* that pointed to a deliberate and imminent Bolshevik coup.

It was still before the dawn of another grimly overcast day when employees of the printing plant ran breathlessly into the Smolny Institute to report what had happened. Trotsky and the leaders of the Military Revolutionary Committee had been on the alert there all night, and had already received alarming reports of the approach of new troops toward Petrograd. A proclamation was just coming off the Smolny printing press to warn all of Petrograd, "The counterrevolution has raised its criminal head. The Kornilovists are mobilizing their forces to suppress the All-Russian Congress of Soviets and break up the Constituent Assembly." Everyone was alerted to possible pogroms, and a list of the regiments and their phone numbers was appended so that people could contact them in the event of disorders.

The report of the Cadets' seizure of the printing plant, recalling the fate of *Pravda* in July, seemed to confirm all the Bolsheviks' fears and warnings about a counterrevolutionary strike, and cata-pulted them into a frenzy of activity. By phone and leaflet the alarm was spread for all the pro-Soviet forces in the capital, and a stream of orders began to flow to the commissars of the military units and the leaders of the Red Guard to alert their forces for any eventuality. "The counterrevolutionary plotters have taken the offensive," an-nounced one leaflet after another, without the slightest distinction between Kerensky and the rightists. "The campaign of the counter-revolutionary plotters is directed against the All-Russian Congress of Soviets on the eve of its opening, against the Constituent Assembly, against the people. . . . The Military Revolutionary Committee will direct resistance against the attack of the plotters. The whole gar-rison and the whole proletariat of Petrograd are ready to deliver a crushing blow to the enemies of the people." Garrisons in the out-skirts of Petrograd were ordered to block the movement of any hostile forces into the city, "by force if necessary." Specific orders to reopen the Bolshevik printing plant went to the nearest reliable troops, the Litovsky Regiment and an engineer battalion quartered in an imposing neoclassical barracks near the Tauride Palace. The troops responded in something less than company strength and got to the press towards midmorning. They easily thrust the police guard aside and opened the premises. By eleven o'clock the workers had *Rabochi Put* rolling off the presses again.

The vigor of the MRC response unsettled its SR contingent and the cautious Bolsheviks as well. Speaking for the Left SRs, Kamkov warned, "We did not enter the MRC for an uprising. The power must be created by the Congress of Soviets." Yielding to these misgivings, the MRC adopted a statement for the press: "Contrary to all kinds of rumors and reports, the MRC declares that it exists not at all to prepare and carry out the seizure of power, but exclusively for the defense of the interests of the Petrograd garrison and the democracy from counterrevolutionary encroachments."

While the MRC was handling the emergency, the Bolshevik Central Committee met to consider the expected attempt to suppress the party and the Soviet. Nine members and two candidate members assembled for their first meeting as a party body in the Smolny In-stitute, hitherto strictly Soviet territory. Kamenev was among them;

he had felt no reason to go through with his threatened resignation. Under the pressure of the morning's events, the Central Committee abandoned its prepared agenda; its first steps were to approve the dispatch of forces to reopen the newspapers and to forbid its own members to leave Smolny (probably for fear of arrest). The main policy question was relations with the All-Russian Central Executive Committee. Trotsky wanted the Bolsheviks to go to the CEC session scheduled later in the day and denounce the CEC for "undermining the cause of revolutionary democracy." Because of the closing of the newspapers Kamenev was prepared to repudiate the negotiations they had been conducting with the CEC, though he wanted to pursue talks with the Left SRs. Trotsky proposed a set of emergency assignments for the Central Committee members—Bubnov to keep in touch with the railroad workers, Dzerzhinsky to be responsible for the post office and telegraph, Milyutin to work on the food supply problem, Sverdlov to keep watch on the movements of the government. (How Sverdlov was expected to handle this broad assignment in addition to all the rest of his responsibilities was not explained.) Kamenev was assigned to negotiate with the Left SRs, and Lomov and Nogin were directed to leave for Moscow to inform the Bolsheviks there of the new turn of events. There was some discussion of the location of an auxiliary party headquarters in the event that government forces captured Smolny; Trotsky's suggestion to designate the Peter-Paul fortress was adopted. With this, the total recorded substance of the Central Committee's last meeting before the revolution was completed. This was the meeting which the official historiography represents as the occasion of the final decision to launch the insurrection, but there is no evidence that the committee had anything in mind yet except to stave off the blows of the government until the Congress of Soviets convened. . . .

All afternoon the Military Revolutionary Committee was mobilizing its forces for the expected government drive. The garrison units and factory committees were everywhere responding to the appeals of the MRC by passing resolutions to support the assumption of power by the Congress of Soviets. The Vyborg district Red Guards assembled with rifles in hand on Sampsonievsky Prospekt outside their headquarters.

The fighting qualities of these forces remained an unknown factor.

The French journalist Claude Anet, who lived near the Pavlov bar-racks, commented, "It would take only three thousand resolute men to rout the whole garrison of Petrograd. I would pay well if anyone showed me the phenomenon, unknown here, of the hero, the demi-god of bolshevism—a man ready to give his life for his faith in Lenin, for the triumph of the extremists' ideas. The soldiers are rebel-ling only so they will not have to go to the front." But morale on the government side was worse. Around 4 p.m., in the first of a fatal series of defections, the bicycle company stationed at the Winter Palace abandoned their posts.

A dependable machine-gun unit finally arrived at Smolny and set up its guns. As they dragged their equipment, clanking and rumbling, through the corridors, the last Mensheviks and SRs of the All-Rus-sian Central Executive Committee, who had maintained their offices in Smolny right up to the last minute, finally abandoned the building. The government had set aside quarters for them in the District Head-quarters. Trotsky wrote, "We were now in full command of the building that was preparing to rear a Bolshevik head over the city and the country"—but it was a strange revolution that did not control its own headquarters until the armed struggle was almost underway.

By afternoon a special subcommittee of the MRC was finally ap-pointed, according to Antonov's account, consisting of "Podvoisky, Lashevich, and myself, to work out a plan of struggle with the Pro-visional Government." The plan, if there was one, was simply to close the bridges and assert control over as many strategic build-ings as possible—the railroad stations, the bridges, electric power plants, the telegraph, the telephone exchange, the news wire service, and the State Bank. The idea initially was simply to dispatch com-missars to each point to proclaim the authority of the MRC, much as had been done in the military units.

The first attempt to do this occurred in the afternoon, when a Bolshevik delegate to the Congress of Soviets, Pestkovsky, was assigned to the Petrograd Telegraph Office. Here is his account:

> *Dzerzhinsky ran up to me with a paper in his hand: "You and Comrade Leshchinsky are instructed to take over the main telegraph. Here is the mandate of the MRC that appoints you commissar of the telegraph. Go right away!"*
> *"How do I take over the telegraph?" I asked.*

"The Kexholm Regiment is on guard there, and they are on our side," answered Dzerzhinsky.

I didn't question any more. The assignment at first didn't seem very hard to me, since I was the director of our Petrograd postal-telegraph cell and knew almost all our Bolsheviks there. I found Comrade Leshchinsky, and we set off together. Neither of us had a revolver. When we were getting in the car we both had the same strange, tormenting tension in our minds: here it is, the decisive move of the proletariat that we have been waiting for for decades. How will it end?

Could it still be defeated?

The bitter experience of the July days did not give us complete confidence in victory.

We decided to work this way. The Provisional Government's commander of the telegraph was a personal acquaintance of Leshchinsky— Staff-Captain Longva, at the time a Menshevik-Internationalist, now a Communist. We would have to talk with him and make sure of his cooperation. Then we would talk with our cell and at once proceed with the "seizure."

It turned out somewhat differently. Comrade Longva, "having no directive from his organization," refused to cooperate with us and only promised "not to interfere." And at the conference with the cell we realized that in the whole telegraph office, among three thousand employees, there was not a single Bolshevik, and only one Left SR, Khaurov; he reported to us that the whole mass of employees was very hostilely inclined against the Bolsheviks. [Unknown to Pestkovsky, all the Bolshevik members of the union were Post Office employees.]

The situation was extremely difficult. But at this point Comrade Liubovich arrived from Smolny to help us. The three of us felt stronger and went to talk with the guards.

When the guards, headed by some lieutenant, saw our mandate from the MRC, they promised to cooperate with us. Then, on October 24 about five o'clock, we three, accompanied by the commander of the guard, went into the main hall of the telegraph and up to the president of the union of postal and telegraph workers, Mr. King (a Right SR), and declared that we were taking over the telegraph. King declared that he was going to throw us out. Then Comrade Liubovich called two Kexholm men and stationed them at the transmitter.

The women working in the office began to scream and cry. The representatives of the "committee" deliberated and arrived at a compromise. They would agree that "the commissar could sit in the room" on condition that we withdraw the soldiers from the room.

We agreed. I "held forth" in the telegraph office, Liubovich went out "to strengthen" the guard, and Leshchinsky went off to the room of the union, in a neighboring building, as a "reserve."

At 8 p.m. of the same day a guard of Cadets, specially ordered by the Petrograd Military District, arrived to "replace" the Kexholm men. The

Kexholm guard, "cultivated" by Liubovich, declared they wanted to go on guarding the telegraph.
The Cadets left.

As the two sides were sparring for control of the bridges, Trotsky addressed a meeting in Smolny of Bolshevik delegates arriving in Petrograd for the Congress of Soviets. He began by hailing the political momentum gained by the party's moves of the past few days, even though some Bolsheviks did not feel ready for provocative action: "A clash was inevitable, and it developed out of the order to summon the garrison to the front." What he meant by "clash," evidently, was the same "insurrection" Kerensky referred to, not anything new that had happened on the 24th, but simply the MRC's assertion of military authority.

At this point Trotsky was interrupted by a message that a delegation from the City Duma had come to Smolny to learn the Soviet's intentions regarding public order and safety. He left the assembly hall and conferred with the visitors for half an hour or so. "I told them," he reported, "that if the government starts the iron going, naturally we will answer with steel," though the Soviet would welcome any cooperation from the old city authorities in maintaining order. But basically the question of violence depended on whether the government would lie down and die quietly: "All Power to the Soviets—this is our slogan. In the days ahead, while the All-Russian Congress of Soviets is in session, this slogan must be put into effect. Whether this will lead to an uprising or a move will depend not only or so much on the soviets as it will on those who in spite of the unanimous [*sic!*] will of the people may try to keep governmental power in their own hands."

Returning to the assembly hall, Trotsky told the delegates what had transpired and went on to describe the precautionary military movements that the MRC had ordered. "The military situation for us is favorable in the highest degree. Now everything depends on the congress." He did not want to preempt the responsibility of the delegates, certainly not openly, yet he made it clear what the party expected of them when they convened formally the following day: "The only salvation is a firm policy of the congress. The arrest of the Provisional Government is not on the agenda as an independent task. If the congress sets up a power and Kerensky does not submit to it, then it would be a policing question rather than a political one." If Trotsky is to be believed by what he said before the revolution rather than after, the Bolsheviks were still waiting for the Congress of Soviets, and did not yet suppose that they could destroy the government beforehand.

Following Trotsky, the Bolshevik delegates heard a report on the pre-parliament and its vote against Kerensky on the land and peace issues. Then Stalin came on, to say that the Bolshevik papers were being printed again after the attempt to close them. He did mention that there was some dissension in the leadership—"In the Military Revolutionary Committee there are two tendencies: one, immediate uprising; two, to concentrate our forces at first"—but, he assured the delegates, "The Central Committee of the Bolshevik party adheres to the second." He said the Left SRs had demanded to know whether the aim of the MRC was to maintain order or launch an insurrection; if the latter, they would pull out. "Of course," Stalin reported, "we answered, order, defense. And they left their men in." After the meeting Trotsky talked with the delegates from Kronstadt. He sent them off to the base with instructions to return at dawn with the whole Kronstadt force, "for the defense of the Congress of Soviets." . . .

At 7 p.m. the Petrograd Soviet did in fact convene and Trotsky repeated his affirmation that the Bolsheviks planned to move before the Congress. "The MRC," he said, "arose not as an organ of insurrection, but on the basis of the self-defense of the revolution." He described all the steps of the MRC in the past day as defensive responses to the government's initiatives, the net effect of which was to prepare the ground for a take-over by the Congress of Soviets. The government, according to Trotsky, had become "a semi-power which the people don't believe in and which doesn't believe in itself, for it is dead on the inside. This semi-power is waiting for the sweep of the broom of history, to clear a place for a genuine power of the revolutionary people." The adherents of the Soviet had demonstrated their ability to control the garrison and the fleet in defiance of the government's orders.

Tomorrow the Congress of Soviets opens. The task of the garrison and the proletariat is to place at the disposal of the congress the accumulated force against which the governmental provocation may smash itself. Our task is to deliver this force to the congress unsplit and unimpaired. When the congress says that it is organizing the power, it will be completing the work that has been going on all over the country. This will mean that, freeing themselves from the power of the counterrevolutionary government, the people are convoking their congress and setting up their power.

This was Trotsky's fullest and most direct statement of his strategy of using the Congress of Soviets to vote power into the hands of the Bolsheviks with a minimum of military risk and a maximum of popular support. The government was playing into his hands perfectly with its ineffective attacks. "If the pseudo-power makes the risky attempt to revive its own corpse, then the popular masses, organized and armed, will give it a decisive rebuff, and the rebuff will be the stronger, the stronger is the offensive of reaction. If the government tries to use the twenty-four or forty-eight hours that are left to it to stick a knife in the back of the revolution, then we declare that the forward units of the revolution will answer blow for blow, steel for iron." The blows were beginning already, and would soon prove so successful for the revolutionaries that there would be little left for the Congress of Soviets to do as the elected representatives of Russia. Trotsky's strategy was about to be invalidated by its own success. . . .

When Kerensky's cabinet meeting broke up [after 1:00 a.m. October 25], the patrols of the Pavlov Regiment stationed on Millionaya Street—the thoroughfare running eastward from the Winter Palace to the Champs de Mars and the Troitsky Bridge—"had their attention especially drawn by a large number of automobiles leaving the Winter Palace through the Palace Square." So recalled Commissar Dzenis.

They set up roadblocks, and were given directions henceforth to stop and question all automobiles and people passing through, to check their documents and detain suspicious individuals. Not five minutes had gone by after this order was given when a medium-height grey-haired man in civilian clothes was brought into the regimental club (where I had set up the operational headquarters of the regiment along with the regimental committee). It appeared that he had been detained along with his automobile as he was leaving the square onto Millionaya Street. I asked for his documents. It appeared that he was Lieutenant Colonel Surnin, head of the counterintelligence of the headquarters of the Petrograd military

FIGURE 4. Leon Trotsky. (*The Bettmann Archive*)

district. I immediately sent him in his own automobile to Smolny to put him at the disposition of the Revolutionary Committee.

I had just managed to send him off when they brought in two new people, one after the other—the minister of religions Kartashev and an associate of the minister of finance. Arrest them or not? Up to now the MRC had been stubbornly silent in the face of our insistent inquiries: evidently they didn't have time. I decided—once you have begun you have to keep on.

The regiment moved its patrols forward and captured isolated Cadet sentries. A whole crowd of people, officers and civilians, began to fall into the hands of the Pavlov men. They were quartered in a temporary jail—the buffet of the regimental club. Smolny still had no telephone service and the response to the arrests had to come back by courier:

Finally two notes written by Podvoisky arrived, one after the other. The first: the Revolutionary Committee is highly satisfied by the arrest of the head of counterintelligence Surnin; it appears that they have already put him where he belongs. But the second note is a surprise: the Revolutionary Committee feels that it has been confronted with the fact of a clash too early; it still does not know when operations will begin, but no matter what, not before the next day, i.e., October 25. The arrests, especially of such important figures as ministers of the Provisional Government, it considers premature actions that will evoke alarm and attention on the other side. They propose that we cease the arrests and remove the roadblocks. However, the circumstance that our reconnaissance (though it is weak, we have nonetheless succeeded in organizing some reconnaissance service) has noticed animation among the troops of the Provisional Government, who are also preparing very seriously for a clash, compells us this time to disobey the Revolutionary Committee and execute its orders only in part.

This is how, in a fit of enthusiastic insubordination, the "insurrection" began. Dzenis goes on:

The apprehension of people leaving the palace and the government buildings adjacent to it continues. The people we arrest are put in the regimental club; by noon on October 25 up to two hundred people have been collected there. But my comrades do not want to confine themselves just to the arrest of passersby, and ask permission to take the Cadet outposts. It appears that the Provisional Government has already set up outposts on

*its side too. I had to agree, but without the right to start shooting. The
results spoke for themselves.*

*Here is the picture on Millionaya Street. Not far from our roadblock,
twenty-five or thirty paces, stands a guard detail in a sentry box. Three
Pavlov men sneak up on them from the rear and suddenly appear from
behind. There is a shout, "Hands up. Drop your rifles!" and the Cadets
are both taken alive, without any noise. During the night we managed in
this way to capture a whole series of outposts at various points (including
the Pevcheskaya Chapel on the Moika). About three o'clock in the morning a guard detail in a sentry box and along with them the commander
of the guard were captured in the same way.*

In the meantime, the MRC finally decided to approve what the troops
were doing anyway. Dzenis wrote:

*About two o'clock I got a note from the MRC that it was necessary to
strengthen the roadblock and organize actual control over passersby and
traffic. But it was already too late: in the palace they had come to, and
none of the more influential people decided to leave it.*

So went the whole night of October 24–25.

Despite all the appearances of a systematic take-over, the Military Revolutionary Committee made no recorded decision for a
general attack on the government before dawn on October 25.
Until Lenin appeared at Smolny each move of the MRC had come in
response to a government initiative—the removal of the troops to
the front, the strike at the press, the raising of the bridges, the movement of troops from the military schools and the front. The Bolsheviks could still well imagine that the Congress of Soviets and
their own party headquarters were prime targets of the military, so
much so that they were ready to negotiate and temporize right up
to the last minute. The movement of their forces were precautionary
and limited. What the Bolsheviks could not calculate was that the
government's forces would give way so readily, that the Cadet
guards would yield everywhere without a fight, that the Cossacks
would refuse to come out, that the commander of the military district
was perhaps betraying the prime minister. In short, the Bolsheviks
had naturally but grossly overestimated the strength of the government, almost as much as the government had overestimated itself. . . .

Aside from these anecdotes, the most significant moment of the
October Revolution is one of the least documented, for reasons that

FIGURE 5. V. I. Lenin after the October Revolution.

can only be guessed. The memoirists are unusually vague and contradictory about Lenin's arrival at Smolny and the impact it had on the course of events. Obviously it must have electrified the entire Soviet Headquarters. There is reason to believe that Lenin, by direct command or perhaps by his mere presence, had a decisive effect in changing the orientation of his lieutenants from the defensive to the offensive.

If the operations of the MRC during the night are carefully followed, it is apparent that a marked change in tone and direction occurred after midnight. A new spirit of bold and systematic attack appeared, exemplified in orders to military units to seize outright the public institutions that were not yet under the control of the MRC. Up to this point the moves of the MRC had all been peaceful or defensive. The committee had twice turned down Lenin's idea of returning to Smolny—because they could not protect him, or feared his presence would provoke the government, or feared that he would upset their expectation of waiting for the Congress of Soviets. But the masses of men they had set in motion to counter the government already had most of the city under their control; it was no longer easy to see the distinction between defense and offense. Lenin, apparently, provided the catalyst to turn the soviets' cautious defenders into the aggressive heroes of insurrection.

One memoirist, Lomov, comes close to the probable truth. Lomov had not yet left on his mission to Moscow, and was busy at Smolny. Before Lenin's arrival, he wrote, "Neither we nor Kerensky risk taking the path of a final engagement. We wait, fearing that our forces are still not sufficiently encouraged and organized. Kerensky is afraid to take the initiative in his own hands.

"Thus things go on until eight or nine o'clock in the evening" —Lomov was off three or four hours on the time. "Suddenly Comrade Lenin appears. He is still in his wig, completely unrecognizable. Everything decisively changes. His point of view triumphs, and from this moment we go over to a determined offensive."

"To work!" said Antonov to himself when he saw Lenin. "Our leader is with us! Full speed ahead!"

Until he arrived at Smolny Lenin had no information that the MRC was responding to his demand to seize power before the Congress of Soviets. In all probability they were not trying to do this up to the moment of his return; they were stumbling into power all over the city thanks only to the total ineffectiveness of the government. But it could very well be that none of them dared confess to Lenin their defensive intentions, nor did they need to, since the state of affairs looked well enough like an offensive. Lenin was still angered by the reports he had read of the MRC's agreement wtih headquarters the day before. "His first question as soon as he arrived," Trotsky recalled, "was: 'Could this be true?' 'No, it's to cover up the game,' we reassured him." From that time on every Bolshevik who was in the revolution had to represent the party's hedging tactics as some sort of ruse to fool the opposition and pave the way for a coup.

* * *

The first of the new orders apparently prompted by Lenin's return was given to a member of the MRC, Lashevich. He was instructed to get troops from the Kexholm Regiment and seize the telephone exchange, the State Bank, and the Treasury. "For the MRC," Lashevich recalled, "it became clear that the moment had come to act." He drove across town to the Kexholm Barracks near the Nikolaevsky Bridge, roused the regimental committee, and demanded two companies. The commander of one of the companies, Lieutenant Zakharov, described his reaction:

> Late in the evening, when I was already asleep in my clothes on a divan in the officers' meeting room, I was waked up by Lieutenant Smirnov of our regiment, a member of the regimental committee, and told that by order of the regimental committee, I must immediately go out with my company and assume the guard at the Petrograd city telephone station, and that as a member of the regimental and brigade committees I must do this without special orders from the regimental staff. I quickly went to my company and found the men already lined up with their weapons. The chairman of the regimental committee, Sergeant Smirnov of the machine-gun unit, informed me that I was being given responsibility to take the telephone station, which was being guarded by Cadets of the Vladimirsky military school, and he added that I must do this as quickly as possible and if possible without fighting. Two commissars were assigned to work with me. Of course, I understood that my move was the beginning of a "coup d'etat" (the definition I thought of at that moment), but I decided not to refuse the assignment but to carry it out as best I could, especially since the mood of the soldiers was very reliable—I felt this at once with my first glance at them.

Led by Lashevich, the detachment moved out along the embankment of the Moika Canal around 1:00 a.m. They met a few Cadet sentries and disarmed them. Nearing the telephone building, Zakharov and his men made a dash to the open entry way and captured the armored car that had been parked there. But it was useless to them: none of the men could handle its machine guns. In the courtyard of the building they met the Cadet guards rushing out of the guardroom. There was a moment of tension as the hostile forces confronted each other and shouted deadly threats back and forth. Lashevich parleyed with the guard commander and reached an agreement to avoid bloodshed: the outnumbered Cadets could leave with their arms, if they promised not to fight for the government. Without a shot, the Bolsheviks had the telephone office. They promptly reconnected Smolny and cut off the phones of the Winter Palace.

Leaving one company of the Kexholm Regiment to guard the telephone station, Lashevich moved on with his other company and some sailors from the Second Baltic Fleet crew who had caught up with him. His next objective was the State Bank, on the Catherine Canal. It was about 6 a.m. when they found the back entrance, disarmed the sentry, and occupied the building. Lashevich woke up the detail of soldiers from the Semyonovsky Regiment quartered there and announced to them that he was taking over in the name of the MRC. The men replied that they too were for the MRC and insisted that they be left on duty as representatives of the Soviet. Lashevich left a few of his own men with them and proceeded to the Treasury. Here his task was ridiculously easy: "The Treasury was guarded by the soldiers most devoted to us—the Pavlov men."

In the meantime, by the frosty light of the moon, other small forces were occupying the remaining key points. A detachment of Kexholm troops and sailors, with some Putilov Red Guards, occupied the Central Post Office around 1:30 a.m. The Nikolaevsky station, terminus of the Moscow railroad, and the power plants were taken over by similar detachments about the same time; usually the appearance of a Soviet commissar was enough to make the employees on duty recognize the new authority. At 3:30, the *Aurora* anchored at the Nikolaevsky Bridge, already closed by Red Guards and then retaken by a platoon of government shock troops. Backed by the "moral effect" of the cruiser, sailors from the shore units easily cleared away the Cadet guards and secured the bridge. By now the Provisional Government was practically isolated in the Winter Palace. At last the preemptive insurrection Lenin demanded had become a reality. . . .

The October Revolution did shake the world. In the eyes of its followers and its enemies alike, it announced the final battle between the international proletariat and the worldwide system of capitalism, the fulfillment of Marx's prophecy. The October Revolution promised a new dawn in human history, a new era of liberation and equality. Its spirit and its doctrine became a new faith for millions of people all over the world, who looked to Moscow as the new Jerusalem. Fifty years afterwards, Soviet Russia still professes to embody the ideals of the revolution, though its claim to the revolutionary heritage is disputed by the radical leaders of lands won by the Gospel of October more recently.

It is only natural that an event that has aroused such commitments and antagonisms should be viewed by both its heirs and its enemies alike as the result of deep historical forces or a long-laid master scheme. Since the days of the October uprising itself, it has been difficult for either side to take stock of the extraordinary series of accidents and missteps that accompanied the Bolshevik Revolution and allowed it to succeed. One thing that both victors and vanquished were agreed on, before the smoke had hardly cleared from the Palace Square, was the myth that the insurrection was timed and executed according to a deliberate Bolshevik plan.

The official Communist history of the revolution has held rigidly to an orthodox Marxist interpretation of the event: it was an uprising of thousands upon thousands of workers and peasants, the inevitable consequence of the international class struggle of proletariat against bourgeoisie, brought to a head first in Russia because it was "the weakest link in the chain of capitalism." At the same time it is asserted, though the contradiction is patent, that the revolution could not have succeeded without the ever-present genius leadership of Lenin. This attempt to have it both ways has been ingrained in Communist thinking ever since Lenin himself campaigned in the name of Marx for the "art of insurrection."

Anti-Communist interpretations, however they may deplore the October Revolution, are almost as heavily inclined to view it as the inescapable outcome of overwhelming circumstances or of long and diabolical planning. The impasse of the war was to blame, or Russia's inexperience in democracy, or the feverish laws of revolution. If not these factors, it was Lenin's genius and trickery in propaganda, or the party organization as his trusty and invincible instrument. Of course, all of these considerations played a part, but when they are weighed against the day by day record of the revolution, it is hard to argue that any combination of them made Bolshevik power inevitable or even likely.

The stark truth about the Bolshevik Revolution is that it succeeded against incredible odds in defiance of any rational calculation that could have been made in the fall of 1917. The shrewdest politicians of every political coloration knew that while the Bolsheviks were an undeniable force in Petrograd and Moscow, they had against them the overwhelming majority of the peasants, the army in the field, and the trained personnel without which no government could function. Everyone from the right-wing military to the Zinoviev-Kamenev Bolsheviks judged a military dictatorship to be the most likely alternative if peaceful evolution failed. They all thought—whether they hoped or feared—that a Bolshevik attempt to seize power would only hasten or assure the rightist alternative.

Lenin's revolution, as Zinoviev and Kamenev pointed out, was a wild gamble, with little chance that the Bolsheviks' ill-prepared followers could prevail against all the military force that the government seemed to have, and even less chance that they could keep power even if they managed to seize it temporarily. To Lenin, however, it was a gamble that entailed little risk, because he sensed that in no other way and at no other time would he have any chance at all of coming to power. This is why he demanded so vehemently that the Bolshevik party seize the moment and hurl all the force it could against the Provisional Government. Certainly the Bolshevik party had a better overall chance for survival and a future political role if it waited and compromised, as Zinoviev and Kamenev wished. But this would not yield the only kind of political power—exclusive power—that Lenin valued. He was bent on baptizing the revolution in blood, to drive off the fainthearted and compel all who subscribed to the overturn to accept and depend on his own unconditional leadership.

To this extent there is some truth in the contentions, both Soviet and non-Soviet, that Lenin's leadership was decisive. By psychological pressure on his Bolshevik lieutenants and his manipulation of the fear of counterrevolution, he set the stage for the one-party seizure of power. But the facts of the record show that in the crucial days before October 24th Lenin was not making his leader ship effective. The party, unable to face up directly to his brow-beating, was tacitly violating his instructions and waiting for a multi-party and semiconstitutional revolution by the Congress of Soviets. Lenin had failed to seize the moment, failed to avert the trend to a compromise coalition regime of the soviets, failed to nail down the base for his personal dictatorship—until the government struck on the morning of the 24th of October.

Kerensky's ill-conceived countermove was the decisive accident. Galvanizing all the fears that the revolutionaries had acquired in July and August about a rightist *putsch,* it brought out their utmost —though still clumsy—effort to defend themselves and hold the ground for the coming Congress of Soviets. The Bolsheviks could not calculate, when they called the Red Guards to the bridges and sent commissars to the communications centers, that the forces of the government would apathetically collapse. With undreamed-of ease, and no intention before the fact, they had the city in the palms of their hands, ready to close their grip when their leader reappeared from the underground and able to offer him the Russian capital in expiation of their late faintheartedness.

The role of Trotsky in all this is very peculiar. A year after the revolution Stalin wrote, "All the work of the practical organization of the insurrection proceeded under the immediate direction of the chairman of the Petrograd Soviet, Comrade Trotsky. It can be said with assurance that for the quick shift of the garrison to the side of the soviet and the bold insurrectionary work of the MRC the party is indebted firstly and mainly to Comrade Trotsky." This passage was naturally suppressed during Stalin's heyday, but after the de-Stalinization of 1956 Soviet historians resurrected it—as proof of another of Stalin's errors, overestimating Trotsky! In fact they are right, though the whole party shared Stalin's accolade at the time: Trotsky in October was at the height of his career as the flaming revolutionary tribune, yet he shied away from the outright insurrection that Lenin demanded. Trotsky exemplified the feelings of the main body of the Bolshevik leadership, eager for power yet afraid either to take a military initiative or to face Lenin's wrath. Trotsky talked revolution but waited for the congress—until the moment of Lenin's return to Smolny. Then, like most of the party leadership, he persuaded himself that he had been carrying out Lenin's instructions all along; any statement he had made about waiting for the congress became, in retrospect, a political lie "to cover up the game." But in truth there was far more lying about the October Revolution after the event than before.

The Communist Party of the Soviet Union
THE BOLSHEVIK PARTY LED THE MASSES

Over the years the Communist party line has been expressed in innumerable ways by high party officials and the Soviet press. Soviet scholars reiterate this line with varying degrees of sophistication, from the complexities of the party theorist to the primitive simplicities of the propagandist writing for workers and peasants. The source used here, the official history of the party, was compiled and edited by a group of distinguished Soviet professors and academicians headed by a member of the party Central Committee's Secretariat. The explanation of the Bolshevik Revolution and the reasons for its success differs only a little from that of the official history published in 1960, when Nikita Khrushchev was in power, and Khrushchev's version in turn varies only slightly from Stalin's account published in 1938. Thus the document excerpted below comes very near to wielding the kind of weight and authority in the Soviet Union that the Bible enjoys in the Catholic Church.

The work of organizing the insurrection was directed by Lenin. He summoned members of the Revolutionary Military Committee, heard reports of the steps taken, and kept a check to see that everything was being done to insure the victory of the insurrection. V. I. Lenin gave instructions regarding the detailed plan of insurrection and the strengthening and arming of the Red Guard. To him came Bolsheviks active in the army and the Baltic fleet, who received instructions on the use of the fleet and on the summoning of revolutionary units from the front; representatives came to him from

Reprinted from *Istoriya Kommunisticheskoi partii Sovetskovo Soyuza* [History of the Communist Party of the Soviet Union], by B. N. Ponomarev et al., 3rd ed. (Moscow: Politizdat, 1969). Editor's translation.

Moscow with reports on the situation in the city and in the Moscow region.

The Central Committee of the party followed the basic instruction of Marxism—to treat insurrection as an art. Its representatives were sent to various parts of the country to help the local party organizations prepare for armed insurrection. . . .

Lenin insisted that the insurrection be begun without fail before the Second Congress of Soviets, scheduled for October 25. It was essential to forestall the enemy, who had been forewarned by the traitors and who expected action to be taken on the day the congress opened.

"Under no circumstances," wrote Lenin to the Central Committee on October 24, "should the power be left in the hands of Kerensky and Company until the 25th—not under any circumstances; the matter must be decided without fail this very evening or this very night.

"History will not forgive revolutionaries for procrastinating, when they can—and certainly will—win today, while they risk losing much, in fact everything, tomorrow" (*Collected Works,* vol. 26, p. 204).

On V. I. Lenin's proposal, the insurrection was launched on October 24, before the congress opened. The headquarters of the insurrection was in the Smolny Institute, where Lenin arrived late in the evening to direct operations personally. On the instructions of headquarters, Red Guards occupied the previously designated objectives. The Red Guards organized the defense of plants and factories. All approaches to the capital were guarded by revolutionary units, to prevent reinforcements for the Provisional Government passing through from the front. Sailors of the Baltic fleet were summoned to the capital. According to plan all government institutions were occupied, and the Winter Palace, where the Provisional Government had taken refuge, was surrounded. The workers' Red Guard detachments formed the principal fighting force of the insurrection. The sailors of the Baltic fleet shared the glory of victory with them. Side by side with the Red Guard detachments and the sailors, fought the regiments of the Petrograd garrison. The insurrection enjoyed such wide support among the masses, and had been so thoroughly planned, that it was carried out with rare speed and success. By the morning of October 25 the Provisional Government had been deposed. At 10 o'clock in the morning appeared the manifesto "To the Citizens of Russia!" written by Lenin, the genius who had inspired and led the revolution.

"The Provisional Government has been deposed. State power has passed into the hands of the organ of the Petrograd Soviet of Workers' and Soldiers' Deputies—the Revolutionary Military Committee, which stands at the head of the Petrograd proletariat and garrison.

"The cause for which the people have fought, namely, the immediate offer of a democratic peace, the abolition of landlord ownership of land, workers' control over production, and the establishment of Soviet power—that cause has been secured.

"Long live the revolution of workers, soldiers and peasants!" (Ibid., p. 207.)

The government which had been overthrown remained in possession only of the Winter Palace, garrisoned by officer Cadets and a women's shock battalion. V. I. Lenin gave orders for this last stronghold of the bourgeois government to be taken by storm. From the Neva, the cruiser *Aurora* fired a shot, giving the signal for attack. That shot heralded the birth of a new world. On the night of October 25–26 the Winter Palace fell; the ministers were arrested.

In the evening of October 25 the Second Congress of Soviets opened. It represented over 400 of the country's soviets. Of the 650 delegates present, about 400 were Bolsheviks. The majority of the rest of the delegates were Left SR's [Socialist-Revolutionaries]. The Mensheviks and Right Socialist-Revolutionaries, who had till then dominated the soviets, comprised a small group of seventy to eighty people. At the congress itself, this group continued to dwindle; its members deserted either to the Left Socialist-Revolutionaries or to the Menshevik-Internationalists. The miserable remnants of the bankrupt parties of compromise with the bourgeoisie left the congress.

On the first day the Second Congress of Soviets adopted the proclamation "To the Workers, Soldiers and Peasants," written by Lenin.

"Backed by the will of the vast majority of the workers, soldiers and peasants," read the proclamation, "and by the victorious insurrection of the workers and garrison which has taken place in Petrograd, the Congress takes power into its own hands. . . .

"The Congress decrees: all power in the localities is transferred to the Soviets of Workers', Soldiers' and Peasants' Deputies, which must duly ensure genuine revolutionary order" (*Collected Works,* vol. 26, p. 215).

The workers and peasant poor had overthrown the dictatorship of the bourgeoisie and established the dictatorship of the proletariat.

October 25 (November 7), 1917, has gone down in history as the day of the victory of the Great October Socialist Revolution in Russia. . . .

Reasons for the Victory of the Revolution. The International Significance of the Great October Socialist Revolution.

1. The chief reason for the victory of the October Socialist Revolution was that it was led by the working class of Russia. It was the first of all the classes to create its own party. The working class came forward as the leader in the struggle of the whole people against the autocracy and against the dictatorship of the bourgeoisie. The other sections of the working people were convinced that in the proletariat they had the champion of the interests of the whole people, who were languishing under the yoke of the landlords and the bourgeoisie. The proletariat of Russia was the principal moving force of the entire social and political development of the country.

2. The October Revolution was victorious because a social force had been created in Russia—the alliance of the proletariat and the working peasantry—that crushed the resistance of the exploiting classes. During the course of the revolution the Bolsheviks had exposed the traitors to the working-class cause—the opportunists who had argued that the proletariat could seize and retain power only where it constituted the majority of the population. The proletariat had received the full support of the poor peasantry, which constituted the overwhelming majority of the rural population—as much as 65 per cent. By winning a majority of the laboring peasantry over to the proletariat, the Bolsheviks separated the peasant masses from the bourgeoisie.

3. The October Revolution differed from all other revolutions in that the workers created their own organs of power. In the womb

of the Russian proletariat was born a new form of revolutionary authority—the Soviets of Workers' Deputies. The Soviets of Workers', Soldiers' and Peasants' Deputies were a form of organization that embodied the alliance of the workers and peasants under the leadership of the workers.

"Had not the creative effort of the revolutionary classes given rise to the Soviets," wrote Lenin, "the proletarian revolution in Russia would have been a hopeless cause. . . ." (*Collected Works,* vol. 26, p. 80.)

4. The October Revolution was victorious because it had in the person of the Russian bourgeoisie a comparatively weak enemy. The whole course of the historical development of Russian capitalism, its backwardness in comparison with that of the leading capitalist countries, and its dependence on foreign capital explain the political flabbiness, cowardice and inadequate experience of the Russian bourgeoisie. The compromisers too—the Socialist-Revolutionaries and Mensheviks—were proved powerless to aid the Russian bourgeoisie. In the course of many years of struggle the Bolsheviks had exposed them as agents of the bourgeoisie. On the eve of the October Revolution these parties openly went over to the camp of the counterrevolution.

5. A decisive circumstance that made the victory of the revolution possible was the fact that at the head of the masses stood the experienced, militant, revolutionary party of Bolsheviks.

While the revolution was being prepared and carried out the party performed an enormous amount of theoretical work, enriching Marxism with new propositions. In the works of V. I. Lenin, in the resolutions of the April Conference and the Sixth Party Congress, and in the decisions of the Central Committee were given the theoretical substantiation of the concrete plan for the development of the bourgeois-democratic revolution into the Socialist Revolution.

In its fight against the opportunists the party worked out and upheld the theory that socialism could be victorious in Russia. V. I. Lenin developed the Marxist theory of Socialist Revolution, discovered, in a republic of soviets, a political form for the dictatorship of the proletariat, substantiated this view, and further developed Marxist theory on armed insurrection, developing them into lessons on uprising. The party was guided by the advanced theory of the working class, the theory of Marxism-Leninism.

The Great October Revolution is a splendid example of the practical application and implementation of Lenin's theory of Socialist revolution.

The toiling masses had seen all the other parties in power, separately and in various combinations. They had seen the Cadets, representatives of the bourgeoisie; they had experienced the rule of a coalition of Cadets, Socialist-Revolutionaries, and Mensheviks; they had tested the Socialist-Revolutionaries and Mensheviks by their deeds, when they were in a majority in the soviets. During the course of the revolution, all the bourgeoisie and compromising parties had discredited themselves, revealing their counterrevolutionary essence. The working parties turned away from the parties of compromise with the bourgeoisie, and, using their right of recall, they banished from the soviets those who had betrayed their confidence, electing Bolsheviks to their places. Thus the Mensheviks and Socialist-Revolutionaries were isolated from the masses. The party of the Bolsheviks was a united party, inseparably leading the revolutionary struggle of the proletariat, of all workers.

The Bolshevik party succeeded in uniting all the diverse revolutionary movements and in directing them toward a single goal—the overthrow of imperialism: the movement of the whole people for peace, and the peasants' struggle for the land, the national-liberation struggle of the oppressed peoples of Russia, and the struggle of the leading force in society—the proletariat—for socialism. Under the leadership of the Bolshevik party, the workers and poor peasants overthrew the government of the bourgeoisie and established Soviet power.

Such were the fundamental domestic reasons that ensured the success of the revolution.

Among the reasons of an international nature that ensured the success of the Great October Socialist Revolution, was the fact that the revolution began in the period of the imperialist world war. Neither the Anglo-French bloc, nor the German bloc could give direct armed assistance to the Russian bourgeoisie. They helped it materially and by organizing plots, but were unable to provide it with any significant military forces. The Russian bourgeoisie, left face-to-face with the proletariat at the head of all the working people, could not stand before the onslaught of the masses.

Suggestions for Additional Reading

The chief purpose of this bibliographical note is to provide a very small list of some of the most interesting and useful works on the revolution available in English. Many of the books mentioned here provide extensive bibliographies for the student who wishes to go further in the study of a specific topic. Annual listings of new books and articles are also to be found in the *Slavic Review, The Russian Review,* and *Soviet Studies.*

Anyone wishing to understand the Russian Revolution and its significance should know something about theories of social change and revolution. The best small work on the processes of change in human society is C. E. Black's *The Dynamics of Modernization* (New York, 1966). Chalmers Johnson's *Revolution and the Social System* (Stanford, 1964) is a brief, succinct and highly successful effort to define the causes and the types of revolutions, and his *Revolutionary Change* (Boston, 1966) is undoubtedly the most balanced and penetrating analysis that has been published on this subject. In "Theories of Revolution," *World Politics* 18 (January 1966): 159–176, Lawrence Stone presents a clear resumé of contemporary theoretical approaches to the study of revolutions.

Some of the best general accounts of the Russian Revolution (Chamberlin, Trotsky, and Daniels) have been excerpted in this book. However, there are several others that have much to offer. Bertram Wolfe's *Three Who Made a Revolution* (Boston, 1948) makes an eloquent and fascinating introduction to the development of Marxist revolutionary thought and organization in the years leading up to 1914. *The Fall of the Russian Monarchy* by Sir Bernard Pares (London, 1939) is a moving account of the monarchy from the beginning of the twentieth century to the tsar's abdication and death; its overemphasis on politics and court life may be balanced by reading Michael T. Florinsky's *The End of the Russian Empire* (New Haven, 1931). The last ten chapters of the Florinsky book, *Russia: A History and an Interpretation* (New York, 1953), set forth an overall account which makes exhaustive use of monographic literature. The several volumes of *The Bolshevik Revolution, 1917–1923* (New York, 1951–1953) by E. H. Carr are quite useful where they actually touch upon the events prior to November 1917, but for the most part these volumes deal with the years after the revolution.

Victor Chernov's *The Great Russian Revolution* (New Haven, 1936) is a thoughtful study by the Socialist-Revolutionary leader who was also minister of agriculture in the Provisional Government. The work by George Katkov, *Russia 1917: The February Revolution* (New York, 1967), is an interesting study of the complex events leading up to the February Revolution, and Alexander Rabinowitch's book, *Prelude to Revolution: The Petrograd Bolsheviks and the July 1917 Uprising* (Bloomington, Indiana, 1968), is a full and well-informed examination of the July uprising. *Revolutionary Russia: A Symposium,* edited by Richard Pipes (New York, 1969), brings together a number of valuable papers by outstanding authorities on many aspects of the events in 1917. Finally, the *History of the Communist Party of the Soviet Union* by B. N. Ponomaryov and others (Moscow, 1960) is the latest of such official histories to be translated. Although emphases in the party line have been shifted, the interpretation of the causes of the revolution and the reasons for Bolshevik victory remain fundamentally unaltered.

Of particular value for an understanding of the peasant, his problems, and his perception of the revolution is the book by Sir John Maynard, *Russia in Flux* (New York, 1949); the useful but more specialized work by Launcelot Owen, *The Russian Peasant Movement, 1906–1917* (London, 1937), places much of its attention upon agrarian events between March and October of 1917.

There are many richly informative eyewitness reports. One of the best, a classic in the field, is *Ten Days that Shook the World* (New York, 1935) by John Reed. Reed was an extremely talented young American journalist with a flair for being at the right place in Petrograd during 1917 and a burning enthusiasm for the Bolsheviks. *Raymond Robin's Own Story* (New York, 1920) by W. Hard recounts the experiences of an American colonel of the Red Cross who through the second half of 1917 had close contacts with the revolutionary governments. Two ambassadors have written superior memoirs. In *My Mission to Russia and Other Diplomatic Memories,* 2 vols. (London and Boston, 1923), Sir George Buchanan reports his conversations with the emperor; and in *An Ambassador's Memoirs,* 3 vols. (London, 1923–1925) Maurice Paléologue of France provides penetrating and thoughtful analyses of the political and social decadence of the imperial regime. Of the numerous accounts by Russians it is almost impossible to select the best, but among the first of these is the work by N. N. Sukhanov, *The Russian Revolution, 1917* (London, 1955). Alexander Kerensky's *The Prelude to Bolshevism: The Kornilov Rebellion* (London, 1919) and *The Catastrophe* (New York and London, 1927) are prejudiced but valuable accounts by one of the principals. *Survival Through War and Revolution* (London and New York, 1939) by Dmitry Fedotoff White is a naval officer's description of events in the fleet at Petrograd in 1917 which gives a fine flavor of the revolutionary temper of the Bolshevik sailors.

It is, of course, quite impossible to understand the revolution without knowing a great deal about Lenin and his special variation of Marxism, subjects best learned by studying the pre-1917 development of the man and the theory. Of the immense literature that has grown up around these topics, the book by Wolfe mentioned above is a lively and very human account. Leopold Haimson's admirable book, *The Russian Marxists and the Origins of Bolshevism* (Cambridge, Mass., 1955) is a brilliant and penetrating study of the development of Marxism into Leninism, which unfortunately ends at 1905. Alfred G. Meyer's *Leninism* (Cambridge, Mass., 1957) is one of the best scholarly monographs available and is essential reading. V. I. Lenin's *Collected Works,* 45 vols. (London, 1960–1970) provide the primary sources of information about his ideas. Volumes 23 through 26 present his 1917 speeches, letters and articles and graphically depict both his analysis of events during the crucial months of the struggle for power and his forceful efforts to drive the revolution forward. For a detailed but somewhat over-critical study of the trials and tribulations of Lenin's Socialist-Revolutionary opponents, see Oliver H. Radkey's *The Agrarian Foes of Bolshevism* (New York, 1958).

Far too many biographical works written about the men involved in the revolution have been too superficial or biased to be of real worth. Isaac Deutscher's study of Stalin, and *The Prophet Armed: Trotsky, 1879–1921* (London and New York, 1954) are both authoritative and readable. The biographies of Lenin tend to adulate or condemn. David Shub's *Lenin: A Biography* (New York, 1948) while useful, does not go very deep and tends to emphasize the sensational. An outstanding recent study is by Adam Ulam, *The Bolsheviks: The Intellectual and Political History of the Triumph of Communism in Russia* (New York, 1965). Others worthy of attention are: Louis Fischer, *The Life of Lenin* (New York, 1964), and Stefan Possony, *Lenin: The Compulsive Revolutionary* (Chicago, 1964). *Reminiscences of Lenin,* by his wife, N. K. Krupskaya (New York, 1970), provides fascinating insights into the Bolshevik leader's personal life.

One of the mysteries that every student must try to solve for himself is the question of Rasputin's significance for Russia. *The Reign of Rasputin: An Empire's Collapse* (London, 1927) by the former president of the Duma, M. V. Rodzianko, is an unbalanced account by a man obsessed with hatred for Rasputin, but it very clearly points up Rasputin's malevolent influence. *Rasputin, the Holy Devil* (New York, 1929) by René Fülop-Miller contains documentary evidence concerning Rasputin's almost unbelievable personal character. No better picture of Rasputin's influence or of the characters of Emperor Nicholas II and his wife Alexandra can ever be drawn than that which they have sketched themselves in *Letters of the Tsaritsa to the Tsar, 1914–1916* (intro. by Sir Bernard Pares; London, 1923) and *The Letters of the Tsar to the Tsaritsa, 1914–1917* (introd. by C. T. Hagberg Wright; London, 1929).

The foreign affairs of Russia in 1917 and their influence upon the internal situation are described by Robert D. Warth in *The Allies and the Russian Revolution* (Durham, N. C., 1954), which strongly supports the thesis that had there been no Kornilov revolt the Provisional Government might have been more successful against the Bolsheviks. A very full bibliography of secondary and source materials in English makes this book especially useful for the student investigating this special area.

The importance of the nationalities movements, which has too often been missed by writers who tend to see only the dramatic events in Petrograd and Moscow, is clearly delineated by Richard Pipes in his *The Formation of the Soviet Union: Communism and Nationalism, 1917–1923* (Cambridge, Mass., 1954). *The Ukrainian Revolution, 1917–1920* (Princeton, 1952) by John Reshetar, Jr., is an authoritative monograph which develops in detail the revolutionary activity of one such minority movement; a similar study of another area is *The Struggle for Transcaucasia, 1917–1921* (New York, 1951) by Firuz Kazemzadeh.

Among the standard documentary collections several are of major value. *The Bolshevik Revolution, 1917–1918,* edited by James Bunyan and H. H. Fisher (Stanford, 1934), contains a mass of materials ranging from excerpted memoirs and personal statements by the participants to the records and orders of government and party officials. *Documents on Russian History, 1914–1917* (New York, 1927) by Frank A. Golder is of similar value, and the work edited by Z. A. B. Zeman, *Germany and the Revolution in Russia, 1915–1918: Documents from the Archives of the German Foreign Ministry* (London, 1958), presents the documents dealing with Lenin's journey through Germany in early 1917. The principal documentary account of the Provisional Government, badly skewed by Kerensky's biases, is the three-volume work by Robert Browder and Alexander Kerensky, *The Russian Provisional Government, 1917: Documents* (Stanford, 1961).

1 2 3 4 5 6 7 8 9 10